WHY DEMOCRACY IS OPPOSITIONAL

WHY DEMOCRACY IS OPPOSITIONAL

→ ←

John Medearis

Harvard University Press

Cambridge, Massachusetts

London, England

2015

Library of Congress Cataloging-in-Publication Data
Medearis, John.
Why democracy is oppositional / John Medearis.
pages cm
Includes bibliographical references and index.
ISBN 978-0-674-72533-1
1. Democracy.   2. Equality.   3. Opposition (Political science)   I. Title.
JC423.M3875 2015
321.8—dc23   2014033457

For Jessica and Max

CONTENTS

WHY DEMOCRACY IS OPPOSITIONAL

Drat the reformers, I say. And I wish there was no Parliament;
so I do. What's the use of all the voting, when it means
nothing but dry bread and cross words?

—Jane Bunce, in *Phineas Finn* by Anthony Trollope

Democracy as we know it is an inspiring but perpetually troubled endeavor, a difficult, ongoing struggle with no clear outcome in sight. When Trollope was writing *Phineas Finn,* a great deal of democratic trouble centered on radical heirs to Chartism who challenged the political domination of landed and high bourgeois classes. These efforts were threatening enough to prod both Liberals and Conservatives to compete doggedly for working-class support. Yet the Second Reform Bill, a product of that competition, enfranchised just a little more than a third of adult males and did nothing for women at all. And so on it went. Today, a range of democratic troubles, a variety of uncertain struggles for popular management of society, are readily apparent. Runaway financial markets have nearly slipped the bonds of the modest democratic control that developed in the midst of the Depression of the 1930s. Facing deeply entrenched resistance, the antiauthoritarian movements that flared up across the Arab world in 2011 too often have been outmaneuvered, or have been beaten back, or have lost their way. Decades after the passage of the Civil Rights Act, many African American men are again denied full democratic citizenship, not because of old-style segregation, but because of mass incarceration and the racialized war on drugs. Post-9/11 security states have developed an array of fantastical powers for surveillance and war-at-a-distance that can be exercised with hardly an effect on the Western publics whose role we generally assume is to monitor and oversee them. And these are just a few examples.

If the democratic ambition is collective, egalitarian management of the institutions and forces that shape our lives, each of these situations includes an element of the opposite, a spiraling loss of such control or an inability to exert it. It would be wrong to say that democratizing forces are absent. Movements, politicians, and ordinary people have tried to regain some democratic restraint on finance, and publics fitfully set limits on military behemoths. Still, democracy seems at best an ongoing struggle with phenomena like these, not a victory over them. Or that, at least, is what I wish to argue in the following pages. Yet neither dismay, nor resignation, nor retrenchment in the face of these democratic troubles is warranted. The democratic path, according to this view, simply is continuous oppositional exertion, without any expectation of transcendent victory.

A political vision like this one, stressing the continual struggle to recapture runaway social forces, wherever we find them—one emphasizing opposition, conflict, and tension—may strike some people, like Trollope's character Jane Bunce, as a promise that democracy will never offer more than "dry bread and cross words." In *Phineas Finn,* Bunce's husband, a copying journeyman, trade unionist, and reformer, survives on jail food for a week after being arrested during protests outside Parliament for the secret ballot. This experience, too, is the very stuff of democratic struggle. I do not mean the arrest and jail, specifically. I mean that democracy in this episode of Victorian English history was not to be found in an unrepresentative Parliament. Nor was it to be found in some pure expression in the crowd outside, or in a remote future that the demonstrators projected, in which every democratic deficiency would be alleviated. Democracy in this instance was precisely the tense interchange between crowd and Parliament, new challengers and Old Regime. But why should such contests be perpetual? What is their character? Why should we not take democracy as a kind of perfection and see the more unpleasant aspects of this scene—the dry bread in jail and the cross words in public—as exceptional, or at least external to democracy's true meaning?

That would be a more customary approach. Democratic theory often focuses on ideal scenarios and new beginnings. But there can be no virgin birth for democracy, which always emerges in a world that is already troubled and uncertain. Democratic action, I argue, responds perennially to apparently untamable wars, sclerotic bureaucracies, racial caste systems, and runaway markets. It persists uneasily alongside these refractory institutions and forces, which resist and make democracy precarious. Redeploying an old term from the political theory lexicon, I refer to these sorts of social structures and forces as *alienated*. I mean two things by this. First, they deeply overshadow ordinary people's capacities to act, while they provide means for some people to oppress others. At the same time, crucially, these forces and institutions are not external ones, confronting the mass of people from outside, but the by-product of the same people's own varied collective activities. They are, in a certain social science vernacular, *reproduced* by these activities. Because democratic action continually struggles to maintain egalitarian control over the social world that our shared activities constantly reproduce—because alienated institutions and forces are a persistent, constantly renewed challenge—democracy is perennially oppositional. And we must recognize this oppositional quality if we are to join realism about democracy's recurrent challenges with a renewed understanding of its highest aspirations. An oppositional approach treats democracy as struggling from inception against aspects of a social world that have already taken shape and that frequently resist popular management. It views democracy neither as a distant ideal nor as a completed reality, but as a continual, active process of becoming. For these reasons, an oppositional theory encompasses contentious politics and social movements—from Chartism and the American civil rights movement to the post–World War I council movement and Occupy Wall Street—viewing the tasks they undertake not merely as possibilities to be tolerated, or as instrumental for achieving real democracy, but as central to democracy and its life.

In presenting this case in the coming pages, I do not propose a "model" of democracy, as the term is sometimes understood. I do not argue that a single institutional framework, like liberal democracy, is always right. Nor do I claim to demonstrate that a certain practice, enshrined in elaborate norms—whether deliberation or something else— is democracy's essence. Instead I try to demonstrate something important about the conditions faced by anyone enacting democratic ambitions. And I try to show that those conditions ought to shape our perception of what it is we are doing whenever we set out to act democratically. In showing why democracy is fundamentally oppositional, why it is a constant struggle we should not expect to move beyond, I try further to vindicate much of the familiar, conflictive life of democracy as we know

3

it. I try to show that a variety of political practices deserve democratic approval, even though many of them may seem mundane and others troublingly contentious.

In calling democracy *oppositional* I mean most of all that democratic action opposes alienation, opposes the tendency of our common activities to escape our common control and reproduce malign social structures and forces. Democrats do have opponents, but it is best to see this fact in the context of broader shared activities and social structures. Similarly, it is of course possible to identify some of the contemporary institutions that are most prone to alienation. In this book, I discuss markets, the security state, and racial caste systems, among other examples. But I do not rest my argument on a permanent division of the social world, between unalienated and alienated, with genuine democracy inhabiting one ideal institutional setting, pitted against some other social structure or realm that is forever inherently undemocratic. Rather, alienation is an ever-present possibility throughout the social world. The point is to oppose the phenomenon of alienation—wherever we find it—not some structure we assume to be intrinsically alienated. And this often means not disdaining but forcefully redirecting and restructuring institutions or forces that exhibit alienation. By the same token, although there will probably always be people who oppose democratization, democratic opposition is not reducible to a struggle against enemies. Pogo's declaration—"We have met the enemy, and he is us"—would exaggerate my point about common action and alienation, but it can be a useful corrective to visions of democracy that portray intergroup antagonism as in itself foundational. The effect of linking democracy to alienation should not be to foreground enmity—nor even the overcoming of enmity—but to highlight why, exactly, democracy is a perpetual struggle.

I come back repeatedly to examples from the history of democratizing movements, from civil rights to Occupy Wall Street. There are movement activities that ought to be recognized as democratic, even though they are not among the more widely accepted democratic practices, like voting or deliberation. These include disruption, demonstrative assembly, and boisterous expression, as well as recruiting, organizing, and planning. Still, the point is not that movement tactics and undertakings alone are the real heart of democracy. Many approaches seem to see democratic theory's task as elevating one practice over all others. In contrast, I promote a pluralistic view of the kind of activities that should be embraced by democratic theory. The challenging, oppositional quality of many movement tactics simply calls attention to the alienated resistance all democratic action confronts. All genuinely democratic activities, that is, derive much of their significance from the fact that they challenge alienated social forms. For all that movements illuminate, democratic theory should also not be preoccupied with valorizing movements as democratic heroes any more than it should focus primarily on identifying democracy's adversaries. Movements are most important as exceptionally acute examples of democracy as struggle. They stand near one end of a continuum. And the frequency with which movements arise to challenge overshadowing social forces or remake oppressive institutions is also an indicator of alienation's persistence.

My focus on democracy as a struggle against alienation can be understood as an attempt to circumvent the distinction sometimes made between ideal and nonideal theorizing. I do not project democracy as some pure practice that can only be expected to thrive in the distant future, or that can only be conceived imaginatively. While inspiring and principled, democratic life is also present in the politics we know, intimately engaged with persistent, inhospitable social phenomena. The vision I propose of democracy versus alienation, to be clear, is neither ideal nor nonideal. It finds its democratic values enmeshed in actual political experience, and thoroughly connected to what resists democracy. An oppositional approach does not assume that what resists democracy can be understood, negatively, as just an absence, a simple negation of democratic values. It places a great deal of emphasis on theorizing the problem of alienation itself. And it treats the many forms of domination and oppression as an integral part of democratic theorizing.

My approach entails criticism of assumptions and concepts embedded in leading scholarly approaches to democracy, especially the models with the most present adherents, elite theory and deliberative theory. The critiques are especially prominent early in the book, but they reverberate throughout. It is also true that the democratic theory offered up here is not the only one that considers democracy to be in some sense oppositional. It would hardly be a good thing if my approach hinged on something no democrat had ever felt to be part of his or her experience. With some interpretive spadework, it is possible to see how canonical theorists like Karl Marx and John Dewey contributed to an alienation-and-opposition understanding of democracy. And in different ways, I think participatory democracy, agonistic democracy, and fugitive democracy have oppositional elements. In some cases, these oppositional elements have to be uncovered. In others, there are significant differences between my oppositional approach and those of other theorists, either because I portray the origin and nature of "opposition" quite differently, or draw contrasting conclusions from it. I also consider other thinkers' explorations of issues such as the character of domination, the dangers of markets, and the best way to respond to state alienation.

It is easiest to understand these engagements with other theorists in light of the detailed arguments of the book. But before turning to a chapter-by-chapter preview, it may help to illustrate my approach to democracy with an example of a single oppositional episode, one both ordinary and vivid. In 2012, on the day after Thanksgiving, a crowd of about a thousand assembled in the parking lot of a Walmart store in Paramount, California, fifteen miles or so southeast of downtown Los Angeles. Participants began slowly to file, three or four abreast, past television news trucks and along the front of the store, down a side-street sidewalk, to a boulevard already closed off by sheriffs' cruisers, anticipating what would happen next. At the entrance to the Walmart store, the marchers' line was periodically broken to let through shoppers ready to join what is now an often frenzied annual ritual, looking for purported bargains on "Black Friday." Calling attention to management retaliation against activist workers, the protesters chanted about justice, unions, and *la lucha*.[1] Reaching the middle of the boulevard, they thronged and stayed put for a while—then finally receded to the curb, leaving nine sitting protestors to be arrested for failure to disperse, the customary misdemeanor of American civil disobeyers. Similar actions, most of them smaller, played out across the United States the same day, from Boynton Beach, Florida, to Portland, Oregon.

Walmart emphasized to reporters that day that many of the protestors across the country were not employees protesting their own work conditions. That was both true and perspicacious. For this single, taut engagement between protestors, corporation, and police was emblematic of something broader than just Walmart, something about democracy and the shape of America's contemporary "Walmart economy." For many ordinary people, not just Walmart employees, the system emblematized by Walmart is wild, harsh, and disempowering. It is, in short, characterized by alienated economic forces that make most of us look feeble. Workers' strength, especially, is often dwarfed both by employer power and by overwhelming market forces that threaten their autonomy. The practice of forcing Walmart employees to work in locked stores overnight, with no keys to get out in case of emergency, has reportedly stopped (Greenhouse 2004), but it exemplifies the relative powerlessness of so many economic actors. So do the many low-wage workers who find they are too vulnerable and unorganized to resist the now widespread employer practice of wage theft.[2] The formidable weapons many corporations wield to prevent their workers from having an organized voice on the job are equally symptomatic. And vulnerability in the workplace is of a piece with exposure to all the uncontrolled forces and upheavals that have led to Gilded Age levels of inequality, economic and political, in much of the contemporary West. It is not just low-wage workers who find themselves overmatched in this economy, but also ordinary homeowners and borrowers, such as those who suffered foreclosure, or just severe blows to their net worth, in the recent Great Recession. Unfair as these widespread troubles may be, however, the first focus of an oppositional approach to democracy, as I posit it, should not be to condemn anyone for the unjust acts involved. It should instead be to explore the alienated conditions that make such acts possible.

No one publicly represented Walmart management outside the store that day. So next to the demonstrators, the other most significant players apparent in the vignette were the customers, so very like Walmart employees themselves, making their way through breaks in the marchers' line. The harsh conditions and low pay that are for many characteristic of the contemporary economy help to create a population of consumers who rely on discount stores to make their budgets balance. Walmart said that just from the time it opened its doors on that Thanksgiving evening through the following morning, it had sold, nationwide, 1.8 million towels, 1.3 million televisions, and 250,000 bicycles (Zimmerman and Banjo 2012). And just as low-wage employment creates a class of bargain hunters, all that cut-rate buying strengthens retailers and thus helps perpetuate the difficult conditions of low-wage labor. As I have suggested, the antiunion exertions and wage theft too common in the "Walmart economy" are significant for democracy less because they show that particular corporations or managers are callous or dishonest, and more because these incidents help reveal the shape of the economy and the distribution of power it entails. And that power distribution owes its continued existence, in no small part, to those who shop at the discount chain or others like it. The irony, then, is that these people's own actions together help sustain an economy that undercuts many of them. But it is not just actual Walmart shoppers who are at issue. In this example, they simply stand in for all of us, in a sense. And this requires us to recognize the degree to which so many of us sustain similar alienated conditions, however inadvertently or unwillingly. They suggest that democratizing society is not, finally, so much about grabbing someone else's powers as taking back our own. It is less about inhibiting someone else's actions and more about regaining some control of ours. It involves struggle, not only because it pits democratizers against those who stand to lose from their efforts, but also because it requires us to confront, collectively, the results of practices in which almost all of us engage. This is a second key aspect of the oppositional democracy viewpoint I wish to explore.

A third concerns the character of democratizing efforts to confront serious inequalities of power and to enhance ordinary people's control over their communal life—to bolster, in turn, their individual autonomy as workers, consumers, students, or caregivers. These campaigns involve all kinds of activities, not just the marching, chanting, and civil disobedience on display the day after Thanksgiving in Paramount. They involve organization building, electioneering, lobbying, legal skirmishing, agitation, and participation in wide-ranging public debate. The efforts include union organizers, politicians, nonprofits, and clergy members, as well as retail employees themselves. Still, the protests that day were a clear evocation of the character of all the democratic activity involved—its oppositional quality and the challenges it faces. Even the strictly electoral or legislative aspects of the effort to democratize the "Walmart" economy involve constant grappling with considerable resistance. Multinational corporations and big banks and wealthy heirs turned activists resist such campaigns with tremendous entrenched political power. Moreover, the goal of such democratic endeavors is not just to ease economic hardships. These efforts necessarily threaten unequal power. They attempt fundamentally to restructure an unbalanced set of social relations some people would rather see maintained. And from the perspective of those marching and getting arrested in Paramount that day, there is something else to be said about democratic activity. Many of them would likely say that their exuberant, turbulent deeds—even the tense exchanges they frequently involve—are not just regrettable political necessities but are a crucial part of how they understand and experience democratic life. Much of what follows is intended to vindicate that view.

Chapter 1 begins this vindication by chronicling how some of the best-known and most influential scholarly models of democracy have responded to the rich history of democratic movements. That they have done so may not always be apparent. But Joseph Schumpeter crafted his version of elite theory partly in reaction to working-class movements that he feared would usher in democratic socialism. And at their best, deliberative democrats aspire to account for the new ideas and values social movements have contributed. Yet while responding to movements, democratic theorists have also often adopted conceptions that make it nearly impossible to understand such movements' challenges, their tactics, and above all, their democratic significance. In tailoring their understanding of movements to fit the idealized forms of "democratic" behavior they posit, theorists have portrayed movements in ways that their participants might not even recognize. Or they have made much movement activity seem futile or irrelevant to democracy's true meaning. The problematic conceptions pervade democratic thinking, broadly. For example, both deliberative theory and elite theory envision democracy separated by walls from the realities of ordinary politics—in one case, protected as a refuge, in the other, enclosed as a quarantine. It is difficult to imagine many movements accepting either of these intramural conceptions, one of them suggesting that they should devalue the sort of struggle for which they are most known, the other that they should cede politics to more competent elites. And the other tropes I discuss—democracy as special relationship among citizens, democracy as an institution, democracy as decision making, and democracy as noncoercion—fare no better in helping us understand the experience of democratic movements. I also endeavor to show that even when deliberative theorists have tried to incorporate more of what movements really do and experience under the heading of nonideal theory, they have not made things better. In fact, resting on a sharp distinction between ideal and nonideal can actually accentuate some of the difficulties associated, for example, with eschewing coercion.

My conceptual critique of these dominant models of democracy points toward the need for another approach that would foreground democracy as a form of active engagement with the many undemocratic tendencies at work in society—not a retreat behind walls or a special form of interaction between ideally situated citizens. It would emphasize democracy as an ensemble of activities and recognize the potential of broad-based movement action to reshape society and politics. But it would also recognize the intrinsic limits of all common action, including democratic action, and emphasize the fact that movements form because new challenges to democracy arise again and again. A conception of democracy that relates it to the limits of common action and to the genesis of alienated structures and forces is best equipped to meet these demands.

Alienation has a rich history and a broad range of meanings in political thought. In Chapter 2, I focus on Karl Marx and John Dewey, who each in a different way reflected on a phenomenon I emphasize, one in which people's own common activities generate malign consequences and reproduce institutions or social forces that are overpowering or destructive to them. Especially interesting is the fact that both also conceived of democracy as a response to this phenomenon. Georg Wilhelm Friedrich Hegel's complex ruminations on alienation set the stage. Marx's contribution, I contend, was to democratize Hegel's "alienation," to hone the concept and make it a useful part of democratic thinking. My interpretation of Marx differs from ones that stress his theory of alienation but that do not connect it integrally to democracy, or that emphasize Marx's theory of democracy but do not connect it to alienation. Dewey, in contrast to Marx, did not emphasize the term *alienation*. But after his own fashion, Dewey did recognize something quite like the same phenomenon and tried to think through a democratic response to it. As against interpretations that depict Dewey as concerned mainly to improve the quality of democratic communication, I argue that he understood alienation as "the public's *other* problem." Dewey argued that Americans in the early twentieth century often lost track of the public consequences of their common actions. They failed to see that the impersonal forces that buffeted or ruled over them were in large part the unintended consequences of their own shared practices. The remedy for this, in Dewey's view, was not just better talk but robust, democratic collective action to counteract such dominating forces and institutions. Despite their strengths, Marx's and Dewey's explorations also show, in different ways, that those who emphasize alienation face a risk of positing a utopian escape from it. To continue in the direction pointed out by Marx and Dewey, while at the same time resisting these utopian temptations and showing why alienation is a persistent threat we should never expect to see abated, I elaborate in Chapter 3 a contemporary theory of alienation grounded in a sober view of human agency and its limits.

Chapters 1 and 2 in a sense preview and prepare the way for my own elaboration of a vision of alienation and democratic opposition, first by showing how such a theory responds to weaknesses in contemporary democratic theory, and second by exploring some of its historical roots. But some readers may want to skip directly from this introduction to the third chapter and then continue with the rest of the book before returning to the early parts, treating those chapters as elaborations of the core argument rather than as its underpinnings.

A proper view of *alienation* needs a realistic and nuanced understanding of *action*—as well as of its role in the reproduction of institutions, forces, and social relations. The importance of getting action right should not be surprising. Democratic theory has often been a debate—a flawed one—about action or agency. In Chapter 3, drawing on Dewey, Pierre Bourdieu, Anthony Giddens, and Roy Bhaskar, I lay out a conception of action that highlights reflexivity and structuration. That is, it emphasizes that as agents, we do not generally carry out plans that we have crafted in full, ahead of time. Action, rather, is a continuous process in which intentions arise through critical and active reflection on what has been done and experienced. And this perspective also builds on the insight that action has a reciprocal relation to social structure—which enables and constrains action, but is also reproduced as a largely unintended consequence of it. These arguments set the stage for understanding both democratic action and alienation. It prepares the way for grasping democratic action because, like all action, it cannot be understood in terms of clean slates, original plans made ahead of time and then executed. It only intervenes in ongoing events, arriving late and already burdened. The arguments about structuration and reflexivity set the stage for understanding alienation because some of these social forms, though reproduced by human activity, can at the same time *dominate* people, or deeply overshadow their ability to act. I treat alienation, in sum, as the phenomenon that exists when people's social action reproduces institutions, social relations, or social forces that confront them in dominating and potentially oppressive or exploitive forms.

Alienation, I argue, is a chronic condition of social life, a crucial feature of the terrain on which we try to enact our highest democratic aspirations. After elucidating the basics of a contemporary theory of alienation, I emphasize the importance of the fact that, although structures enable and constrain, they do not enable and constrain everyone equally. This is important for the oppositional dimensions of democracy, because while the effects of alienation may be felt widely, disparate agents experience domination and oppression from different sides and in varying degrees. I also reflect on the contrast—and the relationship—

between personal and impersonal relations of power. Chapter 3 begins and ends with explorations of economic alienation. The early sections review the way ordinary people reproduced the institutions and helped generate the forces that, in turn, overwhelmed them and made them vulnerable during the Great Recession. The concluding pages explore in more detail what it means to analyze markets as potentially alienated, distinguishing this critique from other contemporary ones, such as those that hold that being bought or sold corrupts certain goods.

Chapter 4 elucidates what it means to say that democracy is oppositional. I begin with a vivid historical example of oppositional democratic action: the post–World War I council movement, which resisted unbridled militarism and tried to democratize the oppressive and dominating institutions that had fueled war. Then I set out to explicate this example, turning to democratic action, a distinctive form of social action, one directed toward managing crucial institutions, relations, and forces collectively, in a way that strives for equality of power. Like all action, the democratic sort is interventionary and reflexive. And more particularly, as earlier chapters illustrate, democratic action always arises surrounded by many other different kinds of social action and by the refractory institutions and social forces such forms of action often reproduce. Because of its aims, democratic action is arrayed, above all, against *alienated* social forms that overshadow the agency of ordinary people, impose necessities upon them, and provide opportunities for oppression. It is because so many of democracy's most endemic challenges are oppositional that social and political movements are so important to democracy. And incorporating movements and opposition expands the repertoire of activities recognized by democratic theory. Democratic action consists of more than just voting and deliberating, the favored activities of the dominant modes of democratic theorizing. It includes, in particular, all the activities that are part of the hard work of collectively resisting alienation, from marching, to agitating, to striking, to building organizations, to publicizing and debating, whether these are undertaken by movements or not.

In the last sections of the chapter, I deepen aspects of my approach through encounters with other resonant democratic theories. Reflection on participatory democratic theory prompts recognition that an oppositional approach like mine similarly entails placing value on a kind of active political flourishing. It also helps expand upon an oppositional dimension to participatory theory by asking how participatory institutions might be established and maintained in social environments that are not hospitable to them. I turn next to agonism. While the distinguishing mark of agonistic theory, broadly, is justified skepticism about the idea of fixed social identities, such an analysis, alone, cannot sustain a progressive, oppositional democratic politics. Finally, I discuss why the principled democratic confrontation with alienated social forms should be seen as perpetual, not extraordinary and "fugitive."

Chapter 5 explores problems of democratic action and the alienated state. There is a long history of progressives and leftists criticizing liberal welfare states for resisting democratic control, for secretly (and not so secretly) serving the interests of just a privileged few, especially business and financial interests. Occupy Wall Street offers just a recent expression of this critique. Some of these progressives have hoped that democratic forces might seize the state and wield it for egalitarian purposes, others have argued for "breaking" the state and replacing it with a form of unalienated political power, and still others have advocated just for keeping one's distance from the state to nurture democracy elsewhere. The ultimate goal, regardless of which of these possibilities these critics have chosen, has been a definitive achievement of democracy. All these critics have rightly seen that the state is perennially prone to alienation. But I argue that in this instance and others we should think of democratization not as a process that can be finite in duration, decisive, and singular in focus, but one that is continuous, provisional, uncertain, multiply challenged, and without a foreseeable end. This viewpoint is bolstered by a couple of decades of scholarship—critical theorizing that goes beyond the old focus on the political advantages enjoyed by business and finance to explore welfare states' deep involvement in creating and maintaining undemocratic race and gender relations. This work shows again that welfare states, by reinforcing and reproducing unequal forms of social and political membership, have often failed to live up to broadly social democratic values of equality and full citizenship. It also demonstrates that welfare states have a wider range of democratically significant, democratically troubling, properties and capacities than previously thought. States are prone, for this reason, to many more forms of alienation than older theory understood. But this analysis, along with the historical record of movements that have sometimes compelled states to reconstruct undemocratic social relations, suggests the need for more direct and contentious engagement with welfare states, not less. A democratic response to the welfare state and its integral relationship to race, class, and gender, I suggest, must involve struggling both against and with the power of the state. Such an approach would look for democracy not in any ideal place or time, but here and now, imperfect but striving, in shifting forms of opposition and contestation.

It is not just the welfare powers of the state that can foster alienation, however. I argue in the epilogue that modern security states show increasing signs of alienation, vastly overshadowing the powers of citizens, while acting in ways that escape their comprehension. Dewey could have penned the diagnosis: through a variety of shared practices, ordinary people enable the security state, yet they do not fully experience the effects of what it actually does. Since 9/11, new forms of warfare and spying have only exacerbated these tendencies. Among the most prominent examples are drone warfare and private military contracting, both of which thrive on gaps between the experience of Western publics and those who live in war zones, between civilians and those who fight in their name, and between soldiers for major powers and soldiers in the developing world.

Of course the number of contemporary worries and evils that could be explored from an alienation-and-opposition approach is much greater than I can address in this book. I can only suggest the form such inquiries should take. For decades now, democratic thinking has been dominated by two modes of thought: ever-shifting, highly detailed reflection on how citizens should talk to each other, on the one hand, and complacent adherence, on the other, to a much older view that citizens cannot say much or accomplish much, anyway. To the degree that my understanding of alienation and opposition provides a purchase on our democratic predicaments, the grip of these modes of thinking should be loosened. We need a debate that emphasizes critical democratic study of the overwhelming operations of markets, states, and social relations of all kinds; an approach that recognizes that democracy's fragility is not just rooted in the permanent incapacities or ethical lapses of citizens; and a theory that looks much more sympathetically on the quotidian experience of ordinary democratic actors, including the many and varied activities in which they engage, in order to recapture social forces that would otherwise tend to escape their common management.

1

THE IRONIC PLACE OF MOVEMENTS
IN DEMOCRATIC THEORY

→ ←

Traveling by train to Chicago in the summer of 1894, John Dewey met a union organizer. During the spring, the Pullman Palace Car Company had summarily fired employees who were protesting drastic pay cuts. By late June, about a quarter million sympathetic workers were taking part in the American Railroad Union's boycott of trains pulling the company's sleepers. With the strike growing, President Grover Cleveland moved to back the railroad companies with force. Just two days before the U.S. Army deployed to Chicago to quell the strike, Dewey wrote to his wife and described his response to meeting the organizer. "I only talked to him 10 or 15 minutes," he recounted, "but when I got through my nerves were more thrilled than they had been for years" (quoted in Westbrook 1991, 86). The way the union activist captured Dewey's imagination that day is not really surprising. A supporter of labor, he had already revealed his sympathy for strikes in an essay three years earlier. And throughout Dewey's career, social movements and dissenting activists, from Progressives to Socialists, riveted his attention and offered crucial material for his conceptualization of democratic life.

Movements had a similar influence on John Stuart Mill, who is often viewed as the preeminent nineteenth-century English theorist of democracy, much as Dewey is seen as the quintessential twentieth-century American democratic thinker. Mill was enlisted as a youth to his father's political radicalism and was already immersed in debates with Owenite socialists before he turned twenty. He later paid close attention to the work of feminists and Chartists, and even had contact with the International Working Men's Association. And all these groups and struggles colored his broad understanding of democratization, a project that included proposals for reforming not just elections but also marriage, land tenure, and industrial organization—all in ways that paralleled the proposals of egalitarian activists of his time.

And movements have continued to provoke or inspire more recent democratic theory, as well—for good reason. But despite a need and interest on the part of democratic theorists to understand movements,[1] some of the conceptions that characterize their work have prevented a full reckoning of the significance of movements for democracy. Even in responding to movements, theorists have often adopted conceptions that make it difficult to understand the challenges, tactics, and place of movements in democracy. They have made some movement activity seem valueless, or at least irrelevant to the true meaning of democracy—or in fitting movements to fixed ideals, portrayed them in ways that their actual participants would hardly recognize.

The contradictory record of democratic theory's grappling with movements does not just point to a need to bring movements back in as historical exemplars. It underscores the need for a better way of conceptualizing democracy. The right sort of democratic theory would locate both the challenges and the value of democracy here and now, in the troubled political foreground in which movements make their stands. And it would make a crucial place within democratic theory for common action—both its potentialities and its limits—neither denying, with many elite theorists, that ordinary people can act effectively in politics, nor treating political action as an uninteresting prelude or sequel to deliberation and decision. In addressing these issues, the needed conceptualization would also help explain why it is that social movements have so often been crucial to democratic life. And it would seek to explain why democracy is always an ongoing and unfinished challenge.

In the early sections of this chapter, I show that, despite the inclination to respond to movements, a great deal of democratic theory—especially, but not exclusively, theory in the deliberative and elite modes—has overemphasized familiar, taken-for-granted conceptions about democracy that undermine this aim. These conceptions include ideas that pervade a great deal of democratic thinking, such as the view of democracy, narrowly, as a way of making decisions, or the envisioning of democracy as something that must be walled off from the rest of political and social life. The conceptualizations also include ones particular to a single approach, such as deliberative theory's elevation of noncoercion to a defining feature of true democracy.

16

Some more recent democratic theorists, deliberative ones in particular, seem to have recognized these weaknesses, and have gone further in explaining and even embracing aspects of movement action. And so after laying out my initial appraisal of these problematic conceptions in democratic theory, my argument continues by exploring newer attempts to think about movements and democracy, each responsive in some way to the difficulties of the previous one. Much of the relevant debate about democracy and movements has made use of a distinction between *ideal* and *nonideal* theory. In particular, some theorists have argued, in effect, that nonideal politics may require movements and their tactics, even though a truly ideal democracy would neither need nor value them. I reflect on the nature of this alluring ideal/nonideal distinction, and then show how it fails to remedy—how in some ways it actually accentuates—the difficulties highlighted earlier. I then explore the possibility of holding on to the ideal/nonideal dichotomy, but putting as much emphasis on nonideal political strategy for the present as on an ideal vision of the democratic future. The crucial example is an illuminating study (Stears 2010) that argues that movement intellectuals in twentieth-century America adopted this very approach. I argue, though, that the history and literature in question is susceptible to a different (and in my view, more promising) interpretation: many of these radical democrats seem to have avoided positing a sharp separation of ideal from nonideal politics, or democratic ends from democratic means.

This potential reinterpretation prepares the ground for a forward-looking survey of ways to transcend the conceptions that have made it so difficult to recognize or appropriately value the democratic significance of movements. A better approach, I argue, would dispense with the ideal/nonideal distinction and focus on what makes democracy precious and precarious in the here and now, and presumably for the indefinite future. It would foreground democracy as a form of active engagement with the many undemocratic tendencies in society—not a retreat behind walls, or a form of interaction between ideally situated citizens. The term *active* is also crucial. The approach I have in mind would emphasize democracy as a kind of action, recognizing the frequently demonstrated potential of movement activities to reshape society and politics. In so doing, it would avoid elite theory's tendency radically to deprecate the agency of ordinary people and deliberative theory's tendency to lose sight of political action, broadly understood, in its overwhelming emphasis on pauses and spaces for ideal decision making.

Of course, if the raw potency of democratic action were the whole story, the recurrent need of movements to resist undemocratic social and political forces would seem inexplicable. So although movements provide the impetus of my argument in this chapter, it is not just movements, finally, that are at issue, but the nature of the challenges they face. The failure to conceptualize movements properly reflects ways of thinking that misunderstand the broader conditions of democratic action. The approach I favor would make a place for democratic action even while theorizing its limits, and the obvious tendency for new challenges to democracy to arise again and again. All this, I argue, points toward an understanding of democracy as a recurrent, active struggle against "alienated" social structures and tendencies. Such a vision, the subject of the rest of this book, would also show why movements are not merely contingently useful or instrumental in creating democratic conditions. Movements do not somehow *define* democracy (as some would say voting or deliberation do). But they do exemplify the ongoing challenge of acting democratically in a world characterized by alienation.

Movements in Democratic Theory

Joseph Schumpeter wrestled with the problem of movements from his first writings on democracy because of his lifelong concern with the transformation of liberal capitalist societies.[2] Although he is known primarily for his elite theory, which presents democracy as a stable form of elite rule, his writings in fact display a keen attention to the way the spread of democratic beliefs and practices might alter societies fundamentally. World War I and its aftermath sparked the spontaneous election of popular "councils" in central and eastern Europe, the spearhead of a movement whose leading organizational innovation was the injection of democratic practices into military, political, and industrial hierarchies.[3] Schumpeter was soon arguing, in surprising harmony with socialist writers of the time, that self-managing councils could eventually be the means of a democratic transition to socialism. During World War II, long after the council movement had faded, but in the wake of fierce unionization battles in the United States, Schumpeter argued that the labor movement and its pursuit of industrial democracy were undermining a main pillar of capitalism, the hierarchical workplace. Schumpeter's ultimate response, though, was to consolidate a revised elite theory of democracy that suggested further dangerous democratic transformations could be warded off.

Deliberative democracy's encounter with movements has developed quite differently. It is not the product of sweeping reflection on history and democratic change. It is rather a sustained exploration of an acute dilemma: the desire to embrace the democratic aims, values, and discursive accomplishments of many movements, coupled with principled disapproval of the decidedly nondeliberative methods and arguments so often used by movements. John Rawls, in particular, was drawn to the examples of the U.S. abolition and civil rights movements, which sought to overturn institutions that radically undermined any claim of America to be democratic. The difficulty for Rawls was that so many activists for these causes made arguments and mobilized adherents based on religious views that not everyone could share, rather than using arguments drawn from more widely shared "public reason," as required by his understanding of deliberation (1996, 247–254). Other deliberative theorists have referenced different movements, but it is less the specific causes or claims of movements that account for theorists' attention than it is awareness of the repertoire of tactics that have characterized modern democratizing protest. Iris Marion Young lists some of these: "demonstration and direct action"; "street marches, boycotts, or sit-ins"; as well as "picketing, leafleting, guerilla theater, large and loud street demonstrations, sit-ins, and other forms of direct action, such as boycotts" (2001, 670, 673).

Beyond the particular aims and trajectories of elite and deliberative theory, there are, in fact, quite good reasons why democratic theorists of all kinds should reflect on political and social movements. First, movements of one sort or another have been crucial in shaping the measure of democracy now enjoyed in countries like the United States and France, or the Philippines and Tunisia. Movements have also introduced and popularized much of the institutional repertoire of democracy upon which theorists, in turn, reflect, from universal suffrage to participatory management. There are also, of course, the democratic values—above all, equality and freedom—that have been posited, enriched, and made more concrete by prominent movements. And taking a wider view, movements have often democratized the whole culture in which contemporary political theory takes its small place. These movement contributions are something more than just examples. They have been preconditions, sometimes unacknowledged, for democratic thinking.

Still, all these contributions may be seen, of course, as merely contingent or instrumental. Some would surely argue that democracy is one thing and the struggles of movements to enact it quite another. Movements might have been important—even necessary—for achieving universal suffrage, but one could still argue that universal suffrage defines democracy while movements do not. In making such arguments, philosophers have at their disposal an alluring set of dichotomies. We must not confuse what is intrinsically valuable with what is only instrumental, some would say, nor ends with means, nor the causes of democratization with democracy's true meaning. In the case of democracy, at least, there are some real drawbacks to thinking in this binary way. And in fact, there is something about democracy itself that should elicit an approach that avoids the opposition of ideal and nonideal.

Bringing Movements Back In: Conceptual Missteps

Although Schumpeter and a substantial number of deliberative theorists have strived to account for movements, their efforts have often misfired. In large part, this is due to problematic conceptions or frames. These ideas are widespread, appearing within a number of different scholarly "models of democracy," as well as in wider political discourse. They are not flatly wrong, but partial and limiting—distorting when accepted uncritically, without an acute sense of their limits. The fact that these conceptions are shared by the two leading scholarly approaches—elite and deliberative democracy—despite their otherwise stark differences, illustrates how widespread they are.

In order to grasp the problems with these different frames, it may help to consider first the sort of periods in which so many democratizing movements have been active. These are historical periods that are both stimulating and troubling for democrats to study, marked at the same time by democratic failure and democratic promise. The civil rights movement exemplified skillful, sometimes virtuosic democratic action while challenging the enduring racial caste system of the American South. Movements like those that brought down East European communist regimes in 1989 were marked by a similar contrast, in this case between vibrant mass action and dominating, ossified states. The council movement, likewise, was a creative attempt to reclaim public influence over runaway social forces in the midst of capitalist crisis and at the end of an extraordinarily destructive war waged by crumbling, despotic empires.

In short, the kind of historical periods I have in mind are characterized by two features. First, during these critical periods, many people have been subject to institutions or social forces that diminished their political agency, hindered their collective capacities to manage their lives, forced necessities on them, and enabled oppression. Yet, second, despite such harmful social forms, these critical democratic periods were also characterized by democratic promise, sometimes because there were arenas in which ordinary people managed their common affairs on terms approaching equality and freedom, and sometimes because of robust movements that sought to achieve democratic goals, not in spite of but in response to the injurious forces and institutions. Because of these glaring deficiencies, on the one hand, and the democratic promise, on the other, we may say that such critical democratic eras were marked by an inter-acting duality in which, for example, some people struggled collectively to tame runaway economic forces in the public interest. The ability to come to terms, theoretically, with such critical epochs is one rough marker of success for any conception of democracy.

Deliberative Theory and the Problematic Conceptions

Deliberative theory claims that a special form of political discourse—deliberation—is the heart of democracy, the practice that makes it legit-imate.[4] Proponents depict deliberation in various ways, but most portrayals stress something like Bohman and Richardson's formulation: "the idea of publicly giving reasons to justify decisions" (2009, 253). The main emphasis of the deliberative literature, then, is on the norms that should govern individuals as they reason with others about political deci-sions. And these often take the form of quite stringent prohibitions. "Classic" deliberative theory has been "defined in opposition" to many of the most familiar and pervasive features of modern politics—in con-trast, that is, "to self-interest, to bargaining and negotiation, to voting, and to the use of power" (Mansbridge et al. 2010, 64).[5] Deliberative theory, because of its characteristic concerns, is disposed to cast move-ments in a very particular light. Movements are generally understood to be collective challenges to dominant groups, ranks, and structures in society mounted by relatively weak or excluded people. Deliberative theory understands the difficult situation of movements largely discur-sively, suggesting that they represent those people excluded from or dis-advantaged in political discourse.[6]

Deliberative theory's banishment of many of the ordinary conditions and practices of politics as we know it points to its adoption of a problem-atic conception of democracy, the first that we shall consider and one that informs several other such conceptions. This is the view of democracy surrounded by fortifications that separate it from the rest of the political world—in deliberative theory, the view of democracy as a refuge. This intramural vision of democracy can find different expressions. Proponents interested in fostering current attempts to deliberate may emphasize the "design of deliberative institutions" today for "the exclusion of extra-political or endogenous forms of influence, such as power, wealth, and preexisting social inequalities" (Bohman 1996, 36). Or, like Jürgen Habermas, they may posit civil society itself as a sort of barrier that can "absorb and neutralize the unequal distribution of social positions and the power differentials resulting from them" (1996, 175). The design of deliberative experiments by scholars, foundations, and governments offers a practical illustration of this wall-building approach. Deliberative conditions are so different from ordinary politics that these assemblies require painstaking construction, including careful selection of deliberators from the general public, judicious production of briefing materials, random assignment of deliberators to small groups, and the empowerment of moderators—all to ensure an institutional context favoring deliberation (Ackerman and Fishkin 2004; Fournier et al. 2011).

But if the "refuge" idea stands out in the work of those who consider how it might be possible to introduce deliberation now, it is just as much a part of those arguments that treat deliberation primarily as a set of ideal norms quite distant from present practice. In these cases, however, it is not space and institutional walls, but time and imagination that project democracy as a distant refuge. Consider, for example, Jack Knight and James Johnson's frank admission that the "sort of equality" required for democratic deliberation to begin includes conditions almost unimaginable today—namely that "asymmetries in the distribution of power and resources" not cause anyone "to vote or act in any way contrary to her unconstrained preferences," and that no one be "unable . . . to participate in the process of mutual influence" (1997, 293). This is a remote "ideal scheme," they admit, and they "are under no illusions about the prospects for moving existing arrangements toward" it (1994, 287).

Before deliberative theory had been widely recognized as a distinct tendency, and well before it had achieved its near-hegemonic status, Nancy Fraser questioned the assumption that it is possible to build "barriers" around public discourse that would "bracket status differentials" (1990, 62, 65) in deliberation. And most movements have not lived such a sanctuaried democratic existence. A central feature of the sort of critical democratic epochs to which I have pointed just above is active engagement pitting democratic movements against threatening institutions and social forces—against social forms that undermine or overshadow the collective political agency of relatively less powerful groups in society. That could describe the efforts of Chartists who planned a subversive procession to carry their petition to Parliament, the sailors' councils who deposed their commanders and occupied the port in Kiel to stop another naval mission, the sitdown strikers in Flint in 1937, or the freedom riders who took their challenge to the strongest bastions of Jim Crow. In these cases, democratic life and action were not sheltered from forces and institutions that could undermine them. They challenged those threatening forces and institutions directly.

What is at issue, though, is not merely an empirical criticism rooted in the unfortunate facts of limited historical periods. For there is little reason to think the movements just named would have preferred, as a matter of principle, to look inward, if only they could have, to the perfection of democratic ideals within protective fortifications. Rather, their practice and ideas were substantively attuned to challenging overshadowing social forces. Preoccupation with walls simply fails to capture certain such vital democratic aspirations. Moreover, as long as social forces and institutions that undercut democracy persist, envisioning democratic refuges encourages us to project democracy, as we have seen, as a distant and always retreating ideal, a demand for something out of the reach of those who live in this world. And this may lead us to overlook democratic life and action as it actually is at many times for many people, a kind of active struggle with threatening forces and institutions.

Even while emphasizing refuge imagery, deliberative democrats, like others, also frequently envision democracy as an ideal relationship among citizens—another problematic conception. I mean, first, that deliberative democracy highlights a set of norms that should govern political discourse among individuals. And second, these norms essentially define citizenship for deliberative theory. "Citizens and their representatives," according to one account, are "expected to justify the laws they would impose on one another" (Gutmann and Thompson 2004, 3). This is meant to illuminate "the process of deliberation" but also to provide "substantive standards of free and equal citizenship" (48).[7] Deliberative theory focuses, above all, on an ideal "ethics" that, as one interpreter puts it, "outlines the citizen's responsibilities and duties" (Green 2010a, 59).

Of course, the shape of any polity, democratic or otherwise, entails a type of citizenship, a characteristic form of membership and participation.

Democracy's vision of what citizens can or should be able to do is crucial, as is the inclusive, egalitarian aspiration that every adult resident of a polity be recognized as a citizen. And different "models" of democracy can be distinguished in terms of varying views of citizenship. But viewing democracy primarily as an ideal relationship among citizens, however attractive and familiar, risks two sorts of reductionism, each with its own perils. First, envisioning a person chiefly as a citizen involves something like synecdoche, first thinking of the whole person as just one of her social roles, and then envisioning society chiefly as a relationship among such role-bearers.[8] If a synecdoche of this sort becomes second nature, it can distort our thinking. Not everyone democrats should care about meets the legal requirements for citizenship. And even those who do qualify always inhabit or live out other roles as well, roles worthy of democratic scrutiny.[9]

During certain critical historical periods for democracy, many of the most significant and democratically troubling social relations and antagonisms could not be fully theorized as relations among citizens. Such a view would clearly drain much of the democratic meaning from feminist struggles, for example, since it is well recognized that much of what feminists have had to say about gender and democracy could not be straitjacketed into a claim for equal citizenship.[10] It would be naive, in theorizing critical epochs—or indeed any epoch—to concentrate on relations among people in their citizen roles while neglecting the way that the citizens, as a whole (or workers or consumers or migrants) have often seen their agency dwarfed by institutions and forces such as Gilded Age railroads and trusts, Eastern bloc state bureaucracies, military juntas, or global corporations.[11] The point here is not entirely distinct from the one about democracy as refuge. One might think about the connection in the following way. Deliberative democrats could reply: however unequal and unfavorable the terms on which consumers or workers face corporations, the point is that all these people should also face each other a certain way *as citizens*. But this is akin to saying that there is or should be a kind of democratic sanctuary, separate from the rest of the political world, where ideal citizens interact.

The other reductionism in viewing democracy as a relation among citizens involves translating and condensing what we desire to be true about social relations and structure into aspirations concerning citizens, their traits, and their behavior. The reduction of democracy to the way citizens should relate entails the danger of reducing the critique of social

24

institutions and forces to the critique of individuals and their conduct. In deliberative theory more broadly, this reductionist danger is obvious in a basic contrast between what is highly developed in the approach and what is generally (but not always) neglected. Much of deliberative theory, as I have pointed out, consists of injunctions directed toward individuals and groups. Indeed, Marc Stears has criticized deliberative democrats for "specifying often in numbing detail the precise behavioral commitments citizens of . . . an ideal society should have" (2010, 211). Far less common are detailed explanatory critiques of existing undemocratic social, political, and economic institutions. Deliberative theorists, Carole Pateman observes, devote little attention to explicating and criticizing "structural features of the wider society" (2012, 10).

A third problematic conceptualization is an institutional, often governmental view of democracy. That "democracy" means "a form of government" is an assumption of many models. It is "an idea that has been taken for granted now for about 200 years by political science," and it may seem to many people to be little more than a truism (Held 2006, 1; Manicas 1987, 34). Deliberative theory, in its highlighting of discourse, seems to point away from an institutional conception, but noted theorists reinstate the emphasis by suggesting that deliberation is simply the best practice for democracy, viewed again as a regime. Rawls, for example, explains that his deliberative theory is meant for a "modern constitutional democracy," a term he uses interchangeably with "democratic regime" (1996, 11). Jack Knight and James Johnson, echoing Schumpeter, likewise define democracy as a particular kind of "institutional arrangement" (1997, 279). And other prominent deliberative theorists similarly identify democracy as "a form of government" (Gutmann and Thompson 2004, 7; Rawls 1999b, 132, 139) and deliberation as a practice that is particularly "appropriate" to it (Bohman 1996, 24).[12]

When we consider critical democratic epochs in all their imperfection, however, we face a quandary in applying institution-centered conceptions. If, according to some definition, we say that the political institutions of such an epoch—say, the United States of the civil rights era—qualify it as a democracy, we risk complacency, relegating democratic restructuring to the status of nonessential reform. Things are no better if we simply reject the democratic-regime label. Even when political institutions are oppressive or exclusive, democracy may be manifested in some form in these eras, often in movements themselves. Writing off the polity of a critical era as *not a democracy* returns us to a problem mentioned above: "democracy" is made to seem like little more than a distant end, an ideal whose most notable characteristic is its remoteness from concrete conditions, an ideal that therefore stands in uncertain, undertheorized, relation to movements' actual situations. The governmental view of democracy is particularly problematic when democracy is taken to mean a definite, predetermined set of institutions. Democracy can take on quite a variety of institutional forms, some emphasizing representation, others emphasizing meaningful participation, and so on. The democratic ambition, one might think, faces a constantly shifting set of challenges, to which any particular institutions are merely provisional responses.

Focusing on whether a set of political institutions should count as a democracy can also direct attention away from something that ought to be part of any assessment of democratic health and vibrancy: democracy as it is actually enacted, experienced, and lived. It is crucial that we transcend democracy as an institution or structure and consider democracy also as activity or action. I do not mean just that certain democratic activities should be specified and described. Rather, democracy should be theorized in light of a balanced general conception of action. Of course, institutions and structures are sustained by action, and action relies on structural, institutional prerequisites.[13] So in conceptualizing democracy we cannot dispense with institutions. But by itself, the emphasis on whether a set of institutions is democratic is one-sided.

A fourth common but limiting conception accepted by deliberative theory treats democracy as a way of reaching decisions. A familiar bombastic trope—the voters decide!—pervades quadrennial election journalism in the United States. And a similar decision-centered frame (without necessarily the fixation on voting) has nearly as strong a hold on many scholars.[14] Among deliberative theorists, Knight and Johnson define democracy as an institutional arrangement "for making binding political decisions" (1997, 279). John Dryzek likewise argues that the deliberative approach focuses attention on "the ability of all individuals subject to a collective decision to engage in authentic deliberation about that decision" (2000, v).[15] All this is in contrast to participatory approaches that, as R. W. Hildreth (2012) and Harry Boyte (2011) argue, put more emphasis on democracy as action.

No one would want to argue that democracy has nothing to do with decisions. Democrats of all kinds want decisions, when they are made, to be made in certain ways. But the potentially distortive effect of *decision*

26

as an exclusive way of explicating critical democratic epochs becomes clear as soon as we recognize that little of what seems most troubling about these periods is reducible to how actual decisions were made. Neither the Depression of the 1930s, nor the runaway forces of war leading up to the rise of soldiers' and sailors' councils in 1919, nor the culture and relations of sex and marriage before second-wave feminism are attributable simply to malign decisions or poor decision making. Yet large numbers of people were actively involved, perhaps unintentionally, in producing or maintaining these social forms. And such undemocratic forces and institutions, inherited from the past, often accepted as natural or unchangeable, also constituted unacknowledged preconditions, shaping and hindering political action.

There are really two issues involved here. First, conscious decision is just one possible moment in the always ongoing flow of social action. And reflective, joint decision making, viewed as a distinctive common activity, is just that: one form of activity among others. Public decision making should be democratic, of course. But even in the best of times, much of social and political life flows on without distinct efforts at public reflection, let alone preauthorizing decision, by those involved. This entails a set of important democratic concerns. Without deciding to do so, people are almost always collectively reproducing their social world, including undemocratic institutions and runaway forces that escape their collective control. Many of these things are taken for granted or accepted as natural and unchangeable—not even subject to potential decision. So to employ the language of an old debate in political science, the challenges to democracy often have to do with "nondecisions" (Bachrach and Baratz 1970, ch. 3), a term I shall use to refer broadly to the unintended consequences and unacknowledged preconditions of social action. In addition, democracy involves all kinds of worthy activities, like organizing and rallying, that are not captured by the idea of making "decisions" together. Democrats should care about sustaining them.

An exclusive focus on ideal decision making, far from being ethically too stringent, may be insufficiently ambitious for democratic theory. Democratic critique must consider directly issues never subject to or even proposed for proper decision making. And it should reflect critically on democratizing the whole ongoing, tumultuous process of social action, that is, not just the exceptional moments of reflection and decision, but also unacknowledged enablements, constraints, and unintended consequences of common action.

27

The conceptualizations discussed so far are related to yet another, this one unique to deliberative theory: noncoercion as a democratic ideal. Perhaps the most cited formulation in the deliberative literature is Habermas's claim that principled communication "rules out all external or internal coercion other than the force of the better argument" (1990, 88–89). Deliberation, writes Dryzek, values "persuasion rather than coercion, manipulation, or deception" (2000, 1).[16] Of course, coercion—compelling others to act through force or threats—pervades actual politics. It is openly coercive for an interest group to threaten that it will support a challenger over an incumbent. Likewise, it is coercive even for cyclists to pack a city council meeting to show the depth and fervency of support for new bike lanes. Such action always implies a kind of threat. So it is no surprise that deliberative theorists end up treating noncoercive democratic association as a refuge from ordinary politics.

The connection of noncoercion to the view of democracy as an ideal relationship among citizens is also quite close. To see why, we should consider the distinction between coercion and power. Though integrally related to power, coercion is by no means identical to it. Power is what allows or enables people to coerce. Power refers properly to "those capacities to act possessed by social agents in virtue of the enduring relations in which they participate" (Isaac 1987b, 80). It is not a kind of act, like coercion, but a capacity for action derived from social structures (Ball 1978; Isaac 1987a; Isaac 1987b; Wartenberg 1992). Political actors can decide to coerce or not to coerce, as emphasized by deliberative theory, but they cannot simply decide to have more or less power. Now deliberative democrats do not necessarily all eschew writing about power—especially power in the guise of capacities to engage in deliberation. But they have generally chosen to frame deliberative democracy around the norm that citizens should not coerce each other, rather than a critique of unequal social power relations. For the most part, they have not even emphasized a commitment to equal empowerment, especially if equal empowerment means equal ability to struggle with others in ongoing political contestation. The ideal of noncoercion is also entangled with the deliberative focus on decisions, as well. For its proponents, as I have suggested, deliberation is not a contested activity, a kind of political struggle for which they would like participants to be adequately empowered, but a decision process in which coercive exercises of power are ruled out of order. It is a pure way of reaching decisions in which, again, the only force should be "the force of the better argument." Or as

Rawls puts it, in principled deliberation, people reach common decisions "for the right reasons," not just because of an assessment of the "balance of political and social forces" or the possibility of "sanction" (1996, xxxix–xl, xliv, 143).

For much of the period when the deliberative paradigm was rising to dominance in democratic theory, its proponents denied that there was any discrepancy between noncoercion and the historical practices of movements. They portrayed Martin Luther King Jr., for example, as a committed deliberative democrat who used only powerful arguments as weapons—and all for the benefit of deliberative "public reason" itself (Dryzek 2000, 51, 101; Dryzek and Dunleavy 2009, 219; Gutmann and Thompson 1996, 133; Rawls 1996, li–liii, 249–251).[17] According to Gutmann and Thompson, King's practice "exemplifies a politics of deliberative engagement" because he "publicly" invoked "values that all Americans could acknowledge as important" and merely called on "American citizens to live up to their professed principles" (1999, 254). Missing from this portrayal is recognition that King was a gifted strategist: nonviolent but well versed in the economy of coercion, he faced entrenched racism from opponents who certainly did not "acknowledge" his cause and resistance even from sympathizers who denied the need to do anything soon about racial caste. More generally, the movements active in critical democratic eras, as deliberative theorists argue, have indeed challenged people to live up to certain widely professed values and have engaged in other communicative practices. But these discursive practices have usually been integrally connected with nondeliberative actions. In pursuit of immediate democratizing change, they have engaged in disruptive civil disobedience that forced others to alter routines and to act differently, they have provoked crises that undermined some people's interests and challenged others' complacency, and they have staged actions that threatened governments with a loss of credibility. And movements have not used coercion solely to bring about better discourse. Very often they have achieved recognizably democratic goals, both structural and discursive, through coercive action. Increasingly, certain deliberative theorists have felt at least some of the force of this objection, as we shall see.

Elite Theory and the Problematic Conceptions

Elite theories of democracy have roots in the work of Vilfredo Pareto and Max Weber, as well as that of Joseph Schumpeter. And aspects of elite theory have found wide expression, as well, in works by Friedrich Hayek and Samuel Huntington. In political science, however, it is Schumpeter's formulation in *Capitalism, Socialism and Democracy* ([1942] 1976) that has proved to be the touchstone. And it is in political science that a form of elite theory continues to have its strongest, though sometimes implicit, hold.

Schumpeter claimed that elite domination of politics was all but inevitable because ordinary people lacked the necessary capacities for meaningful participation. This dim view of ordinary people's political agency—their "will," as he put it—undergirds his own versions of the widely shared problematic conceptualizations we have been considering: democracy behind walls, democracy as a relationship among citizens, democracy as a regime, and democracy as a way of making decisions. Schumpeter contended that any "common" will—any reasoned plan of action by a public—would have to be constructed from the will of individuals. But psychology and economics, he said, had exploded the idea of "a definite will that is the prime mover of [individual] action" ([1942] 1976, 256). Even under the best circumstances, individuals often did not really know what they wanted, were buffeted by whims and ill-considered fancies, and did a poor job translating these into action. People acting in groups were worse off (257). So it was madness to entertain any theory of democracy that assigned a central role to reasoned public will-formation. The only political act of which ordinary people were capable, Schumpeter contended, was accepting leadership, and so democracy could signify just one thing: a political "method" of acquiescence, an "institutional arrangement for arriving at political decisions in which individuals acquire the power to decide by means of a competitive struggle for the people's vote" (269). The only role for the public was voting occasionally for new leaders.

We already have a good idea of the general limitations of intramural democracy, democracy as decision making and so on. Here I need only note that Schumpeter's negative assessment of popular political abilities gives his version of each of these widely shared conceptualizations a deeply pessimistic, at times almost misanthropic, character. For example, Schumpeter did not just argue that ordinary people were incapable of the political feats purportedly assigned them by traditional democratic theory. He thought that it was best as well that there be barriers between the general population and those really making decisions on behalf of the public. Hence he advanced a different fortified, intramural view of democracy—but democracy as quarantine rather than democracy as refuge, as in deliberative theory. Democracy was "rule of the politician" ([1942] 1976, 285), and this required that a small cadre of inspired leaders manage politics while most people were kept out of the way: "The voters outside of parliament must respect the division of labor between themselves and the politicians they elect . . . [O]nce they have elected an individual, political action is his business and not theirs" (295). This ruled out, of course, formal sets of demands made by citizens of their representatives, but Schumpeter insisted that even "bombarding [politicians] with letters and telegrams" should be excluded. Popular participation needed to be confined to particular moments and places, lest it interfere with the healthy functioning of political leadership.

And of course, Schumpeter was hardly alone in this. Out of a fear of the growing power of the employed masses, specifically, Hayek also envisioned mass participation confined to particular institutions and limited intervals, with reliable elites carrying out essential political tasks, curtailing the danger of populist contagion infecting either the state or the economy. Hayek's vision, however, was more institutionally distinctive than Schumpeter's, and in his later work he called for most significant legislative powers to be confined to an upper house elected by a very narrow segment of the population (1979, ch. 13). Similarly, Samuel Huntington's analysis of a crisis in the United States attributed it to "democratic distemper," which he said proved the need to protect elites from "democratic politics" itself (1975, 73, 102, 106).

The same skeptical view of collective agency characterizes Schumpeter's adoption of a version of democracy as an ideal relation among citizens. Schumpeter's dim view of mass capacities gave him little reason to regard restrictions on suffrage as objectionable. "Every *populus*" should be allowed to "define himself," Schumpeter argued ([1942] 1976, 244–245), and he well understood that this self-definition could mean excluding women, "Orientals," "Jews," and "Negroes" (244, 244n12). What could it matter if some people were denied political rights that they could not meaningfully exercise anyway? No such exclusion from suffrage, however broad—nor any imbalance of power between citizens and elected politicians—could violate the conditions of democracy as long as the right relationship pertained between those actually deemed citizens.

Schumpeter's negative judgment of popular "will" is also entwined with an institutional, governmental view of democracy. Given the view of mass agency articulated in *Capitalism, Socialism and Democracy*,

Schumpeter could hardly define democracy there in terms of meaningful common action, let alone in terms of the realization of democratic values. So it is little surprise that Schumpeter adopted a minimalist, government-centered definition, one of the most influential and most often repeated: democracy as an "institutional arrangement," in Schumpeter's well-known phrase ([1942] 1976, 269).

Finally, it is due to a sour assessment of popular agency, as well, that Schumpeter's theory incorporates a particular version of democracy as a way of making decisions. According to Schumpeter, the "democratic method," gave certain elite individuals "the power to decide" ([1942] 1976, 269). The fact that Schumpeter denied ordinary people this power of political decision making, then, should not obscure the fact that he simultaneously assigned it to professional politicians of the kind he admired, such as William Gladstone. Schumpeter was not rejecting the idea that democracy is primarily about decisions or arguing that the "decision" frame is misleading for democratic theory, but simply arguing that the public does not decide—that in fact, the public had to kept away from decision making.

The influence of this way of thinking in empirical political science, broadly, is well established.[18] Perhaps more surprising is its lasting power in "normative" democratic theory, even at a time when deliberative theory dominates. Jeffrey Edward Green's *The Eyes of the People* (2010a) is an especially interesting case. Green's intellectual genealogy emphasizes Weber over Schumpeter, but that fact reinforces an important point: Schumpeter's elite approach is illustrative of a wide tendency in democratic theory. The most novel aspect of Green's provocative book is his advocacy of an "ocular" model of democracy (3–31), in which ordinary people are cast not as true actors but as spectators whose gaze disciplines politicians. This he prefers to a "vocal" model (64–119), in which "citizen-governors" (32) make political decisions through their representatives. But much of Green's critical, deconstructive work is done by arguments deeply resonant with Schumpeter's critique of the "will" of ordinary voters (though Green is careful to avoid Schumpeter's contempt for ordinary people). Indeed, in aligning himself with Schumpeter, Green emphasizes "the very real sense in which most citizens on most issues lack opinions, preferences, interests, and values waiting to be represented" (2010b, 269). He adds later, "nonparticipation, nondecision, hierarchy, nonpreference, [and] spectatorial passivity" are "foundational features" of contemporary democracy (273).

32

The mature form of Schumpeter's elite theory of democracy has, for those who understand his trajectory, an ironic cast. His offensive against the supposed "classical" theory of "collective action" ([1942] 1976, 265) is far more destructive than perhaps he realized, and easily demolishes, with its intended target, any basis for crediting the agency of democratic movements. But Schumpeter had at one time shared with the council movement's most ardent admirers the view that the councils represented an extraordinary bottom-up organizational innovation that had the potential to transform capitalist societies into democratic socialist ones. It is difficult to know how this could be accomplished by the same people who, in their guise as an "electoral mass," were "incapable of action other than a stampede" (283). Schumpeter's project finally led him to the political arguments for which he was most famous, but which also seem to deny the premises and concerns that caused him to start on his intellectual journey in the first place.

Ideal and Nonideal Theory

To find that there is a gap between the way things are and the way, on consideration, we think they should be, is a fundamental experience of political life. What exactly should we make of this gap in democratic theory? One answer is to posit a sharp, genuine, and meaningful distinction between a pure, distinct theory of the way things should be and the subsidiary study of the many ways in which the world does not live up to these stringent demands. In contemporary ethics and political theory, this distinction is often described as one between ideal and nonideal theory. However intuitively appealing, though, this dichotomization does not help resolve the conceptual problems I have been exploring concerning democracy and movements. In fact, in some ways, relying upon it exacerbates them. So ultimately it makes sense to try to frame democratic theory in a way that does not rely on the distinction.

According to many who champion or just take for granted the ideal/nonideal distinction, it is obvious that the ideal view necessarily takes philosophical priority over the nonideal. In *A Theory of Justice,* for example, John Rawls insists that "ideal theory" provides "the only basis for the systematic grasp" of nonideal problems (1999b, 8). But what, precisely, is the "ideal" theory that lays claim to this primary status? It not simply normative theory, as Charles Mills points out (2005, 166, 170). All critical thinking is normative, or value laden, in spirit. Nor is ideal theory merely ideal in the sense of being *abstract*. All social theory requires some kind of abstraction, as well (Mills 2005, 166, 173), some simplification, some standing back from the concrete complexity of social life. "Ideal theory" really utilizes, in particular, what Mills terms "the ideal-as-idealized-model," a "model of how [some phenomenon] should work," including, comprehensively, "what people should be like," "how they should treat each other," and "how society should be structured" (168).[19]

Just as important, positing "ideal theory" of this kind means positing its alternative, "nonideal" theory, too. This dualist vision, however justified, often posits ideal theory as a field or phase of inquiry, distinct from sociology, psychology, history, and political science.[20] Many proponents suggest that ideal theory should be completed first—before worrying about how the political or social world really operates or is constructed. Rawls writes: "Non-ideal theory presupposes that ideal theory is already on hand" (1999a, 89–90). The "nonideal," it seems, should be understood only as an application of "ideal" theory to the findings of sociology, history, and so on. Mills puts it this way: "Ideal theory either tacitly represents the actual as a simple deviation from the ideal, not worth theorizing in its own right, or claims that starting from the ideal is at least the best way of realizing it" (2005, 168). Given this alleged priority for the ideal, Raymond Geuss calls this approach "ethics-first" (2008, 1) and Bernard Williams contends that it treats political thought as just "applied moral philosophy" (2005, 77).

The distinction between "ideal" and "nonideal" theory can slip readily into other related ones, such as the positing of moral "ends" as one set of activities or experiences, and the mere practical, political "means" of achieving them, as quite another—the view that some experiences or actions are valuable in themselves, intrinsically and always, while others are never more than instrumental in realizing those truly desirable ends. In the realm of democratic theory, these dualisms often support an apparent distinction between democracy as an ideal set of valued practices and relations, and democratization as no more than the contingent process or means of achieving ideal democracy.

The ideal/nonideal distinction pervades deliberative democracy, especially deliberative theorists' response to criticism that draws on the experiences of movements (Stears 2010, 8–9). For Rawls, deliberative "public reason" is "an ideal conception of citizenship" that presents "how things might be," not how they are (1996, 213). Gutmann and Thompson contrast "the ideals of democratic deliberation" with "the nonideal cir-cumstances of politics" (1996, 3). And their definition of deliberative democracy (2004, 7) clearly constitutes an idealized model in Mills's sense. Archon Fung refers to deliberative democracy as a "revolutionary political ideal," not because it emphasizes a theory of revolutionary action (it doesn't) but because it stands in radical contrast to "the decidedly non-ideal circumstances that characterize contemporary politics" (2005, 397, 398). Of course, this does not mean that recent deliberative scholars have taken no interest in "nonideal" theory. Some of the most interesting recent deliberative work contains both ideal and nonideal aspects—but carefully distinguished from each other. Mansbridge and her colleagues, for example, differentiate between the rule that "coercive power" be "ideally absent" from "decision-making"—"a regulative ideal, impos-sible to achieve"—and the way the world actually works (2010, 80).[21]

The ideal/nonideal dichotomy, turned on its head, structures Schumpeter's work, too. He shunned arguments that prioritized ideal over nonideal theory. He was ferocious in deriding "the classical doc-trine of democracy" as "patently contrary to fact" and thus tenable only as a kind of "religious belief" or, tellingly, an "ideal schema of things" ([1942] 1976, 264, 265, 266). Proponents of "classical" democracy, he said, insulated themselves from both fact and logic, and looked neces-sarily on criticism "not merely as error but as sin" (266). In contrast, he said he founded his own theory of elite democracy on facts "known to all," a vision of politics that was "truer to life" (265, 269).

Deliberative theory, it is worth noting, does not merely embrace an ideal/nonideal distinction or contain a pronounced strain of ideal theory. The idealizing strain is, in addition, usually centered on how individuals should act. This is evident, as I have suggested, in the view of democracy as an idealized sort of relationship among citizens. To the degree that pro-ponents wish to argue for some sort of improved deliberation now—under nonideal social and political conditions—they must emphasize delibera-tion in terms of norms describing how deliberators should behave in the present. The structural aspiration that participants in deliberation should have "equal opportunity to influence the process" and "equal resources" (Mansbridge et al. 2010, 66) may presently be utopian. But ideal theory can still urge people now to "treat one another with mutual respect and equal concern," "listen to one another, and speak truthfully" (66).

The ideal/nonideal framework gives deliberative theory several ways of responding to the critiques I have made of democracy as refuge or quarantine, democracy as a relation between citizens, democracy as a set of institutions, and democracy as decision making. Those critiques, as I have laid them out, are all based on the observation that these conceptualizations exclude the democratic practices and challenges of movements in critical democratic eras. The first and most characteristic response, as I have pointed out, has been to stand the ground of ideal theory alone by insisting (unconvincingly) that certain favored movements have actually embodied deliberative ideals, redescribing their conduct (tendentiously) in deliberative terms.[22] Another response might be to dismiss critiques like mine as misdirected nonideal objections to ideal theory. But either of these retreats to the high ground of the purely ideal naturally tends to limit the scope and present relevance of deliberative theory, as some proponents themselves have admitted. As one deliberative scholar puts it, emphasizing the need for dramatic "egalitarian political, social, and economic conditions" as a precondition to deliberation "offer[s] little guidance regarding the responsibilities of deliberative democrats in the decidedly nonideal circumstances that characterize contemporary politics" (Fung 2005, 398). Similarly, ideal deliberative theory might provide the tools for criticizing some of the opponents of movements in critical eras—whether antilabor Pinkerton agents or southern White Citizens' Councils—as *undeliberative*. But this epithet sheds little light on the substantive challenges or the contributions of movements.

Some deliberative theorists, then, have begun to entertain the doings of movements as part of nonideal deliberative theory—to suggest in general that nonideal circumstances may sometimes justify nonideal behavior, even though this should not change anyone's view of deliberative ideals themselves.

The ideal/nonideal framework itself—what Geuss terms the "ethics-first" approach to political philosophy—is vulnerable to a number of broad critiques. One is that it often seems to deny autonomy to properly political theorizing, treating politics as just a special case of ethics, and relegating crucial concepts concerning power and conflicts of interest to secondary significance, behind purportedly pure ethical principles (Shapiro 1999b; Williams 2005, 77). Valorizing ideal theory necessarily assigns less importance to the substantive analysis of the nonideal, to the texture and operation of racism, patriarchy, exploitation, violence, or the bureaucratic state. But these are problems, as Mills points out, that cannot just be derived from idealized models by "*modus ponens* or some other logical rule" (2005, 178). And so the prioritization of the ideal may tend to put off indefinitely the turn to nonideal theory, a phenomenon of which there are many examples (Mills 2005, 179–180).

Some critics have done more than champion the distinctive importance of nonideal theory. They have contended, most sharply, that where ideal theory is concerned, there simply is no there there—no possibility of a distinct, purely ideal standpoint, established first, from which to judge the actual, nonideal world. If so, those who think they are beginning elsewhere than in the real, imperfect world can easily fall prey to one kind of delusion or another. Practitioners of "ethics-first," in Geuss's estimation, are in danger of succumbing "to a kind of fetishism, attributing to a set of human conceptual inventions a significance that they do not have" (2008, 16).

These are powerful arguments, and they deserve recognition, but my goal with respect to the problem of the "ethics-first" approach is not to resolve conclusively a pervasive difficulty in political thinking but to make some progress in democratic theory, specifically. Some deliberative theorists have tried to answer critiques like those outlined above. They have tried to work through the challenges faced by movements in critical democratic eras—while holding on to the dichotomous conceptual structure that distances ideal from nonideal theory. But this effort entails its own difficulties.

Incorporating Movements in Nonideal Democratic Theory
Struggling toward Democracy, Part I

A number of advocates have acknowledged the difficulty that deliberative democracy traditionally has had in coming to terms with the challenges and strategies of social movements. A dozen years ago, Iris Marion Young (2001) highlighted the tensions between deliberative and activist citizenship, with considerable sympathy for the latter, under actually existing conditions. And more recent articles by Archon Fung ("Deliberation before the Revolution," 2005) and Jane Mansbridge and colleagues ("The Place of Self-Interest and the Role of Power in Deliberative Democracy," 2010), in particular, are illustrative of attempts to acknowledge and remedy the vulnerability of deliberative theory to what Young (2001) termed "activist challenges."[23] To a greater extent than many of their deliberative predecessors, Fung as well as Mansbridge and colleagues look unflinchingly at certain coercive and nondeliberative tactics in the social movement repertoire. But while they seek a richer and more sympathetic understanding of "nonideal" situations, they abandon neither the ideal/nonideal framework itself nor the ultimate priority of ideal deliberative theory.

Fung, it is clear, has an acute understanding of the limits of ideal theory when it stands on its own. He emphasizes that the achievement of a truly deliberative democracy would require "dramatically more egalitarian political, social, and economic conditions than exist in any contemporary society" (2005, 397). He also admits that such an emphasis on the disparity between actual and ideal offers "little guidance" to democrats in the here and now (398). No one wants simply to say that "all bets are off 'before the revolution,'" he says (399).[24] So Fung tries to find a way through this dilemma—not by jettisoning the ideal/nonideal distinction that structures it, but by offering "principles to guide the political actions of deliberative democrats who act in a wide range of suboptimal circumstances" (400). The result is a set of semi-ideal principles for nonideal times—"fidelity," "charity," "exhaustion," and "proportionality"—along with a nuanced discussion of how to apply them. Topically, the scope of the piece by Mansbridge and colleagues is broader, acknowledging the conditional legitimacy of self-interest, nondeliberative negotiation, and voting in real, nonideal democracy. In this context, the coauthors argue that it may be ethical for movements to use coercive tactics like the strike, especially to create "the conditions for good deliberation" (2010, 82–83).

An initial hint of the difficulty even these more tolerant deliberative theorists face in coming to terms with movements and critical democratic eras can be found in the discussion of "coercive power" in "The Place of Self-Interest." The coauthors present an uncertain and inconsistent conceptualization of power, the partial result, it seems, of an attempt to hold fast to an ideal value—noncoercion—while opening the door to a fuller nonideal vision of a political world that is structured by stark differences in power.

Two different vocabularies intertwine in the key passages. One is a vocabulary of "power as capacity."[25] The other is a vocabulary of causal acts or exercises of power.[26] There is a real distinction to be made between these sets of terms. It is one thing to refer to a potential or a capacity, and quite another to refer to its actualization. We normally distinguish, for example, between gravity and an object actually falling, or between an athlete's ability and her performance in a particular race. If we did not, it would be difficult to justify pushing a vase away from the edge of a table, and incoherent to note that someone has declined or failed to do something we think they could do. I have already argued that the most cogent and convincing treatments of power define it as a capacity, the capacity to act bestowed on an agent in virtue of her place in society.[27] And such an understanding of power makes sense of the two vocabularies just mentioned. According to this view, coercion, usually defined as compelling by force or threat, is properly understood as an exercise of power rather than as power itself.

Viewed this way, it is fair to say that on the whole deliberative theorists have traditionally had much more to say about coercion than about power. Their approach, that is, has generally been to advocate the rule that deliberators should not coerce. But "The Place of Self-Interest" illustrates how difficult it is to retain this exclusive emphasis when considering, sympathetically, the position of movements in politics as we know it. No account of democratic movements and the critical eras in which they were active can be complete without exploring the fact that such movements generally have occupied far less powerful positions in society than their opponents, and that they were therefore quite concerned to enhance their power and to use it in various political efforts. So there is a strong motivation even for some deliberative theorists to incorporate, alongside the critique of coercive conduct, a language of power as "potential" and of "power as capacity," the power that accrues to those who "occupy" the status quo (Mansbridge et al. 2010, 81).

But the response of Mansbridge and her coauthors to this imperative is unstable. At one point, they posit power, confusingly, as *either* "actual or potential" (2010, 80n44). At other points, however, they seem to adopt a version of the behaviorist understanding of power, built around hoary illustrations of "A" causing "B" to do "what B would not otherwise have done" (80). But the behaviorist approach to power was meant precisely to deny that one could coherently talk about power as a potential.[28] "Power," according to this decades-old view, could only properly be invoked when one agent was actively causing another to do something. According to this definition, power was by no means "actual *or* potential"; it was exclusively actual. This empiricist conceptualization, then, cannot work for Mansbridge and colleagues, and so they do not adhere to it consistently. They stipulate, for example, that merely "occupying the status quo gives one power."[29] But if so, then power is, after all, something possessed in virtue of one's position in some social relation or structure (81). And once possessed, it is something that may or

39

may not be exercised.[30] This suggests that fixing solely on the coercive *exercise* of power touches only the surface of democratic troubles.

It is crucial to recognize, behind the shifting positions, the real dilemma at hand. It concerns whether to focus democratic theory on the critique of unequal power relations in society or on criticizing agents who, contrary to certain ideals, exercise the power they have. It is about whether movement tactics are always to be seen as an uncomfortable contradiction with ideal democracy or whether, in light of power relations, they may sometimes be seen as an enactment of real, living democracy.

This brings us back to the problematic conceptions discussed earlier and the way they are handled in this more recent work. I have argued that traditional deliberative theory—what Mansbridge and colleagues term "classic" deliberative theory—tends to posit democracy as a refuge, a haven from many of the typical features and practices of politics as we know it. But this is hardly less true of some of those who have tried to incorporate movements—and the coercive strategies they often use—within the nonideal domain. The purely ideal gestures of deliberative theory sometimes seem to portray deliberation as a practice for a future on the far side of revolutionary change. But nonideal inclusions of movements call on contemporary actors to create distinct deliberative sanctuaries in the present. "Improving deliberation," Fung insists, does not require altering "deep structures of inequality" (2005, 413). But how to honor deliberative ideals, then? When inequality divides people who otherwise are willing to deliberate, he says, it is incumbent on deliberative activists *"to bracket the effect of these inequalities on deliberation by appealing to the goodwill . . . of participants"* (406–407)—that is, to create a deliberative refuge of a particular kind.

In a similar vein, Mansbridge and colleagues argue that deliberative theorists "might" justify strikes—even though they are coercive—if they are undertaken to create "the conditions for good deliberation" between labor and management (2010, 82). Notice that this is quite different from recognizing the value of strikes, the most familiar of all tactics in the labor movement repertoire, as protecting or enacting the autonomy of one's life activity, as a way to develop one's political agency, as politically educative, as a uniquely appropriate form of political action and participation for workers within the institutions that are most crucial to them, as a way of permanently improving the economic and political power of workers, or just as a way to redress economic inequality, regardless of whether this is accomplished through changed discourse. Mansbridge and her coauthors in fact call on strikers to create a most remarkable kind of deliberative refuge. If the ideal goal of a strike is really, as they say it should be, just proper deliberation—discourse that itself is not touched by coercion—then to be successful, this nonideal *deliberative* strike, though in itself coercive, would have to somehow bring about a decisive break with the coercion-tinged, power-infused past. After the strike, power and coercion would have to cease to affect discourse between labor and management. Management would not act or agree, as they might have done in the past, because of the threat of another labor action. Rather, the strikers' hope would have to be that management would at once forget about strikes and sincerely acknowledge the justice of demands they had previously denied. To put this differently, within the deliberative refuge to be created by the strike, there could be no consideration of or reference to the world "outside" deliberation, in which labor and management can sanction each other, a world in which they confront each other with differing powers.[31] Each side would look at the other only as an equal, ideal deliberator. So this apparent nonideal concession to movement tactics yields in fact an even more rigorous version of deliberation as refuge, one that contains an extraordinary demand that coercion spontaneously negate itself—that it form, in itself, the barrier behind which future noncoercive deliberation can thrive.[32]

Deliberative theory traditionally focuses, we have seen, on democracy as an ideal relationship among citizens. This obscures democratically significant interactions between people in their noncitizen roles and risks reducing questions of how society is or should be structured to questions of individual conduct. So much I have already argued. The work of some deliberative theorists in trying to open up a wider space for nonideal conditions also reflects a problematic citizen-relations emphasis. Fung, for example, agrees that "many claims of deliberative democratic theorists relate to the obligations of political actors and institutions under highly favorable circumstances" (2005, 398). His intervention is different chiefly in elucidating the "responsibilities of deliberative democrats" not in general but in "nonideal circumstances" (398). The discussion of strikes in "The Place of Self-Interest" shares this focus. It is not directly an exploration of how the actual structure of the existing economy may undermine democracy, but about whether or when political agents may justifiably strike. Either way, the main question is: how should certain political agents behave? This demand for a certain kind of deliberative-friendly behavior under nonideal conditions is what leads

Stears to point to a "paradox of politics" in deliberative theory: the creation of an ideal deliberative future seems to require tomorrow's ideal deliberators to be active today (2010, 10–11).

The ideal citizen-relations focus in nonideal deliberative theory—the emphasis on judging political agents for whether they follow certain norms—is not limited to scrutinizing the behavior of deliberative activists themselves. These activists' "choice of means," Fung argues, should in turn be "scaled according to the extent to which political adversaries and opponents reject the procedural norms of deliberation and the substantive values that ground it" (2005, 403). But this way of framing the problem entails the danger of reducing structural barriers to democracy to individual, essentially volitional, acts on the part of adversaries. Movements face opponents who enjoy a more advantaged position in society and politics. Should movements assume that these opponents, in making use of their unjust advantages, do so with conscious malice, so to speak—that they explicitly "reject" the proper democratic norms? If so, then according to Fung the range of justified actions for deliberative activists widens considerably. But if, as seems more likely, no one can prove such conscious malice, it seems that the same activists must patiently put up with their structural political disadvantages.

So here the bifurcation of ideal and nonideal theory combines with the fixation on norms governing the conduct of citizens to produce a sharp divergence. Most of Fung's article centers on how to act with "charity" and "proportionality" in certain nonideal cases. But when opponents "use their status or position" to close off deliberation, even these modified principles lose their force, according to Fung (2005, 404), leaving activists almost without guidance. And there is little reason to think that such a condition would be an unfortunate rarity, since Fung judges that such a lack of "willingness" on the part of many political actors "to accept deliberative transformations . . . accurately describes a large portion of political reality" (415).

The limitations of democracy-as-decision are also not transcended in these attempts to incorporate nonideal alongside ideal politics. Mansbridge and colleagues reaffirm that "democracy is a practical form of decision-making" (2010, 84). So political action, the challenging actions of movements, takes a more noted place in this work, but generally only as a prelude or sequel to what is really important: the right sort of decision making. Of course, this does not mean that there is nothing different about the decision focus of these works. In fact, alongside decision, the problem of nondecision makes an appearance. But an incomplete acknowledgment of the problem of nondecision creates another kind of instability in deliberative arguments.

First, it is important to establish how "nondecision" enters these deliberative reflections on nonideal politics. "Nondecision" can serve as a helpful contrast to "decision," as long as we recognize that it refers not to a singular event or act (Isaac 1987a) but to all the ways in which unintended consequences and unacknowledged structural preconditions affect what happens in politics and social life. "Nondecision" is, or should be, closely related to the idea of "occupying the status quo"— holding an advantaged social or political position. But for Mansbridge and colleagues, "occupying the status quo" is generally cast as a volitional act, a "use of force" or a "threat of sanction"—and so is an active violation of the norms of deliberation. And they argue that "deliberative democrats" (again the example is strikers) do not have to "cleave to the norms of deliberation when opposing parties who do not meet those norms" (2010, 83). So in this case, failing to meet deliberative norms seems to refer, narrowly, to acting deliberately to coerce or to maintain a recognized unfair advantage.[33] But if so, then in those cases where powerful opponents do not exercise their power to make threats or use force—or are not aware of violating norms by coercing or acting to maintain unfair advantage—other political actors would presumably have to stick to deliberative practices, no matter how disadvantaged they are under the structural status quo. But it is obvious that some of the most contentious debates in contemporary politics—from overcoming historical racism, to determining the causes and remedies of economic inequality, to examining the role of money in politics—turn at least as much upon whether unfair structural advantages even exist as upon what to do about them. Powerful interests often sincerely (if wrongly) deny that they have unfair or objectionable advantages and can enjoy them without actually exercising power. With this in mind, one could, as the authors of "The Place of Self-Interest" sometimes seem to suggest, broaden the meaning of *not meeting norms* to embrace instances in which preservation of the status quo is "automatic" or "unintended"— where it functions "whether or not anyone is conscious" of it (Mansbridge et al. 2010, 81). But if so, then in a very wide range of existing cases, political actors would seem to be quite free from deliberative obligations—and so, for these theorists, quite free from democratic obligations, generally.

Running through these recent deliberative reflections on real politics and movements is also a version of the problem of categorically distinguishing "means" from "ends," which I have argued is linked to the ideal/nonideal dichotomy. Since, in this work, the end remains the achievement of rigorous deliberative ideals, the movement activities that attempt to achieve them are assigned the status of mere means. So it is, for example, with strikes, as we have seen, but also, more surprisingly, with mobilizing "popular demonstrations" or "media attention" (Fung 2005, 403, 408). These are "means," Fung says, whose "choice" should be "scaled" to the challenges and carried out just to "advance deliberation" (403). This may seem like an obvious deduction from the primary value Fung places on noncoercion and deliberation. But there would seem to be more to strikes and mobilizing than instrumentally employing coercion. They may represent an insistence on autonomy in expending one's labor. They may help participants enlarge their capacities to act politically, to cooperate actively with like-minded people, or to express themselves, deliberatively or not. They also teach them to become proficient at what Max Weber called "the slow boring of hard boards": all sorts of mundane activity that, while possibly unglamorous to scholars, require skill and are the stuff of day-to-day political work. The enlargement and exercise of such basic political capacities might seem to union activists to be democratic goods.[34] But, from a deliberative standpoint, mobilizing a "disadvantaged population to participate" or developing "persuasive skills and capacities of particularly promising 'leaders'" count only as *means* to deliberative *ends* (Fung 2005, 403).[35] And so it is even with political empowerment. Even in their nonideal addition to deliberative theory, Mansbridge and colleagues place a quite secondary value on "equal power"—in particular, the equal power of the vote—even though they recognize "power in general" may mean the "capacity to act" (2010, 89, 81). Again, this equal political capacity seems valuable for them only as a means, a "practical and reasonable step" toward better deliberation (89).

Struggling toward Democracy, Part II

In *Demanding Democracy* (2010), Marc Stears takes a different approach to these same issues, an approach at once more historical and less idealizing. His starting point is the frame that has occupied the last few pages: ideal and nonideal theory and how the choice between them helps shape democratic theorists' encounters with movement tactics. Deliberative theorists, Stears argues, have addressed "what an ideal democracy would

44

look like" (11), while realists like Geuss and Williams have identified "serious imperfections in the political present" in terms he finds "depressingly pessimistic" (12). But neither side gives sustained attention, he complains, to "how citizens should behave in the here-and-now if they wish to transform the imperfect present into the better future" (11). Rather than address these mirror-image deficiencies through further critique of contemporary political theory, however, Stears looks for a way out of the dilemma in an exploration of the history of left-wing American political thought from the Progressive era to the 1970s. This leads to the central claim of his book: that in these movements and the leading figures who wrote for or with them, it is possible to identify a tradition holding that "a new democracy in the United States could be built but only if Americans cast aside many of the traditional behavioral constraints . . . and became willing relentlessly to campaign, protest, and to struggle for democratic reform" (4).

Stears's book both adopts and transcends the terms in which the debate comes to him. He determinedly gives equal weight to ideal and nonideal dimensions in the American radical tradition. So he avoids one danger of ideal theory, "reliance on the idealization to the exclusion, or at least marginalization, of the actual" (Mills 2005, 168). He also argues that his protagonists resisted Fung's solution of counting on ideal (or perhaps semi-ideal) activists in the present, an approach that founders, he argues, on the "paradox of politics."[36]

The key, for Stears, is to "disentangle" his subjects' "ideal democratic theory" from their "short-term political strategy" (2010, 23). Figures like Herbert Croly and Walter Lippmann looked ahead, in Stears's view, to the creation of "vibrant national discussion," "togetherness," and the identification of "shared goals and common values" (28–29). But in the imperfect present, in order to achieve that sort of community, they were willing to embrace "the politics of manipulation, of coalition building, and even of factional mobilization" in tactics such as the strike (26–29, 37–39, 48–53). Similarly the civil rights movement, in Stears's view, sought "a democratic political order reaching 'the majestic heights of understanding and brotherhood,'" (159) even while engaging in frankly coercive tactics designed "to reveal the fact of domination and to illustrate its locations and its mechanisms" (155) and to cause "oppressors to see the limitations of their strength" (156).

This approach to democratic politics, in giving equal weight to ideal and nonideal, does not assign such priority to the former that there is no time for the latter. Stears also shows that his subjects' approach, on its face, avoided half of the democracy-as-refuge error: insisting that democracy in the present is above all to be achieved by building protective walls. Croly, for example, argued that Americans would have to engage directly with the existing political order, "burst the frame apart," in hopes it would "crumble to the ground" (quoted in Stears 2010, 32). Democrats, according to Stears's protagonists, could also not limit their attention to decisions—neglecting either nondecisions or the broader tide of action in which decisions are immersed. It was necessary to think critically about and to challenge a kind of society that had been created, not simply by decision, but by complex historical forces, neglect, and ossified thinking: the new industrial order of the early twentieth century or the Jim Crow South. More than idealized decision making, what was needed was action, "buoyant, crusading, and militant political action" (Stears 2010, 5).

Of course, once again, it remains possible to argue that none of this touches what is truly ideal; it establishes only what is shrewd or prudent in an imperfect political world. But Stears's interpretative effort may point beyond such a conclusion. This is because there are at least two possible readings of the history he puts before us. According to one reading, all these engaged intellectuals, from Walter Lippmann to King and Tom Hayden, accepted the same dichotomous framework of ideal and nonideal, imperfect present and more perfect future, untainted ends and impure means of their achievement. Stears at times encourages such a reading—when he argues, for example, that even while embracing "coercive" means, proponents of the civil rights movement "reasserted" a "fundamental 'means/ends' distinction" (2010, 159), or again, when he discusses a Progressive debate about strikes, in which some participants argued that "in an ideal democracy citizens would behave deliberatively toward each other," but then points out that early twentieth-century America was not an ideal democracy" (50).

Within such an ideal/nonideal framework, banishing democracy-as-refuge, democracy-as-citizen-relations, and democracy-as-decision from the imperfect present would still be perfectly consistent with retaining them as hallmarks of an ideal future. One could even argue that for Stears's American leftists, the conflict between ideal norms and actual present conduct would be extremely sharp because of the equal status accorded nonideal politics. The language Stears uses to describe ideal and nonideal behavior pushes their opposition nearly to the breaking point.

On the one hand, he characterizes his protagonists' view of nonideal move-ment practices as including "the worst characteristics of the citizen body," "coercive politics," "manipulation," "factional mobilization," "devious practices," "competition," "violence," "military-like logistical innova-tion," and "blackmail" (2010, 3, 39, 50, 73, 74). On the other, he pres-ents the ideal as "vibrant national discussion," devotion to the "common good," "togetherness," "the communicative ideal," and "the majestic heights of understanding and brotherhood" (28, 29, 95, 159). As Stears puts it, the former, though possibly necessary for betterment, were "polit-ical strategies and behaviors" that would actually be "undesirable, even illegitimate, in an improved future state" (147). Such terminology seems to suggest, again, that nonideal conduct of this kind is a means only, worthless in itself.

But Stears's rich material may lend itself to another reading—another interpretation of how American radicals understood the collective action they endorsed. First, though the American radicals in question surely advanced democratic ideals, it is not certain that they all posited a true "idealized model" of democracy in Mills's sense—or that their ideals were, in any case, truly deliberative. As Stears notes, the Progressives he highlights thought that American ideas and political institutions were out of sync with new industrial American realities, and that this pre-vented citizens from recognizing common national interests (2010, 25–29). This is a standard Progressive theme. One could interpret it as reflecting a view that existing reality fell short of a fixed ideal model, but one could also understand it as indicating pragmatic advocacy of a proper fit between a society's structure and its leading ideas.[37] Relatedly, Stears's subjects seem to have argued not just that movements and activ-ists are *permitted* to take coercive action of various kinds, but that under present conditions they *ought to* do so. And their nonideal theory, as Stears presents it, seems to have focused, substantially, on developing a critical understanding of the "nonideal" workings of present society—explaining industrialization or the perseverance of Jim Crow—not just judging what individuals might and might not do under pure and impure social conditions.

Most interesting, Stears's book suggests that his protagonists' view of nonideal movement conduct may not be as sour as suggested by con-trasts like "manipulation" versus adherence to the "common good." At a number of points, Stears portrays American radicals arguing, appar-ently, for the value of nondeliberative movement activity in a way that suggests that these activities were to them neither exclusively ends nor exclusively means. Dewey, appropriately, is a particularly strong spokesman for this approach in Stears's narrative. Dewey's advocacy of the search for an "immanent spirit of democracy" in the nonideal present (2010, 99), would seem to undermine the two poles of ideal/nonideal theory from the middle.[38] And such thinking about the interdependence of means and ends would appear to animate other figures in Stears's narrative, as well, including the Progressives who argued that participation in "pressure groups" might promote the growth of democratic capacities (40) and that "trade union activity" was not just instrumentally valuable but could provide "an experience of a vigorous form of fraternity," along with "fine displays of courage and action against adversity" (51). The same goes for the civil rights activists who favored participatory democracy not merely because it was a prudential means to an end—or even because it " 'mimicked' or approximated in the present" certain "ideals of the future"—but because it could "create virtuous and uplifting experiences that were suitable for a time of conflict" (162–163).

Even when they acknowledge a limited role for coercion, deliberative democrats' view of deliberation itself still emphasizes ideal communication, ideal learning, as noncoercive; it sees deliberation as a respite from and distinct prelude to ongoing political action. Political actors reflect and learn through discussion. They decide and then they act. But Stears points out that many in the civil rights movement thought that "the primary purpose of [coercive] direct action" was itself both communicative and educational. He notes: "Marches, demonstrations, and sit-ins worked best, therefore, when they provoked a violent response from officials and from the public, laying bare for all to see the nature of the power structure of the United States" (2010, 155). Stears notes that "interwar radicals" such as those in the Congress of Industrial Organizations had a similar view (156). But this view of what we might call "experimental" political action effaces many of the parallel oppositions that structure the deliberative understanding of democracy and political action, such as coercive action versus noncoercive deliberation and reflective learning versus interventionary doing. According to such a view, coercive political action can have an educative, capacity-enhancing, communicative, epistemological value in the here and now. This perspective challenges the idea that present action in the difficult political foreground is a mere prelude to purer, more effective communication in the future—an instrumental means, intrinsically valueless, toward some valuable ideal future. It even makes experiencing and exercising power an integral part of political communication and learning, instead of something to be walled off from them. It makes protest action part of a continual, immersive, never-ending cycle of political action, result, and reflection.

Toward an Oppositional Theory of Democracy

There is no unique alternative conceptualization of democracy that follows with logical certainty from the critical explorations of this chapter. But I do think that the criticisms of contemporary approaches I have outlined point together in a different direction, toward the need for an approach that both recognizes—and even more, seeks to theorize—the active, oppositional character of democracy as we know it. One could say that while Stears and others have propounded a vision of movements engaged in a "struggle toward democracy," the approach I am suggesting would theorize democracy itself as a kind of struggle.

We need, in democratic theory, to emphasize an adequate conceptualization of agency or action—to theorize democracy as a form of common action not reducible to moments of reflection or decision. Democratic theories that put too much emphasis on decisions can easily forget that explicit decision constitutes just one moment—and a relatively unusual one—in the always ongoing processes of social action. The significance of "decision" is best understood, that is, in the context of a conceptualization of ongoing, reflexive action. "Decision" also can obscure the importance of "nondecisions"—or really, aspects of politics and social life that are not really the result of proper public "decisions" at all. It is crucial that while potential democratic actors may not have "decided" to create these conditions, their actions have often played an active role in maintaining or reproducing them. Moreover, these structures and forces condition what democratic actors can do. In short, such "nondecisions" are both unintended consequences and unacknowledged preconditions of action. In a related way, an intramural view of democracy—democracy behind walls—misses the democratic impetus to engage challenges actively and in so doing to enhance and exercise democratic powers of action. A better approach would envision democracy not as withdrawal from challenges but as active engagement with them, not as the blessed aftermath of an encounter with domination but as the active, turbulent encounter itself.

Of course, it would be easy to adopt too optimistic a view of democratic action. And in fact, there is a corrective drawn from the history of social movements. It may be almost too obvious to see: there have been, and still are, a lot of them. So it is important to consider the continual recurrence of movements; the renewal of the sort of challenges they confront; the reappearance of what I have described as the dualistic conditions of critical democratic eras; the juxtaposition of democratic promise with conditions of domination, necessity, and oppression. If democratic action were a panacea, boundlessly potent, then movements would not recur this way. We would have no occasion to distinguish "waves" of feminism; one would have been enough. "Pullman" might have meaning in the history of the American labor movement, but if so, then not "Flint." More pointedly, were democratic action easy and its outcomes assured, even the "first" feminist or labor or racial liberation movement might never have been necessary. So it is surely important for democratic theory to conceptualize the limits of democratic action—and the continuous reappearance of the problems that call it forth.

One way to approach the limits of democratic action is through closer attention to another theme emerging from the discussion above: power and its manifestations. Power is implicated in the very being and emergence of movements, viewed as collective challenges to dominant groups, ranks, and structures in society mounted by relatively weak or excluded people. The recurrence of the conditions that make movements necessary entails the continuation or return of certain kinds of power relations. It is not as if contemporary democratic theories have had nothing to say about power and cognate issues. Deliberative theory, of course, has emphasized noncoercion, and coercion is a particular use of power. But, as we have seen, the subject is something of an embarrassment for deliberative democracy. In ways both large and small, democratic movement strategies, from strikes to sit-ins to boycotts, are very often coercive. This is a difficulty that cannot be evaded, I have argued, simply by retaining noncoercion as the democratic ideal while accepting coercion as ethically aberrant but necessary in the nonideal present. We can only make sense of coercion by broadening the perspective of democratic theory to emphasize not just coercion but power itself.

A number of my appraisals of shared conceptions in democratic theory also reinforce doubts about sharply distinguishing ideal and nonideal in democratic theory. Such a distinction may seem to be a matter of common sense. But it tends to impose either a framework under which

50

movements as we actually know them are left out of democratic theory entirely—or one under which it is only possible to see movements as nonideal, their tainted activities subordinate to their valued accomplishments. Almost inevitably, that is, the distinction entails treating most of what movements do—most of the activities in which movement participants engage, such as marching and organizing boycotts—at best as mere means toward higher, finer democratic ends. Combined with democracy as principled citizen-relations, or democracy as ideal decision making, the ideal/nonideal approach can also impose a sharp contrast between competing sets of behavior rules for political actors, a chasm between conditions under which rigorous ideal standards of conduct apply, and others under which such standards, disconcertingly, seem to lose their force entirely. All this points to the potential advantages of a perspective on democracy that is neither ideal nor nonideal, one that does not impose an opposition between democratic means and democratic ends. Such an approach would directly theorize what is deeply unsatisfying about contemporary political life without giving up on profound democratic aspirations or consigning democracy to the status of a remote ideal.

The distinction between ideal and nonideal theory has much in common with one between democracy and democratization, a partitioning that is no more innocent than ideal versus nonideal. Much of this chapter has assessed certain conceptions in democratic theory from the standpoint of movements and what I have termed "critical democratic eras." Up to this point, I have written as if these epochs in the lives of democracies can be understood as discrete, and possibly exceptional. Some readers, then, might insist that critical periods and the conditions that characterize them do not tell us about democracy proper, but only about democratization or transitions to democracy. If so, democratic theory proper, *ideal* democratic theory, need not concern itself especially with them. But there are real drawbacks to positing a sharp distinction between democracy and democratic transition. Taking a global viewpoint, if we accept such a sharp distinction, then political theory can offer little more than remote and abstract ideals to the critical analysis of the many countries throughout the world today where democratic institutions and practices are interpenetrated with and often thwarted by undemocratic ones. Even quite mainstream approaches to comparative politics already recognize such interpenetration in countries such as Russia, Honduras, Pakistan, Egypt, Iran, and Venezuela. The widely used "Polity" surveys, for example, show that a sizeable proportion of the world's polities combine democratic and authoritarian features (Marshall and Goldstone 2007). Such interpenetration or duality is obvious when we reflect on the stifling of prodemocracy protests or military intervention in political disputes.

And for reasons that I can only fully clarify in light of the arguments still to come—reasons having to do with what I understand alienation and opposition to be—I think that the dualistic conditions of critical democratic epochs actually pertain quite generally, and we should expect them to pertain for quite some time to come. It may be better, then, to speak of critical *conditions,* rather than critical *eras* or *epochs.* In the view I am putting forth, the existence of democratic practices or movements alongside dominating and undemocratic structures and forces, is not a special case—something far from the core, ideal interests of serious political thinkers—but a very general, enduring condition upon which democratic theory should reflect seriously and directly.

And so we arrive at this. We seem to be in need of a way of conceptualizing democracy not behind walls but actively engaged with threatening forces; a theory not satisfied with viewing democracy in terms of just one social role, that of the citizen; not just focused on decision, narrowly, but on action, extensively; a view of democracy that emphasizes power, comprehensively, not just in one of its manifestations, coercion; a view of democracy that is not bisected by the distinction between ideal and nonideal or between democracy and democratization. The rest of this book attempts to elaborate such a theory of democracy.

2

———————————————→ ←———————————————

The ancient Greeks, some people once believed, lived in deep harmony with their social institutions and laws. They regarded the polis, their city-state, not merely as benign, but as their joint work and their fulfillment—in Georg Wilhelm Friedrich Hegel's words, the product "of all and each" ([1807] 1977, 264). No one, I think, argues that people in the twentieth and twenty-first centuries have generally felt the same way about their social worlds. As I write this, I am studying a reproduction of a 1913 painting by Ludwig Meidner, *Apocalyptic Landscape (Near the Halensee Railway Station)*. It is a city scene dominated by jarring strokes of blue, black, and white. The dozen or so figures spaced along the street that looms in the foreground and curves ahead to the left seem to be staggering or falling, as if the urban ground itself was lurching. In the lower right corner, the ground tilts alarmingly downward, suggesting not only a frenetic motion of the canvas as a whole but the possibility that everything in sight could be swallowed by a vortex. Buildings in the middle distance arch unnaturally toward the viewer. A distant peaked structure at the left center, the painting's most prominent patch of livid pink, hints at the beginning of a conflagration. The jagged clouds, though part of the natural, not the human-made scene, mirror the city's motion and confusion, and they are fed as well by dark smoke from a factory. In short, Meidner conveys a vision of a human world turned monstrous, hostile, alien.

Meidner's scene could as easily be Manchester in 1833 or Shenzehn in 2013 as Berlin in 1913. Depictions of an alienated world such as this have abounded in Western art, literature, and philosophy since the nineteenth century, and they probably reverberate even more widely. They also vary tremendously. Even *Apocalyptic Landscape* itself is complex,

53

open to many interpretations, some social, some psychological, and some religious (Eliel 1989). And as its title suggests, the painting seems to depict not just a human-made world that is hostile and foreign, but also the possibility of events rushing toward some climactic, possibly redemptive, crisis—a distinct idea from that of alienation.

This chapter concerns a particular, political, strain of thinking about alienation. Given the permutations of alienation and the extent of its hold on the late modern imagination, I intend no general survey, no comprehensive overview of the history of the word's many uses and meanings. The scope of this chapter is narrower in a couple of ways. First, I am concerned with figures whose discussions at least include—if they are not limited to—a particular understanding of alienation that links it to the consequences and limits of common action. Moreover, my main interest is in treatments of alienation that place the phenomenon in tight relation to democracy. Many people would recognize Hegel and Karl Marx as leading figures in the history of alienation. And that is as it should be. But I shall focus not only on them but also on John Dewey. This is not because I claim that Hegel, Marx, and Dewey wrote about the same universal, transhistorical philosophical problem. Rather, my point is that, despite their very clear differences, they recognized what I take to be a real and persistent modern social phenomenon and linked it to their theories of democracy.

Marx's and Dewey's theories of alienation and democracy have much to offer. They represent democracy as continuous toil pushing constantly against resistance. They link democracy as we know it not to some distant ideal of which it is a pale reflection but to actual efforts to deal with actual social forces and institutions that threaten to overwhelm the agency of ordinary people.[1] Democratic action, in this way of looking at things, is always preceded and surrounded by much that is threatening and undemocratic.

Besides the insights, there are also problems, of course, with Marx's and Dewey's work. Tracing the inadequacies of Hegel's thinking of alienation, and then Marx's reconfiguring and Dewey's reinvention of the conception, helps locate a starting point for a contemporary deployment of "alienation" for democratic theory. But Marx's and Dewey's explorations also show, in different ways, that those who link democracy to alienation, and who seek the origins of alienation in uniquely modern institutions, face a risk of positing a utopian escape, past or future, from the phenomenon. I explore those problems and others in this chapter, and then follow them into the next.

Alienation, Citizen, Subject

In Hegel's case, we ought to begin in the middle of things, with his portrayal of the citizen of the Roman Empire. No person in history was ever more politically alienated, in Hegel's view. No one was ever more dwarfed and dominated by overpowering political forces partly of his own creation.[2] Roman alienation can best be understood in the contrast, the opposition, between the emperor, in whom all public power and purpose resided, and the corpuscular citizen, shrunk to a spiritually meager, purely private existence. Roman social and political practice, according to Hegel, allowed individuals to interact with each other as rights-bearing equals in commerce. But this came at the terrible cost of ceding all political action to the emperor. Roman citizenship, then, was egalitarian, but politically it was the equality of emptiness, of nullity. By comparison, the supreme ruler was the "lord and master of the world," the "real essence" (Hegel [1807] 1977, 292). For the Roman, then, the political world had "the character of being something external, the negative of self-consciousness," an "alien reality already present and given, a reality which has a being of its own and in which it does not recognize itself" (294). But, Hegel continues, the Roman citizen also helped make, or reproduce, this alien world. "Its existence [was] the *work* of self-consciousness," Hegel explains, adding:

> This external world . . . *is* his work, but not in a positive, rather in a negative, sense. It obtains its existence through self-consciousness's *own* externalization and separation of itself from its essence which, in the ruin and devastation which prevail in the world of legal right, seems to inflict on self-consciousness from without, the violence of the liberated elements. (294)

This is perhaps the most vivid description Hegel offers of the characteristics of alienation in society. And it shows that, for Hegel, alienation can entail both a failure of thinking, the failure to *recognize* the social world as an expression or extension of oneself, as well a failure of action—the self-destructive creation and recreation of social relations that wreak "ruin and devastation."

Behind this portrayal of Roman alienation is Hegel's view of the entire universe as the emanation or expression of a cosmic *Geist* (Spirit) that becomes embodied, by necessity, in concrete human beings and in their social worlds—Spirit that only becomes conscious of itself through humans and their own consciousness, even though they are not, at least initially, aware of their unity with Spirit. According to this account, the embodiment of Spirit in mundane humans and their social relations passes through different stages of development and makes possible myriad forms of separation or estrangement, forms that Hegel links together into a quasi-historical narrative.[3] This latter narrative of alienation begins with the ancient Greeks, reflects on the place of the nobility under absolute monarchy, reaches a terrible crescendo in the French Revolution, and resolves in the central postrevolutionary political vision of the *Philosophy of Right*.[4]

I am particularly concerned with two different, though not necessarily exclusive, ways that Hegel draws on this complex vision. One is to view alienation against the backdrop of a presumed and pregiven spiritual unity—most comprehensively, the unity of Spirit and human beings—a unity sundered many times by a litany of errors of thought and understanding, but capable of being recaptured by fundamental rethinking. According to this conceptualization, human beings must recognize that the universe is and always has been an extension of themselves. The other characteristic approach to alienation in Hegel's work is to emphasize a context of common human action that has in some way gone wrong, creating dangerous or oppressive institutions and social structures, and separating human beings from their potential or powers. In describing the second approach, Georg Lukács notes that Hegel's mature theory of alienation results from the combination of two ideas: "firstly, the belief that the whole of human history together with all the social formations that are born and pass away, are the products of human activity"; and second, that "all these formations get out of the control of man and become autonomous powers with an objectivity of their own" (1976, 82). It is the latter, twofold conception that is useful to democratic theory, while the former, more spiritual and cosmological one, can lead to serious problems.[5]

Marx considered Hegel's narration of human self-creation and alienation an "outstanding achievement" ([1844] 1964, 177). But Marx's searing criticism is also probably the best-known appraisal: the claim that Hegel is never fully able to transcend the realm of mere intellect and abstraction. According to Marx,

> When . . . wealth, state power, etc., are understood by Hegel as entities estranged from the *human* being, this only happens in their form as thoughts . . . They are thought-entities, and therefore merely

an estrangement of *pure,* i.e., abstract, philosophical thinking. The whole process therefore ends with Absolute Knowledge . . . The whole *history of the alienation process* and the whole *process of the retraction* of the alienation is therefore nothing but the *history of the production* of abstract (i.e. absolute) thought. (175)

There is a significant measure of justice in Marx's critique. One of the most dramatic passages of the *Phenomenology* is Hegel's account of Terror in the French Revolution.[6] He interprets revolutionary Terror as resulting from Jacobin refusal to let the social and political world to become in any measure alienated—frenzied, violent insistence, in this case, that no one should be allowed to challenge the public's general will ([1807] 1977, 357–358). The resolution of this terrible period, in the end, was largely exhaustion, followed by a transformation of consciousness— a spiritual advance that apparently made any recurrence of such episodes impossible. Still, characterizing Hegel's alienation narrative as "nothing but the *history of the production* of abstract (i.e. absolute) thought" does not account for the fact that Hegel actually recognizes something more than merely spiritual, intellectual alienation: namely, alienation of a person from her active powers and alienation of political or social structures and institutions from the actors who recreate them through their common activities. These forms of alienation are not simply identical, even for Hegel, with problematic forms of consciousness. This suggests that the resolution to the long epochs of alienation, as Hegel describes it in the *Phenomenology,* fails to do justice to Hegel's own portrayal of alienation, especially the problem of human action gone wrong. The movement of the *Phenomenology* generally involves not merely inadequate ideas but inadequate, self-defeating actions—practices that do not achieve their objectives, that go deeply awry. This is clearly the aspect of Hegel's work that captivates Marx, who praises the *Phenomenology* for focusing on human activity—on human "self-creation" as "process," on human beings' "active orientation," on "labor," and on human "powers" (Marx [1844] 1964, 177). For Hegel, social activity, not merely thought, abstractly, engenders oppressive and dangerous institutions and social relations. And overcoming such forms of alienation would seem also to require common effort, the active recapturing of social activities and creative powers and with them the social structures and forces they produce.

Politically, the enlightened monarchical state described in the *Philosophy of Right* embodies for Hegel aspects of the same sort of resolution to alienation suggested in the *Phenomenology*.[7] And the discussion consequently entails much the same weakness—namely, Hegel's unwarranted satisfaction with resolutions to alienation resting mainly on an intellectual transformation, on recognition of some posited, preexisting unity. In fact, Hegel's depiction of enlightened monarchy is historically a very significant example of this flaw, since Marx criticized such monarchy as an alienated form of political life months before writing the more frequently cited discussion of Hegel and alienation found in the *Economic and Philosophic Manuscripts*.

Hegel argues in the *Philosophy of Right* that the modern state must not appear to citizens to be an alien imposition. The people must be able rationally to identify with it so that they accept its authority willingly. It must, then, be differentiated, so as to reflect in itself the different elements found in every person, every subject, including, crucially, a "moment of ultimate decision" (Hegel [1821] 1991, 313). But lest one think that this idea that the state must reflect the human capacity for self-determination would commit Hegel to supporting democratic sovereignty, he assures readers that he thinks this is a "garbled notion" (319). Thus the subjectivity and personality in which all people share is not to be expressed actively by them in politics but is rather only to be represented symbolically by a monarch (317). And this representation, in itself, is apparently sufficient to satisfy the need of citizens to see their own subjectivity manifested in the state. For all the creativity of Hegel's theory of alienation, his political response—his proposal for the state—really rests on spiritual reconciliation with monarchy.

Democratizing Alienation

A certain conception of alienation was always there to be found in Marx, even in the writings whose familiarity had bred—well, complacency, in any case. Throughout *The Communist Manifesto* and *Capital,* Marx portrays the capitalist economy in general as a product of human action that escapes human control, with disastrous consequences. "Modern bourgeois society" is alienated, he says with Engels: people confront it "like the sorcerer who is no longer able to control the powers of the nether world whom he has called up by his spells" (Marx and Engels [1848] 2012, 78–79).[8] But despite the fact that Marx's reflections on alienation pervade his work, alienation really only began to get its due from his interpreters in the second half of the twentieth century.[9]

Marx's discussion of alienation is nearly as complex and shaded with meanings as Hegel's, and the secondary literature on that discussion is accordingly extensive and diverse. But I am not concerned here to surpass it. Indeed, I draw on a good deal of impressive scholarship. My aim instead is to bring into focus the close connection between alienation and democracy in Marx's writings, a task that also involves highlighting a particular aspect of alienation. Actually, *connection* is not strong enough a term. For Marx, alienation does not merely affect democracy, as if the two were externally related. Rather the close conceptual bond between alienation and democracy, evident in some of Marx's earliest writings, is due to the fact that for Marx, the most profoundly undemocratic institutions are alienated, and democratic action is a primary means of reconquering alienated social realms.

This understanding puts me partly at odds with some prominent, even classic, approaches to Marx's views of alienation and of democracy. For example, some well-known interpretations of Marx present alienation without democracy—or, more precisely, they treat alienation and democracy as if they were only contingently related. Erich Fromm's seminal analysis of alienation is a case in point. Fromm primarily derives from Marx's alienation an understanding of a pervasive social-psychological condition.[10] The problem of alienation in capitalist society, he writes, is the problem "of the socio-economic conditions in modern industrial society which create the personality of modern Western man and are responsible for the disturbances in his mental health" ([1955] 1990, 83). Alienation, then, refers to all the "effects of Capitalism on personality" (120). It designates a "mode of experience in which the person experiences himself as an alien" or "does not experience himself as the center of his world, as the creator of his own acts" (120). This description covers, as it turns out, a diverse array of conditions, attitudes, and pathologies, from "the attitude of the 'owner' of a big corporation to 'his property'" (128) to the tendency of lower-middle-class families to collect "ugly bric-à-brac" (133).

The indirect connection Fromm makes between such alienation and democracy is illustrative of the result of emphasizing a psychological understanding of alienation. Fromm's alienation theory does not directly analyze, for example, the structural relationship between capitalism and politics. Rather, he argues that capitalism creates a certain kind of person, and that sort of person is incapable of fulfilling the role designated for her by democratic theory. Tellingly, Fromm draws deeply on

Schumpeter to make this point, calling him "a keen observer of the political and economic scene" who supports the idea that "the expression of the will of the voter in modern democracy is an alienated expression" ([1955] 1990, 187, 184). Democracy and alienation are in this sense surely associated in Fromm's work, but only in a contingent way. Alienation, a social-psychological phenomenon, simply happens to be the external cause of democracy's present ills, in Fromm's account.

Other interpretations present readers, alternatively, with a view of Marx as a theorist of democracy without alienation. In his systematic study of the depth and significance of Marx's and Engels's practical commitment to democracy, August H. Nimtz Jr.'s (2000) approach is to emphasize their political activities over their philosophical or even their economic writings. He relies on the thesis that the key to establishing democracy, historically, has been the political self-organization of the working class.[11] And promoting this self-organization, he argues, was the core of Marx's and Engels's party activities from their first encounter with the Communist League through their leading participation in the International Working Men's Association. In addition, Nimtz argues that democracy was the overriding goal of Marx's and Engels' participation in the revolutions of 1848, a contention supported by their *Demands of the Communist Party in Germany,* which focuses not on economics, per se, but on universal suffrage and related measures.[12] Nimtz does pay brief attention to Marx's well-known warning to the working class about the alienated state: the movement should not, could not "simply lay hold of the ready-made state machinery, and wield it for its own purposes" (Marx [1871] 1996, 181). Nevertheless, Nimtz's view that Marx's democratic significance lies largely in his contribution to the establishment of liberal, political democracy tends to marginalize what is distinctive in Marx's view, and particularly his linking of democracy to alienation. At times, Nimtz almost seems to suggest that Marx the democrat can be understood as a proponent of modern, liberal-democratic politics, if only because such a political terrain is the most favorable to socialist transition.[13] Nimtz gives us, in this sense, democracy without alienation.

The key, then, is to focus on the close conceptual link in Marx's work between democracy and alienation. In highlighting this internal relation, I am indebted to Paul Thomas (1994). Against those who derive from the *Manifesto* a view of the state as just an instrument in the hands of the capitalist ruling class, Thomas argues that it is essential to understand that Marx viewed the state as alien, and this in two senses. The state, for Thomas's Marx, is alien because it is really no one's conscious, malleable instrument, but rather dominates society as a whole. And it is alien, as well, because it represents the estrangement of democratic citizens from the full experience of democratic activity—preventing civil society from being democratic and relegating democracy to a shadow life.

Background: Philosophy, Action, and Ethical Judgment

At the close of the last chapter, I set forth a few features of an oppositional theory of democracy that would avoid some of the missteps of both elite and deliberative theory. Even without taking into account Marx's theory of democracy and alienation, it is clear that Marx's general approach is quite favorable to two of these, namely, emphasizing democracy as common activity and transcending the supposed gap between ideal and nonideal theory.

Stressing democracy as common activity means resisting two temptations: putting undue emphasis either on democratic institutions or on detached reflection, deliberation, and decision, and thereby extracting any of these from their reciprocal relation or entwinement in the always-ongoing tide of common action. Marx's "Theses on Feuerbach" returns repeatedly to the need for an active perspective for social theory.[14] An active focus is also entwined with the second aspect of Marx's thought that is amenable to the oppositional approach to democracy I am defending: his refusal to divide his subject matter into "ideal" and "non-ideal." Simply in supporting a roughly pragmatic or practice-centered criterion of truth, Marx rejects purely ideal forms of thinking. For Marx, keeping "theory" rooted in "practice" is the alternative to a system of ethical and political thinking as a series of abstract "mysteries" to be probed and revealed by the detached philosopher: "All mysteries which lead theory to mysticism," he writes, "find their rational solution in human practice and in the comprehension of this practice" ([1845] 2000, 173). Of course, many aspects of Marx's thought, especially those related to his inversion of Hegelian idealism, point in the same direction. If the pragmatic aspect of Marx's thinking calls into question the ability to root ethics in detached, universal judgments stipulated *from nowhere,* his materialist conception of history[15] entails the view that those who try to make such judgments are likely just to restate thoughtlessly the moral principles that are woven into the fabric of their time and society.[16]

Democracy and the Alienated State

The generally accepted centerpiece of Marx's theory of alienation is the *Economic and Philosophic Manuscripts* ([1844] 1964). Here Marx presents capital as the archetype of alienation. It exemplifies a situation in which some thing—some social relation—produced by human activity returns to those who produced it as alien, hostile, uncontrollable, and oppressive. According to Marx, alienation can be viewed in four ways: "alienation of the worker in his product," alienation "in the activity of labor itself," alienation from "species being," and alienation or estrangement of "man from man" (108, 110, 112, 114). Since there are a number of very good treatments of these four main aspects of alienation in the *Manuscripts*[17] and since Marx himself describes them quite cogently, I will stress here only several especially relevant points about them. First, although Marx begins by discussing the alienation of the "product" of labor, he argues that it is the alienation of "activity" that explains this alienation: "How could the worker come to face the product of his activity as a stranger, were it not that in *the very act of production* he was estranging himself from himself? The product is after all but the summary of the activity, of production" (110). The emphasis here, then, is on alienation as a consequence of common action, alienation as manifested in social relations or structures that are created by human activity but that confront human beings as something foreign. Of course, what Marx says about capital as the alienated product of labor is crucial. Capital becomes "a power on its own" over the worker and the worker lives in "bondage" to it (108, 109). But Marx immediately explains that this "means that *the life which he* [*the worker*] *has conferred on the object* confronts him as something hostile and alien" (108; italics added).

The second point is that for Marx, alienation is a concrete human and social problem, a matter of observable, conflictive social relations. "If the product of labor is alien to me, if it confronts me as an alien power, to whom, then, does it belong? If my own activity does not belong to me, if it is an alien, a coerced activity, to whom, then, does it belong?" he asks. And he then answers: "If the product of labor does not belong to the worker, if it confronts him as an alien power, then this can only be because it belongs to some other man than the worker . . . Not the gods, not nature, but only man himself can be this alien power over man" ([1844] 1964, 115).

The alienation of some human beings from their activity and its product involves for Marx at the same time the alienation of some human beings from others. So alienation, however far-reaching, is not a problem that confronts all human beings in society in the same way. It is fundamentally a problem of social structure and of the different place of various actors in it. The consequent emphasis here on the sociologically grounded problems of power, conflict, and oppression points toward a third important matter. Despite the prominence of Marx's analysis of alienation from the product of labor, the mere fact that one's activities become congealed into objects—or even social relations and structures— is not in itself a problem for Marx. "The product of labor is labor which has been embodied in an object, which has become material: it is the objectification of labor," Marx allows ([1844] 1964, 108). But it is important to distinguish such objectification from alienation (Lukács 1971, xiii–xiv). Objectification, for Marx, can be found in any society, at any time (Schaff 1980, 75; Ollman 1971, 143). The true problem is not objectification but the fact that under capitalist production "this realization of labor" takes the form of a "loss of realization" and "bondage"—which in turn result in "estrangement" and "alienation" (Marx [1844] 1964, 108).

Although the attention paid to *Economic and Philosophic Manuscripts* is certainly well deserved, Marx actually first drew a connection between alienation and democracy in works he wrote the previous year, the *Critique of Hegel's "Philosophy of Right"* ([1843] 1967) and "On the Jewish Question" ([1843] 2000). Marx composed the first of these in the immediate aftermath of his resignation as editor of a radical journal, the *Rheinische Zeitung,* which had come under strict censorship and severe pressure from the Prussian king, Frederick William IV. Contra Hegel's defense of monarchy—his view that subjects can reconcile themselves to monarchical rule and so overcome alienation—Marx argues in the *Critique* that monarchy is actually the "fullest expression" of political alienation ([1843] 1967, 32). Hegel, Marx writes, erred in positing sovereignty as something in itself, as a subject independent of the people. He should instead have started, Marx states, with "real subjects"—the people—"as the bases of the state" (23).

This claim sets up a passage that is essential for understanding the links in Marx's thought between common action, democracy, and alienation. The unfortunate obscurity of the passage results from the fact that, without explicit warning, Marx uses the term *democracy* in two ways: to signify a constitution or a specific political form (what I will refer to as "Democracy A") and the underlying process of social action, in which many people participate, and which engenders and reproduces every social relation, every structure, every constitution ("Democracy B"). So when Marx argues, paradoxically, that "democracy is the truth of monarchy" ([1843] 1967, 29), he means that even monarchy is created by the common action of the people, that is, by Democracy B. "Monarchy," then, "is necessarily democracy"—again, Democracy B—"in contradiction with itself" (29). Monarchy is, in other words, produced by the people, even though its appearance and ideology emphasize the doings, the agency of the monarch, and even though in monarchy, the people's common action returns to them in dominating, alienated form.[18] "Monarchy," then, "cannot . . . be understood in terms of itself," Marx argues (29). It can only be understood in terms of Democracy B. By contrast, democracy—now he means a political form, Democracy A—presents itself openly as an expression of Democracy B (29). In sum, "democracy"—meaning Democracy B—"is the resolved mystery of all constitutions" (29–30). Of course, this means there is something special about Democracy A, a unique fit between appearance and reality, or form and substance. In Democracy A, "the constitution not only in itself, according to its essence, but according to existence and reality, is returned to its real ground, the real man, the actual people, and established as its own work. The constitution appears as what it is, the free product of men" (29–30).

In "On the Jewish Question," Marx contends that even the establishment of a "republic"—though, significantly, "the negation" of monarchical "alienation"—would not resolve all problems of alienation and freedom. Though liberal democracy, a republic, could only be the result of a "battle of democracy," as Marx and Engels put it in the *Manifesto* ([1848] 2012, 91), it would leave civil society dominated by property relations, and thus unemancipated and significantly undemocratic. The merely political "emancipation" that founds liberal polities, he writes, actually establishes a division of the state from civil society—and a related division of the person into the "egoistic" and often oppressed individual, separated and alienated from the universal citizen, who subsists only in abstract, almost only in imagination.[19] The proper response to this condition, in general, is emancipation. In particular, it is an act of recapturing an alien realm, an act of democratic conquest or struggle. "All emancipation," Marx contends, is bringing back man's world and his relationships to man him-self . . . The actual individual man must take the abstract citizen back into himself and, as an individual man in his empirical life, in his individual work and individual relationships become a species being; man must recognize his own forces as social forces, orga-nize them, and thus no longer separate social forces from himself in the form of political forces. Only when this has been achieved will human emancipation be completed. ([1843] 2000, 64)

This is stirring, of course, but hardly sufficient as a guide to political action. The later political works, especially "The Eighteenth Brumaire of Louis Bonaparte" ([1852] 1996) and the *Civil War in France* ([1871] 1996), elaborate in far more concrete terms the relationship between democracy and alienation.

Marx's immediate subject in "The Eighteenth Brumaire" is of course the political ascent of Louis Napoleon, a puzzling sequence of events, partly because the latter was, in Marx's estimation, a mere con man, a mediocrity—and partly because his rise was aided by the French bour-geoisie's readiness to take a step backward to authoritarianism, to sacri-fice its professed liberal, republican principles along with its right to rule itself.[20] After the armed class warfare of June 1848, the drafters of a new constitution decided that there should be an election to a strong presi-dency even before the rest of the constitution was completed. Louis Napoleon was elected overwhelmingly to fill this position. Over the next few years he suppressed the socialists, rescinded universal suffrage, then reinstated it long enough to be elected to a new ten-year term, and finally declared himself emperor—ruling, Marx contends, on behalf of the bourgeoisie, but not with their participation. As Marx puts it, Louis Napoleon came to guarantee "the security and existence of the bour-geoisie" without actually allowing them to exercise "political power" at all ([1852] 1996, 102).

How, in Marx's view, did this profound alienation of the state from society come to pass? We can imagine at least two possible explanations for an alienated state's resistance to being controlled by society at large: first, that the state is captured by a narrow ruling class and brought under their exclusive control, and second, that the state serves that class's inter-ests without being truly under its (or any class's) control. Marx's analysis in "The Eighteenth Brumaire" generally seems premised on the latter theory. Marx argues that under Louis Napoleon, "the state seem[s] to have achieved independence with respect to society, and to have brought it into submission" ([1852] 1996, 116). In Marx's view, this was possible because successive revolutions and governments had strengthened the state apparatus, centralizing it and refining it to the point that its occupants could operate almost independently of society (115–116).[21] The process began, in Marx's telling, with French absolute monarchies' attempts to hasten "the decline of feudalism" (115). "All upheavals perfected this machinery instead of destroying it," Marx writes (116). This genetic account of state power means that the state, for Marx, does not owe its characteristics only to the present play of forces in society, but also to the unintended consequences of past historical figures pursuing their political ambitions and to forces and capacities inherited from the past.

But Marx does not see a state that defies even bourgeois control as inevitable or as a predetermined outcome. He argues that between the two Napoleons' reigns, the state bureaucracy was something closer to just "the instrument of the ruling class" ([1852] 1996, 116). His explanation of the independence of state power under Louis Napoleon is laid out in terms of institutional capacities (not guaranteed results) and of the human actions that produce and reproduce those capacities. Such capacities can. be exercised for different purposes, and either well or poorly. Marx treats Louis Napoleon with derision but recognizes that he played a role in enhancing the autonomy of the French state. And even this is only half the story. Just as important as the structure and capacities of the state were the capacities of the various classes of mid-nineteenth-century France: their ability to cooperate or unite, their ability to organize themselves politically, the ideas that guided their action, and so on.[22] Marx focuses especially on divisions within the bourgeoisie and the conditions of agriculture affecting the peasantry, who he argues were "incapable of asserting their class interests in their own name" (117).[23]

Obviously a situation in which no group or class in society exercises significant political power on its own behalf is, almost by definition, incompatible with democracy. But the full democratic significance—the democratic response—to this alienated state is best understood in light of Marx's argument in *The Civil War in France,* his eulogy for the Paris Commune, the revolutionary council that ran the city for a few months in early 1871 after Napoleon III's army was defeated, while the city endured and resisted a siege. The Commune was not really socialistic, so Marx praises its radical democratic features, not its social or economic policies. And he praises this radical democracy not so much for its institutional perfection as for the understanding the Communards showed, in designing it, of the need to struggle against state alienation. They recognized, he writes, that they could not just try to seize the existing state and "wield" it, intact, for their purposes. This was precisely because the state machinery, in its present form, was alienated, built not to respond to but to dominate society. The state power seemed to be "soaring high above society" ([1871] 1996, 183); it made itself "independent of, and superior to, the nation itself" (185); like a "parasite," it "absorbed" the forces that were properly those of the "social body" (186). The Commune, Marx contends, was the "direct antithesis" of this. Its constitution would have "restored" alienated social forces to the people (186).

The institutions and practices Marx discusses make sense chiefly in terms of this interaction of democracy and alienation: not as ideal forms of democracy in themselves, but as effective means, under the circumstances, of contesting alienation. Marx groups many of the Commune's main features under two headings: measures intended to minimize the distance between the people and their representatives, such as universal suffrage and short terms of office ([1871] 1996, 184); and measures intended to amputate "the merely repressive organs of the old governmental power" (185), such as replacing the army with a citizens' national guard and stripping the police of political duties (184). Marx never suggests that these are the democratic institutions that would be adopted under imaginary, perfect circumstances by ideal political actors. On the contrary, Marx argues that they were designed for struggle. "The working class did not expect miracles from the Commune," Marx writes, adding: "They have no ready-made utopias to introduce *par décret du peuple*" (188).

The Public's Other Problem

It is now nearly a piece of orthodoxy that John Dewey was a deliberative democrat.[24] One of Dewey's most distinguished interpreters has argued that *deliberative* better describes Deweyan democracy than does *participatory*, the term he himself once used (Westbrook 1997, 138). And others now seem to accept the designation almost as a truism (B. Taylor 2001, 976). Precisely what the "deliberative" label means in this case is not always clear. Certainly Dewey favored free and open democratic communication. But he cannot, obviously, have intended to contribute to the literature on deliberation that burgeoned four decades after his death, or to side with contemporary deliberative theory against its critics. He did not use the term *deliberation* systematically to describe democratic method as he did terms like *intelligence* or *experiment*. Nor does he seem to have shared some of the preoccupations of contemporary deliberative theory, such as the painstaking elucidation of ideal deliberative norms. This categorizing of Dewey as deliberative can never be more than an external description. The question, then, is not so much whether such a designation is "correct," but rather how fully it captures Dewey's approach—and what it leaves out.

Again, there is no doubt that Dewey often seems to have understood the inadequacies of American democracy in terms of communication and discourse, something broadly true of deliberative theory. This is what many interpreters seize upon in casting Dewey as a deliberative democrat.[25] For example, Dewey tells us in *The Public and Its Problems* ([1927] 1954) that "the essential need . . . is the improvement of the method and conditions of debate, discussion, and persuasion." That, he adds, "is *the* problem of the public" (208).

This sounds definitive and exclusive. But Dewey's public, I contend, confronted another crucial problem. Dewey did not believe, that is, that early twentieth-century American democracy was weak only because citizens failed to communicate in the right way about public, political matters, or even because historical developments had made the right kind of communication difficult. The public in his time also faced, roughly speaking, a problem concerning modern forms of action and the troubling ways their consequences returned to citizens. To put the matter simply, the problem was an aspect of the perennial phenomenon that I term *alienation* in this book, though in his writings, Dewey uses different terminology to describe it.

The Deweyan democratic theory I describe here is about action and its consequences, not just about thought and discussion. It treats democracy not mainly as an ideal but as an existing practice, and a possibility to be valued in the here and now, a good to be understood in relation to constant difficulties and threats. Somewhat like Marx, I argue, Dewey recurrently describes the state as a problem, an institution recurrently captured by private interests, always escaping democratic control. The crucial challenge for democracy, according to Dewey's approach, is that people in modern societies lose track of the consequences of their common activities, are unable to trace the genesis of the powers that profoundly affect them. They face seemingly distant institutions and impersonal forces, like the state and like the capitalist economy, which resist popular control and dominate their lives. Democracy, then, is a response to these run-away consequences, these overwhelming forces—an "energetic, unflagging, unceasing" struggle on "many fronts" ([1939] 1989, 132, 134).

Background: Experience, Action, and the Origin of Values

Like Marx's general approach to the critique of politics, Dewey's is favorable to two aspects of the oppositional democratic theory I propose: a focus on activity, broadly—rather than decision or deliberation, narrowly—as the central problematic of philosophy and politics, and transcendence of the supposed sharp distinction between ideal and nonideal in political thought. Both aspects of Dewey's thought stem from "experience," a conception that reflects his denial of a sharp separation of thinking or reflection from activity.[26] (For me, as for Dewey, emphasizing action rather than reflection or decision means taking a broader, more inclusive viewpoint, rather than asserting action as something truly distinct from and superior to reflection.) Deweyan experience is not abstract and intellectual; it is situated and practical. It is Dewey's name for the continual and indefinitely repeated cycle of acting, undergoing the consequences, and then reflecting before moving on to more action. "Intelligence," Dewey argues characteristically, is always "caught up in the actual course of events" ([1917] 1993, 7).[27] Properly oriented philosophy, then, is focused not on reflection alone but on "intelligence *and its place in action*" ([1917] 1993, 8; italics added). In part, this is Dewey's response to what he terms "the spectator notion of knowledge" ([1917] 1993, 4) in modern Western thought. Human beings, he argues, do not gain in understanding of the world from just standing back and observing or reasoning—not even from reasoning together discursively—but from intervening in the world, from acting. Humans are not, he argues, detached knowers, thinkers, or debaters, but "biological" beings whose brains are primarily "organs of action-undergoing" ([1929] 1958, 23). "Every experience," Dewey argues, "is the result of an interaction between a live creature and some aspect of the world in which he lives" ([1934] 1980, 562). In more contemporary terminology, Dewey's theory of experience is a theory of *reflexive* action. For action, Dewey argues, is neither wholly subordinate to nor merely the preformed successor of thinking. On the contrary, for Dewey, reflection and deliberation only emerge when a problem of action is encountered, when action meets "resistance and conflict" ([1934] 1980, 555). For Dewey, Eric MacGilvray writes, "experience is conceived as a seamless flow of action and sensation which proceeds unconsciously until a 'problematic' (i.e., unanticipated or uncertain) situation emerges. At such moments, intelligence intervenes, ideas are generated, experiments performed, the obstacle surmounted or the project abandoned, and unproblematic experience resumes" (1999, 546). Not only does intelligence intervene only after action is already under way, but fruitful thinking, for Dewey, is always followed by more action. This is partly why the pragmatic test of the value of thinking is not conformity with abstract standards of any kind—or with external fixed "truth"—but proof in action.

Dewey's conception of experience leads directly to his avoidance of ideal theory, set up as something self-contained, something sharply distinguished from the quotidian realm of the nonideal. Philosophers make a grievous mistake, he argues, when they posit a world of values as something distinct from the world of day-to-day experience. For Dewey, critical inquiry begins with the ceaseless and continuous flow of action, sensation, and reflection.[28] It begins, that is, with "actual situations of belief, conduct, and appreciative perception" ([1929] 1958, 403). That world of experience, for Dewey, is not calm but troubled, characterized by the "precarious and perilous"; it is "uncertain" and "uncannily unstable" (41). So "all reflection sets out from the problematic and confused," Dewey insists (65–66).

But it is not just risk, danger, and uncertainty that are the stuff of experience. So, too, are "values" themselves, according to Dewey. In the first instance, values "just occur, are enjoyed, possessed" ([1929] 1958, 403). Of course, at any given moment, these ideals, these possibilities, may be thwarted, not fully realized. Still, "they are genuine ideals only in so far as they are possibilities of what is now moving." If not "related to actualities, they are pictures in a dream" ([1929] 1999, 72). Since values are only to be derived from experience, "social life" itself is to be "cherished in behalf of its own immediate possibilities, not on the ground of its remote connections" to distant ideals ([1908] 1993, 67). And since experience is always both infused with values, and troubled, discordant, and imperfect, it is wrong to think that we really know a value when we have conceived of it in flawless, ideal form. The very meaning of a value, for Dewey, is bound up in its relationship to some difficulty. "If there were nothing in the way, if there were no deviations and resistances, fulfillment would be at once, and in so being would fulfill nothing, but merely be," Dewey writes ([1929] 1958, 62). He adds:

Water that slakes thirst, or a conclusion that solves a problem have ideal character as long as thirst or a problem persists in a way which qualifies the result. But water that is not a satisfaction of need has no more ideal quality than water running through pipes into a reservoir; a solution ceases to be a solution and becomes a bare incident of existence when its antecedent generating conditions of doubt, ambiguity and search are lost from its context. While the precarious nature of existence is indeed the source of all trouble, it is also an indispensable condition of ideality. (62–63)

Of course, this does not eliminate or even diminish the importance of critical thought. The "proper business" of intelligence, according to Dewey, is "discrimination of multiple and present goods and of the varied immediate means of their realization," not the "search for the one remote aim" ([1908] 1993, 73). "Criticism" is needed precisely because the enjoyment of valued things is brief and uncertain. That lesson is quickly learned, and as soon as it is, "enjoyment ceases to be a datum and becomes a problem" ([1929] 1958, 398). And "as a problem, it implies intelligent inquiry into the conditions and consequences" of the value or "value-object" (398–399).

Ironically, it is precisely the painful experience of the world as changeable and uncertain, Dewey thinks, that causes philosophers to recoil and posit a distinct realm of changeless, sure ideals. Just as Aristotle "never surrenders his bias in favor of the fixed, certain and finished," Dewey argues, Kant also "assigns all that is manifold and chaotic to one realm, that of sense, and all that is uniform and regular to that of reason" ([1929] 1958, 49). But this is not only an error; it is one that generates a spurious problem, namely the question, "What is the relationship of these two 'worlds'?"—the ideal and the world of experience (394). Once "ethical science" is posited as attending to problems categorically different from social science and psychology, there can be no satisfying answer, no way to bring the two back together.

Dewey is particularly severe in his criticism of a closely related distinction, that between ends and means.[29] "Ends" can be understood, Dewey argues, as just another name for "values" ([1929] 1958, 396), which philosophers often treat as part of an ideal realm contrasted with the world in which we actually live. But in addition to the opposition between the world of values and the world of experience, there is a second, related, opposition discernible here, one between "ends" and other activities that have, supposedly, no worth in themselves, that are only instrumental in the attainment of "ends." Dewey insists that this is a confusion, because ends and means are always interdependent ([1938] 1993). Indeed, sometimes he even sandwiches the two terms, referring to "means-consequences" as part of a single "situation" ([1929] 1958, 397). They are, he suggests, part of the same continuous flow of experience. In this flow, no thing, no activity, is intrinsically or permanently either a means or an end. Today's ends are tomorrow's means of better and richer experiences, a point that Dewey makes most vividly in his educational and aesthetic theory. In proper learning, knowledge is not acquired passively, but through action, and it is not really an end in itself, but rather a means to more fertile future activity ([1916] 1966, 151). "The eternal quality of great art," too, Dewey insists, "is its renewed instrumentality for further consummatory experiences" ([1929] 1958, 365). The sharp separation of means from ends, as when industry is severed from art, Dewey contends, is a reflection of conditions in which many people engage by necessity in deadening, unfree activities. Or, more sharply, it is a feature of social caste, of "the insulated existence of working and leisure classes, of production that is not also consummatory, and consummation that is not productive" ([1929] 1958, 368). The categorical distinction between means and ends, Dewey insists, arises from the practice of slavery, in which some are reduced to mere means, utilized for ends only others perceive ([1916] 1966, 85).

Democratic Struggle against "Dominantly Controlling Forces"

By the time Dewey published *The Public and Its Problems*, he had already written for decades on democracy. In fact, pervading concepts like intelligence and education tie Dewey's democratic thought so intimately to the rest of his philosophy that it can be difficult to determine where one ends and the other begins, if indeed there is any distinct border at all. The democratic theory Dewey expounds is *radical*[30] because he advocates the extension of democracy to the economy and to social life, broadly—and *developmental* because he links democracy to the enlargement of human capacities for action. Dewey also resists institutional, regime-centered conceptions of democracy. Democracy is a "mode of associated living" ([1916] 1966, 87), a "way of life," not merely "something that [takes] place mainly at Washington and Albany . . . under the impetus of what happened when men and women went to the polls once a year or so" ([1939] 1993, 241). Purely political democracy, the sort of existing political regime identified as democratic, in his time and ours, "does not work very satisfactorily" anyway ([1922] 1993, 77), Dewey contends. He was a leader and longtime member of the League for Industrial Democracy (Ryan 1995, 207) and a full-throated proponent of "cooperative control of industry" ([1929] 1999, 64). And as for the developmental side of his democratic thinking, Dewey consistently highlights connections, varied and mutually entwined, between democracy, personal culture, and education. Only under democratic conditions, he argues, can education attain its aim of preparing every person for lifelong growth ([1916] 1966, 100). At the same time, democracy's fulfillment requires a form of education that "makes its chief concern to release distinctive aptitudes in art, thought, and companionship" ([1922] 1993, 79–80). The full meaning of democracy, he writes, entails the "release of individualized capacities" ([1922] 1993, 77). On the other hand, Dewey warns, institutions such as present-day factories, that are organized hierarchically and undemocratically—institutions that force some people to "execute plans which they do not form"—stultify participants, leading to "a depressed body and an empty and distorted mind" ([1929] 1999, 64).

All this, however, is arguably just descriptive. What *is* democracy, really, in Dewey's eyes—and, perhaps more importantly, what is democracy's deepest challenge? (These questions, we have seen, cannot really be distinct for Dewey.) Dewey's mature theory answers this by drawing on his understanding of experience in a way shaped profoundly by his pragmatic understanding of the relationship of ideals and values.[31] It is well known that Dewey wrote *The Public and Its Problems* partly as a response to Walter Lippmann's disillusioned analysis of American democracy, *The Phantom Public*.[32] Democrats went wrong, Lippmann had argued, in counting on "the public" to understand political and social issues and to devise solutions consonant with the common good. Such knowledgeable publics did not, *could not* exist. Real citizens were distracted and uninformed and incapable of such intellectual feats. They were, in fact, not political agents in any meaningful sense of the word, just "bystanders" (Lippmann [1927] 1993, 30–43).

For Dewey, Lippmann's book was disquieting. That the contemporary "public" is a "phantom," Dewey admits, is descriptively, symptomatically, quite correct. Voters, he agrees, are often listless, apathetic, ill informed, and manipulated by political parties ([1927] 1954, 116, 132, 134). But in Dewey's view, this is not attributable to any permanent disability in human agency. Rather, it is a matter of modern breakdowns in the recurring cycle of experience—that is, any disengagement of the public is due to contemporary barriers to fruitful common action and to intelligent reflection on action's consequences.

Lippmann frames democracy's weaknesses in terms of the failure of a true public to emerge. So does Dewey, but rather than simply denying that citizens can exercise the right sort of agency, he seeks an explanation for this failure by regrounding his democratic theory in the problematics of action, his analysis of experience. A crucial aspect of that analysis, we have seen, is the importance of human beings undergoing and reflecting intelligently on the consequences of their actions. But modern societies throw up roadblocks to this phase of fruitful experience. Dewey begins his new exploration of democracy's challenges by observing that actions have two kinds of consequences, private and public. Private consequences affect only those directly involved in a transaction, while public or indirect consequences are broader, touching people who are not immediately concerned ([1927] 1954, 12). Private consequences are of no particular interest to Dewey here, but the public, indirect ones are many, varied, and democratically significant.

Some of what Dewey has in mind in referring to "consequences" can be understood in terms of "ramifying" chains of events, each event seemingly causing the next ([1939] 1989, 51).[33] But this does not fully capture what "consequences" means for Dewey, or perhaps what kind of consequences are at issue. The idea, in the end, remains, admittedly, somewhat indeterminate. Dewey mentions the public consequences of a patient visiting a doctor, and this involves more, he says, than "my health" and "his pocketbook" ([1927] 1954, 51)—more, even, than my missing work while ill, or passing on an infectious disease, apparently. It also seems to involve something to do with the general "exercise" or practice of medicine in society. Or again, his view of the indirect consequences of buying and selling land goes beyond its effect on the value of other people's real estate holdings to include the general shape of property institutions and their "prime importance" to society (51). Furthermore, in a way that Dewey does not quite make perfectly clear, this inability to track the consequences of action is related to overwhelming forces shaping modern society, especially industrialization, marketization, and war.

Though not fully clear, this analysis of action's consequences allows Dewey to introduce his understanding of a public: "The public," Dewey writes, "consists of all those who are affected by the indirect consequences of transactions to such an extent that it is deemed necessary to have those consequences systematically cared for" ([1927] 1954, 15–16). This could involve any activities from steel production to war. So understood, a public could be "unorganized and formless" (67). An *organized* public is a public that in fact recognizes how it is affected by such consequences and that, furthermore, makes sure the relevant consequences are "systematically cared for" and that public "agencies" are put in place to attend to those consequences (16, 131). This leads to Dewey's analysis of the state, which he understands to be an organized public plus those agencies (39).[34] This steady accrual of related concepts, from action and consequences to public and state, might make the state seem benign and the growth of a democratic state seem inevitable. But just because a state exists—just because there are officials who are supposed to look after the indirect consequences of action—does not mean that those officials are democratically controlled or that they truly look after the public interest. The state, for Dewey, is a perpetual problem, "by its very nature . . . something to be scrutinized, investigated, searched for" (31).

The danger that the state might not serve the public is just one example of a broader phenomenon, according to Dewey's analysis: the frequent failure of publics to recognize and care for all the indirect consequences of action, a failure that is a breakdown, a blockage in the circuits of experience itself. As he puts it, "An inchoate public is capable of organization only when indirect consequences are perceived, and when it is possible to project agencies which order their occurrence." But, he argues, "At present, many consequences are felt rather than perceived; they are suffered, but they cannot be said to be known, for they are not, by those who experience them, referred to their origins" (Dewey [1927] 1954, 131). Referring consequences to their origins would largely mean the public tracing its problems to its members' own activities. In modern societies, there are "an indefinite number of ramifying conditions between what a person does and the consequences of his actions, including even the consequences which return upon him. The intervals in time and space are so extensive that the large number of factors that decide the final outcome cannot be foreseen" ([1939] 1989, 51).

We can grasp a part of the phenomenon of failure by turning to Dewey's analysis of "the Great Society." This is not, to use a Deweyism, a *eulogistic* term. It just signifies, for Dewey, a society in which the most important forces people confront are the remote, indirect consequences of their common action. In a "Great Society," in contrast to one characterized by

"face-to-face" interactions—or by associations that are "local and con-
tiguous and consequently visible"—it is "mechanical forces and vast
impersonal organizations" that determine "the frame of things" (Dewey
[1927] 1954, 96–97). A keyword from *Individualism Old and New*
([1929] 1999) refers, as well, to an aspect of this modern tendency: "corporateness." We in the contemporary world, Dewey thinks, are buffeted
by large-scale forces well beyond our control. "The United States has
steadily moved from an earlier pioneer individualism to a condition of
dominant corporateness" (18), Dewey contends. The industrial economy,
in particular, confronts most ordinary people, especially workers, as a
"despotic master" ([1927] 1954, 184), leaving them "hapless subjects of
overwhelming operations" (130) who face "dominantly controlling forces"
([1935] 2000, 42).[35] So "corporateness" refers not only to employment
and business corporations themselves, but to the general phenomenon of
indirect consequences, manifested as "impersonal forces" such as "mass
production" and "mass distribution" dominating "the choices and actions
of individuals" ([1929] 1999, 18, 19). Under such conditions, when "concentration and corporate organization are the rule," the "isolated individual is well-nigh helpless" ([1935] 2000, 65). Much of modern politics,
then, can be understood as the attempt of many to protect themselves
from the "destructive impact of impersonal forces" ([1939] 1989, 54).

These kinds of phenomena are not merely national in scope, nor are
they exclusively economic. Dewey also perceives them as well in connection with World War I. Here he emphasizes the difficulty for a public in
making sense of the "extensive, enduring, intricate and serious indirect
consequences" of war ([1927] 1954, 128). The difficulty arose because
of the many "connections and ties," "political structures," and "intricate and interdependent economic relations" implicated in the war and
all the "overwhelming operations" of these things (128, 129, 130). The
public inability to trace from common activity to consequence, or (in the
other direction) from experienced difficulty to active social causes, led
many people to conclude, wrongly, that "the spread of war" was beyond
human regulation, "like the movement of an uncontrolled natural catastrophe" (128). There were, in other words, phenomena that undermined
the ability of a public to trace the overwhelming problems it experienced
to their social origins, and subsequently to organize itself to deal with
those problems.

This analysis focuses both on publics themselves—including the quality
of public communication, and the ability to use joint inquiry into political

and social problems—and on extremely troubling contemporary social forces that are the result of common activities. Both of these are equally aspects of Dewey's analysis of modern political experience and its challenges. One might say that the alienation in question here refers, on the one hand, to the public losing track (and thus losing control) of the consequences of what it does. Kosnoski is right, in this sense, to emphasize Dewey's view that the shape of modern society "obscures the manner in which one institution, social group, or individual affects another" (2005b, 198).[36] Contemporary publics do not perceive indirect consequences of common activities (Dewey [1927] 1954, 32, 131). But this is not just a cognitive problem, one of grasping and expressing complexity versus simplicity, of understanding and good communication versus confusion. Just deploring the deficiencies of present-day communication and public inquiry does not in itself explain anything about the momentousness of the problems at hand or the difficulty of addressing them. Alienation, for Dewey, is not just the communicative, intellectual problem of losing track of consequences, but just as aptly, the particular uncontrolled nature of the evils experienced. It refers to the sense in which people are dominated by impersonal forces and experience them as "despotic master[s]" (184). These two dimensions of what we might term "alienation" are intimately connected through the continuous cycle of experience, such that the nature of one can only be understood in light of the other.

In light of all this, it should come as little surprise that Dewey's democratic theory is infused with the theme of resistance to these alienated forces—to struggle and to active, ongoing political effort. "The present struggle in this country," Dewey contends, is a struggle "against the destructive encroachments of forces that are alien to democracy" ([1937] 1987, 297). This "struggle for democracy has to be maintained," Dewey writes, on "many fronts" ([1939] 1989, 132). "To form itself," Dewey writes, "the public has to break existing political forms" ([1927] 1954, 31). The modern world, Dewey contends, is characterized by industrial power and physical power "undreamed of a century ago" runaway "forces" that can affect people from "the other side of the world" ([1939] 1989, 126). And under such circumstances the challenge of "freedom" is one of recapturing such powers, "management and direction of the new physical energies so that they contribute to the realization of human possibilities" ([1939] 1989, 128).

There is a similar oppositional emphasis in Dewey's schematic depiction of democratic history, broadly. Even familiar political democracy has to be understood as a reaction to a "historical background," the tendency of governments to be captured by various private interests. The theory and practice of political democracy, Dewey writes,

> represent an effort in the first place to *counteract* the forces that have so largely determined the possession of rule by accidental and irrelevant factors . . . to *counteract* the tendency to employ political power to serve private instead of public ends. To discuss democratic government at large apart from its historic background is to miss its point. ([1927] 1954, 83; italics added)

But is it just the *means* of gaining democracy—not democracy itself— that entails struggle? Given his approach to values and to means and ends, Dewey gives us little reason to reach such a conclusion. Consistent with his general philosophical method, Dewey is at great pains in the very essay just quoted to insist that democratic ends and means should be understood as consistent with each other. (The title of the essay, after all, is "Democracy Is Radical," not "Achieving Democracy Requires Radical Means.") And while the harmony of democratic means and ends signifies, for Dewey, a rejection of violence, he is not arguing that democratic ends are fixed and known and that democratic means must therefore be subordinated to them. (This would be at odds with his whole approach to social theory.) Dewey is deeply suspicious of dogmatic reliance on "class struggle," but he refuses to rule it out as a means of democratization. He insists only that it "has to be justified, on the ground of the interdependence of means and end, by an examination of the actual consequences of its use" ([1938] 1993, 232). Unsurprisingly, he is quite insistent on this point, arguing that democratic means and ends condition each other, that they are "one and inseparable." Democratic faith itself—not just the path to democracy—is oppositional, or as Dewey puts it, "buoyant, crusading and militant" ([1937] 1987, 299). And there is little reason to think that this is a temporary matter, a present, contingent historical fact. Democratic struggle is ongoing; it must be constantly renewed. Since ends cannot be defined separately from daily experience, the "result" we should care about is one attained "today, tomorrow, the next day, and the day after day, in the succession of years and generations." "Democratic method" is both "simple" and "immensely difficult"; it is "the energetic, unflagging, unceasing creation of an ever-present new road upon which we can walk together" ([1939] 1989, 134).

None of this, of course, means that communication—deliberation as contemporary thinkers would say—is not also central to Dewey's understanding of democracy. "Free and systematic communication" is essential, Dewey argues ([1927] 1954, 167). Nor does this mean that it is possible for democratic actors to do nothing but struggle perpetually on exposed terrain against vast, impersonal forces. As a good participatory democrat, Dewey is attentive to the relationship between different spheres of activity, to the way in which practices and skills learned in one can be put to use in another. Dewey praises associational life partly because of the way it can help people better understand and connect to their social worlds (Kosnoski 2005b). As Dewey puts it, "there is no substitute for the vitality and depth of close and direct intercourse and attachment" ([1927] 1954, 213). But life in small, face-to-face associations is no alternative to, no permanent escape from, democratic struggle for Dewey; indeed, its value is in part due to the way it can inform and enable such democratic striving.

Still, in light of everything we have seen, it would also be a serious mistake to think that for Dewey, robust democratic communication is an answer in itself—or something purely discursive, something distinct from or prior to potent common action. Dewey's theory of experience, we know, thoroughly entwines thought and action. Intelligent reflection, for Dewey, is only triggered when action confronts a difficulty, and thought is feeble and stale unless it leads to new action and reflection. Even new ideas were not to be expected from discourse alone; it is "unique modes of activity that create new ends," he argues ([1922] 1993, 77). This is why Dewey insists that "[it] is false that freedom of inquiry and of expression are not modes of action" ([1935] 2000, 69). Given this active emphasis, the sort of communication that is vital to solving political and social problems democratically, according to Dewey, is communication that is thoroughly engaged in active, participatory experimentation. This cannot be reduced to mere discursive, pluralistic openness and self-critical fallibilism, however important these qualities may be to scientific experiment. Dewey is quite clear that discussion, "the comparison of ideas already current so as to purify and clarify them," is insufficient: "Discussion and dialectic, however indispensable they are to the elaboration of ideas and policies after ideas are once put forth, are weak reeds to depend upon for . . . the plans that are required if the problem of social organization is to be met" ([1935] 2000, 73).

So it is political experiment, active intervention in the world and observation of results, that is democratically crucial for Dewey. Dewey's approach entails, as well, that it is not just experts who ought to take part in such intelligent activity. It seems quite clear that this insight is behind Dewey's view of the labor problem. What is needed for a democratic economy is not just a public discussion of the comparative justice claims of unions and management. What is needed is the creation of industrial democracy, "cooperative control of industry," the involvement of workers themselves in experimentally directing industry, which would liberate minds, give them "nourishment," reward knowledge, and promote "initiative and responsibility" ([1929] 1999, 64). And while Dewey is not as clear about this as he could be, it seems fair to assume that his sympathy for the labor movement and for strikes is not merely a matter of the "end" toward which strikers direct themselves—even if we assume that end to be industrial democracy itself—but also a judgment that their "means" are consonant with those ends, that the labor movement, in at least some of its phases, can itself be understood as an example of "buoyant, crusading and militant" democracy.[37]

Limits, Cautions, Clarifications

All interpretations are guided both by an impulse to understand and a reason for trying. I have been concerned in this chapter to uncover and scrutinize a common aspect of Marx's and Dewey's understandings of democracy. My motive for this is that I think they recognized not some transhistorical *philosophical* problem but an enduring aspect of the modern political world, a recurrent challenge for democrats. Uncovering this feature of their thought is not the same task as providing a full and comprehensive interpretation of Marx's and Dewey's democratic theories, much less an exhaustive elucidation of their whole body of work, in which we might properly place the single conception that I have examined. Furthermore, in the remainder of this book I make no claim to be offering an authentically Marxian or Deweyan political theory, in any strong sense. Even the rest of my comments in this chapter concern, not so much Marx's and Dewey's own strengths and errors, per se, as the advantages and risks for those who attempt to build upon their understandings of democracy and alienation.

I argued in the first chapter that the dominant modes of democratic theory share a number of problematic conceptions, and that the difficulties they entail are not solved—in fact, they are in certain ways made worse—by the attempt by some deliberative theorists to partition ideal from nonideal theory. In contrast, Marx and Dewey both avoid treating the task of political theory chiefly as the imaginative construction of ideals in their perfect form, *sub specie aeternitatis*. For Marx, this resistance grows out of his rejection of Hegelian idealism, his adoption of a more or less pragmatic criterion of truth and validity, and his suspicion (rooted also in the materialist conception of history) that those who claim that they are finding ideal values on some ground independent of experience are likely just to be projecting the dominant values of their society into the imagined eternal. For Dewey, this resistance follows from a more fully elaborated, pragmatic theory of the origin of values—a theory that holds that values are simply those things and activities that we value in the here and now, in the imperfect world we actually experience. But what is most important, from my standpoint, is simply the way that the linking of alienation to democracy—theorizing the connection, in itself—entails avoiding the dichotomy of ideal and nonideal. Neither Marx nor Dewey begins with an ideal of what perfect democratic relations would look like. Instead, alienation enters at the ground level of their democratic theorizing. It colors and shapes what democracy means to each of them just as democratic aspirations shape their understanding of alienation. Both alienation and democracy are integral parts of their respective understandings of the problematics of action, their theories of how action can misfire, and what to do about it. In this sense, their democratic theory is neither ideal nor purely nonideal. In any case, the abstention from ideal theorizing pervades their approaches to democracy.

This also has diverse implications for how they avoid undue emphasis on the other problematic concepts I outlined in Chapter 1: democracy surrounded by fortifications, either as a refuge or as a quarantine; democracy conceived primarily as a special kind of relationship among citizens; democracy as a kind of regime or institution; and democracy as a way of making decisions. The refuge/quarantine model of democracy both forgets that democracy as it is almost always encountered is an active engagement, a challenging interaction with powerful opponents and overshadowing forces. It also makes it difficult to imagine valuing that engagement itself. Surely, the refuge approach suggests, true democracy would not be such a struggle, but a practice carried on without the threat of nonideal elements. By casting democracy as the ongoing practice of

81

recapturing the state—and other alienated social forces or structures—and by envisioning democracy as a struggle, perhaps even a "battle"—Marx and Dewey effectively avoid conceiving of democracy as a refuge from the day-to-day, postlapsarian world of politics. Neither proposes creating democratic havens nor even has a vision of what such havens would look like. In fact, Marx disparages merely political emancipation for projecting universal citizenship as part of a political realm so distant and abstract that real human beings never enjoy it.

Similarly, the portrayal of democracy as a special, refined kind of relationship among citizens, I have argued, runs afoul of dangerous reductionism: treating all democratic agents just as citizens and collapsing the critical analysis of democracy into an ideal conception of the citizen. Negatively, so to speak, neither Marx nor Dewey devotes much space to constructing ideal citizens or even ideal relations between citizens. They do not treat the elaboration of democratic norms as a path toward or even an intimation of real democratic enjoyment. In fact, Marx is quite attentive to what is involved in certain portrayals of the human being as a citizen: bifurcating both the person and society, leaving untouched the realm of day-to-day life as a consumer and producer, while relegating life as a citizen to a sphere, again, that no one truly experiences.

Another problematic conceptualization in contemporary democratic theory, I have argued, is an institutional, governmental view of democracy. In itself, this approach tends to deemphasize democratic action, democracy *as* action, but it also creates the quandary of how to classify imperfectly democratic societies. The institutional view, if it centers on a single fixed institutional form, can also make it hard to recognize institutional (and other) variations in democracy that may be needed to cope with varying challenges. Both Marx and Dewey ground their whole approaches to social theory in reflexive action (or as Dewey would have it, "experience"). And not surprisingly, then, they have active conceptions of democracy, especially democracy as struggle, as the constantly renewed effort of taking back alienated institutions and forces. In itself, this undermines an ordinary institutional view of democracy. And Dewey quite explicitly derogates the standard institutional conception of democracy, democracy as a set of familiar electoral and legislative institutions.

Finally, there is democracy as a way of reaching decisions. An exclusive focus on decisions can miss or marginalize a great deal: the ongoing tide of reflexive action in which deliberate decision is just one moment, and the significance of nondecisions, aspects of the social world that condition or limit our choices and that sometimes are taken as natural. Marx is not prone to these errors, nor is Dewey. Indeed, in insisting that ideas can only be verified in action (Marx and Dewey), and that decision making is only a moment of experience, one that is triggered only when action becomes problematic (Dewey), both Marx and Dewey make it impossible to isolate and valorize decisions and decision making this way. At the same time, the emphasis on alienation, on malign, dominating forces produced unintentionally by human action, is in itself a focus on *non*decisions.

This review of constructive, promising aspects of Marx's and Dewey's thought—this tour of problems avoided—in no way means that their theories of democracy and alienation are fully formed or entirely perfected. In both cases, it is necessary to criticize, develop, reconsider, and broaden the scope or extend the logic of different aspects of their approaches.

The most prominent risk in extending Marx's and Dewey's recognition of the interplay of alienation and democracy is thinking that the point of identifying this problematic is to figure out a way to escape it permanently. The legitimately utopian aspect of democratic thought is the desire to identify what is valuable about the democratic experience now and to consider how that experience might be enhanced, enriched, and extended into a more democratic future. But this by no means requires us to imagine what democratic life would be like if it faced no alienated challenges. Doing so would constitute utopian ambition in an illegitimate sense. A different, related utopianism could result from imagining that historically concrete, practical problems of alienation might be overcome with a dramatic shift in thinking alone, apart from the quotidian challenges of practical political experimentation. Hegel gestures in this direction, I think, in his narrative of the French Revolution's aftermath.[38] Some might also hold out the hope that the problem of alienation could be resolved permanently in a new form of society or in a more fulfilling kind of productive activity. This is the potential in Marx's thought, explored in David McLellan's suggestively titled essay, "Marx's View of the Unalienated Society" (1969). Striving to deal democratically with challenges of alienation does not require such an expectation. Finally, there is a possible reading of Dewey, growing out of his contrast between the Great Society and an earlier pioneer America: the idea that alienation would not exist in less complex forms of society than our own, communities characterized by a high degree of social transparency and simplicity ([1927] 1954, 111).[39] All these pitfalls are best avoided, not so much by a close critical examination of different utopias as by extending the sober view of human agency and its limits we can find in both Marx and Dewey—a view that recognizes alienation as both a perennial problem that no form of society is likely to escape permanently as well as a distinct phenomenon that must not be reduced to relatively benign features of social life. This is the work of the next chapters, guided by lessons learned in this one.

Beyond utopian temptations, there are other issues—both potential mistakes to be avoided, or underdeveloped conceptualizations to be expanded upon—that are particular to either Marx or to Dewey, individually. To begin with Marx, it is necessary to consider what is involved, precisely, in viewing alienation as a problem that extends beyond the sphere of production. This is a feature of Marx's own work, surely. "Marx's theory of alienation," Thomas writes, "was never intended to be restricted to the dimensions of a critique of the organization of factory production on the shop floor of the machine age" (1994, 109). So it is worth contrasting two ways in which it might be possible to continue the work of broadening Marx's alienation theory. One is the approach taken by Fromm in *The Sane Society* ([1955] 1990). In this work Fromm attempts to show how a wide range of the most important "disturbances" in the "mental health" of "modern Western man" are due to the alienation that is inherent to capitalist production (83). That such a diversity of ills might be due to productive alienation only seems plausible to Fromm because alienation refers to an underlying social-psychological problem, to the very the shape of modern character under capitalism.[40] According to Fromm, Marx thinks that under alienated labor "man does not experience himself as the acting agent in his grasp of the world" (1961, 44). So, more broadly for Fromm, alienation means "experiencing the world and oneself passively, receptively, as the subject separated from the object" (44). In contrast, the aspect of Marx's alienation I single out for attention concerns particular unintended consequences, harmful structural consequences, of common action in general. I do not assume that every or even most forms of delusion and suffering can be chalked up to alienation. Rather, I suggest we look for particular damaging structural consequences of action in the economy, politics, and society, generally, and consider democracy as a response to them. And this involves elaborating a realistic theory of action and the steps required to progress from such a theory to an understanding of how alienation arises.

This problem of generalizing Marx's theory of alienation, then, is in part the problem of generalizing from an analysis of labor to an analysis of action, generally. Ollman argues that for Marx, work is simply a kind of activity, particularly the kind of activity that produces use values (1971, 99–105). Marx's materialist conception of history clearly prioritizes productive work, but that does not mean that action, generally, shares no important qualities of work, particularly. Indeed, this must be the case if Thomas is right to suggest that Marx did not intend to limit the conception of alienation to the capitalist economy. Work, the production of use values, often entails objectification in one sense, the creation of objects, physical things that, once made, are self-standing and separate from those who use or interact with them. It is important to specify the sense in which action, broadly, can be objectified, and whether objectified action is necessarily alienated action. What, in other words, is objectification, generally, and what distinguishes that which is alienated from that which is objectified?

Running both between and within the four types of alienation classically identified by Marx in the *Economic and Philosophic Manuscripts* is a possible distinction between what could roughly be termed psychological and social-structural meanings of alienation. On the one hand, we have questions about how a person experiences the world, how she contemplates herself and her place in that world, how she feels about this interaction, and what she recognizes about that interaction. One might say that with respect to these questions it is the person who may be alienated—for example, if he fails to recognize that "he contemplates himself in a world he has created" ([1844] 1964, 114). Fromm strongly emphasizes this sort of psychological—or in the terminology used by Schaff (1980), "subjective"—alienation. On the other hand, we confront questions about the qualities of social structures and forces and the sense in which they may escape the control of or dominate over human beings who reproduce them, in which case it is the structures that are alienated. Marx's alienation from the activity of labor, alienation from species being, and alienation from other persons seem to partake, potentially, of both kinds of alienation, psychological and social-structural. Yet, the distinction needs to be clarified so that we can understand what sort of alienation democratic action combats.

A last issue that needs further consideration, as part of a fuller theorization of action and alienation, is a claim Marx makes in "The Eighteenth Brumaire." There he says that the ability of the French state to tower above French society was not simply a result of the contemporary play of social forces but was a legacy from the past, especially of the state-building projects of modernizing monarchs. To those who cling to a simplified base-superstructure scheme for understanding Marx's materialist conception of history, this must be particularly puzzling. According to such an interpretation, Marx sees the state as a reflection, pure and simple, of the capitalist forces of its time. Yet Marx's analysis of Louis Napoleon apparently evades such a characterization. To approach the problem from a different direction, we can best make sense of action and alienation by exploring the problem of *structuration,* which refers, roughly, to the mutual dependency of agency and structure. Structuration, particularly the insight that there can be no structure unless it is reproduced by present action, is sometimes thought to rule out such a possibility of the dead hand of the past exerting a present power. Whether or not structuration theory can support the view that the past is a powerful force in the present will be considered in the next chapter.[41]

Turning to Dewey's conceptualization of alienation and democracy, there is a need to clarify the meaning of the "consequences" of action. One way to approach this problem is to consider two things Dewey tells us about the sort of problems that both provoke and hinder the formation of publics. The first is that publics lose track of the consequences of what they do. The second is that publics face dominating forces, impersonal "despotic masters." But what is the relationship between these two problems? Dewey's argument is suggestive, but not entirely clear. For the most part, Dewey treats "consequences" like ripples radiating from a stone thrown into a pool, as a chain of reactions—perhaps like the Rube Goldberg movement of prodded parrots, rolling balls, and levers, all linked together in one machine. Goldberg machines are not an entirely facetious example, for on reflection, they hint at the right question: how did the machine come to be that converted the motion of my soup spoon into the wiping of a napkin across my lips? Or, to ask a related question, if my action has "ramifying" consequences that affect you, what shapes and directs the spread of these consequences? Some unintended consequences of common actions may not properly be understood as events, at all, but rather as contributions of some kind to the creation of overwhelming forces, social relations, and structures that channel the effects of actions.[42]

This perplexity about Dewey's account is related to the question I raised above concerning Marx's view of the influence of the past in shaping the present. Like many Progressive thinkers, Dewey was quite attentive to the way in which old, outmoded ideas can hinder present progress—for example, the way that a form of "individualism" that made sense in early America can be to the detriment of modern Americans. But his view of ramifying consequences would not seem to support the idea that present action could be shaped, directed, or constrained by the actions of people long dead. The ramifying consequences motif would seem to refer to a more or less contemporary chain of events, perhaps a very long one. So again, a fuller consideration of social structure and its relation to action would seem to be necessary to explain the way the present can be structured by past choices and actions.

Dewey's conceptualization of common action and alienation—or rather its limits—also points to a need to think carefully about how power should fit into such a narrative. Dewey has frequently been criticized for blithely neglecting questions of power. There are passages, it should be said, where he suggests he is not at all unaware of the issue, as when he writes that "liberty" is "power, effective power to do specific things," that the "demand for liberty is a demand for power," and that the distribution of "powers or liberties" is "identical with actual social arrangements" ([1935] 1993, 158, 159). These claims point tantalizingly in the direction of a proper consideration of power. Hildreth, then, is probably right that power is an "implicit" aspect of Dewey's democratic theory—indeed a sufficiently integral one that a Deweyan understanding of power can be reconstructed (2009, 780). But such interpretive work is not my main purpose in this book. I derive the needed conception of power from other, more recent, sources.

In Chapter 3, then, I aim to address some of the difficulties raised in the last few pages by elaborating a contemporary conception of action and alienation. In Chapter 4, I show how such a conception should shape our understanding of democracy and the conditions under which it arises.

3

A CONTEMPORARY THEORY OF ALIENATION

The hydra that took hold of Sheila Ramos and her grandchildren, tore them from a ranch house in Florida, and deposited them to live in a tent in Hawaii menaced her with various heads, some visible, others obscure. There was an enabling mortgage broker, a callous judge, and a long succession of anonymous call-center workers.[1] But the ligaments and body, the whole hydra, was the financial crisis that began to reach around the world in 2007. Confronting its vastness and sinewy strength, Ramos never really had a chance; foreclosure was all but inevitable. Ramos's story has its own particular twists, including a business gone sour and a car crash. Even when at the mercy of wide-ranging social forces, each individual's experience of those forces tends to differ. But a key to the tale is that Ramos used her Florida house as a credit card—not for luxuries but to start a business and to get through difficult straits. When she had trouble making her mortgage payments, she was unable to sell the house to escape her doom. The real estate bubble had burst, and the house was worth less than what she owed. After strenuous efforts to keep it, she gave up, accepted foreclosure, and moved her family to an undeveloped patch of land in the north of the Big Island. By that time it was the only way to avoid homelessness and losing her grandchildren to foster care.

It would be possible to construct a narrative of Ramos's experience that focuses on her particular misfortunes and mistakes. Equally, we could center our attention on those bankers and brokers who were able to exploit people like Ramos and still escape the worst of the crisis themselves. But either approach would risk missing the big picture of the financial crisis, as well as the point that makes Ramos's story so relevant to democratic thinking. Tolstoy says that to understand everything is to forgive everything. That may be so, but for our purposes, it is surely understanding, not judging or forgiving, that matters. Facing financial constraints, and encouraged by her broker, Ramos did something that millions of other Americans did in the 2000s: she used mortgage debt to finance current needs. And that had dire consequences for her and people like her. So the place to start is with a great number of people all doing much the same thing: acting on altered views of homeownership and consumption. Egged on by the financial industry, Americans took on mortgages and home equity loans in order to extract an incredible sum, $1.5 trillion, from their homes, in just two years (Kiel 2012). Their combined activities reproduced a stacked financial system, propped up the economy, and inflated house prices. All that would soon return to devastate many of them.

As in any situation in which overshadowing, threatening social forces rise up, there was not just one sort of person, doing one sort of thing, behind it all. It was, rather, the confluence of different kinds of widespread practices that was responsible. In this case, the millions of overleveraged homeowners were abetted by an army of mortgage brokers, whose ranks swelled by about two hundred thousand during the pumping up of the bubble (Kiel 2012). In order to squeeze as many people as possible into new loans, they engaged in an extraordinary array of new practices such as no-money-down mortgages and loans with monthly payments that failed to cover even interest. Often they just lied or encouraged borrowers to lie about their financial status (Stiglitz 2009, 85–86). But the brokers, in turn, were just representatives of the lenders and insurance companies that profited from these reckless and exploitive new financial practices. They took these dubious home loans and then combined them into what they claimed were sterling investment pools with names whose suffixes—like 2007-MLN1[2]—made them sound, appropriately, like strains of the flu. Other financial institutions bought into these pools, often with borrowed money, the leverage making it possible to enjoy staggering gains on little investment—or to lose far more than the original stake. Still other entities sold "insurance" for these volatile investments—insurance that really was a mechanism for speculators to profit from bets that the whole house of cards would collapse, as indeed it did.[3] All these practices were justified on the theory— discredited many times, but resurgent as the new wisdom of the financial elite—that "unfettered markets by themselves can ensure economic prosperity and growth" (Stiglitz 2009, xiii). It does not really matter whether we call this ideology "neoliberalism" (Crouch 2011) or "market fundamentalism" (Stiglitz 2009). It was entwined with the disastrous refashioning of mortgage banking and the dismantling by politicians, abetted by banking lobbyists, of the regulations that once kept writing mortgages a placid sector of the financial industry.

When the unraveling began, a new, overwhelming dynamic took hold: individuals were forced to take new actions that turned them into unwilling transmitters of spreading economic destruction. The first wave of foreclosures triggered more; the plunge in asset prices caused banks and insurance companies to collapse; each individual's dire circumstances forced her to cut back spending, which led to the next person, and the next, having to do the same. The country was suddenly beset by a bewildering array of intertwined, irresistible forces: waves of foreclosures, spiking unemployment, bank failures, credit constriction, and drastic government budget cuts that magnified the pain. Society was by now, to recall a phrase from Marx and Engels, like the sorcerer's apprentice, unable to control the forces "called up by his spells" ([1848] 2012, 79).

But however widely these overwhelming economic forces were experienced, they did not affect people equally. Many, like Ramos, became easy prey to the unscrupulous. Such people, who are often still feeling the effects of the meltdown years later, are not evenly distributed throughout America but are concentrated in lower-income communities and neighborhoods with large African American and Latino populations (Dreier et al. 2014). And beyond this uneven impact of foreclosures, there is the simple fact that the financial system put some people in the position to mistreat or take advantage of those hit hardest—before, during, and after the crisis. Early on, even as her problems worsened, her mortgage broker, who earned substantial fees at each turn, encouraged her to get in deeper. Later, as they tried to refinance their loans to avoid foreclosure, people like Ramos found themselves at the mercy of a large, complex financial machine, of offices that repeatedly lost paperwork and a legal process stacked against them. And though a few institutions suffered for a while, the financial industry as a whole was able to take advantage of its long-standing political and economic power, its privileged position, to avoid most of the consequences of the disaster.

Of course, the recent financial crisis is hardly unique in subjecting people to overwhelming social powers and making them vulnerable to others. That is, it is not the only example of what I term alienation: the condition that exists when their common action returns to people in the form of social forces, relations, or institutions that dominate some or all of them and enable some people to oppress or exploit others. Marx and Dewey, we have seen, were able to avoid some of the missteps of contemporary democratic theory by conceiving of democratic action in dialectical relation with this recurrent phenomenon of alienation. This way of conceiving of democratic life helped them avoid positing it as a refuge from the hard realities of politics as we generally know it. It allowed them to incorporate more of the practices of real democratic actors into their conceptions of democracy. It made it possible for them to portray domination and oppression not merely as violations of democratic norms, but as ongoing challenges with which democratic action is constantly grappling. It helped them point the way toward a view of democracy not as ideal, de novo decision making but as a continual struggle to recapture and redirect many of the institutions and forces we have already created and are always recreating.

But we cannot just adopt their theories wholesale, for a number of reasons. As the previous chapter made clear, it is important to get "alienation" right. First, it might be possible to theorize democracy's entwinement with alienation but still think that the ultimate goal is permanently to conquer it. Such an ambition is futile, in my view. In this chapter, I try to show why. Alienation, I argue, is a continual danger rooted in the preconditions and limits of human action—indeed in the very same problematics in which democratic action itself is also rooted. As I suggested in the last chapter, the utopian temptation to banish alienation is best resisted by starting with a sober view of human agency and its limits, recognizing alienation as a perennial problem that no society is likely to escape permanently. Even when it is concerned with agency—in this case, democratic agency—social and political critique should avoid a "Promethean exaltation of human mastery," as Jeffrey Isaac argues, and build instead on a view of human agents who are "enabled and constrained by historically evolved social structures which it is possible to understand and consciously change" (1992, 236). Such a spirit informs my approach. More concretely, I also try in this chapter to explore some of the challenges and puzzles not solved by Marx and Dewey, despite their insights: explaining the significance of viewing alienation as a possible tendency of action, generally, and not just of labor; asking how a social-structural theory of alienation may be different from a psychological one; questioning what it means to say that alienation involves the "consequences" of action; working out how a well-formulated conception of power and its different manifestations may be woven into the fabric of a theory of alienation; and accounting for the possibility of past action confronting present actors in alienated form.

In this chapter, I build a contemporary theory of alienation out of component conceptions: agency, action, and their relation to social structure; social forms that dominate or overshadow the agency of a great many people; and the unjust or exploitive acts by a smaller number of people that these social forms foster. I try to elucidate the logic and workings of social structures and forces that resist common management, that overshadow the ability of ordinary people to act, that force stark choices on them, social forms that at the same time make it possible for some people to exercise power over others harshly or unjustly. My interest, ultimately, is not in these sorts of alienated structures or forces alone, but their integral relation to democracy. If alienation is a chronic feature of modern social and political life, then it is an unavoidable, intrinsic challenge for democracy, and a crucial topic for democratic theory. Engagement with alienation is basic to democracy as we have always known it—integral, as well, to democracy as we are ever likely to know it.

In the next section, then, I explore *action* or agency from several aspects. *Action* is the first of a series of building-block terms leading to a conception of *alienation*. So after action, I discuss *objectification* as the tendency of common action to produce or reproduce structures and forces that appear to people to be external to them—in this sense, object-like. *Alienation,* as I use the term, is not identical to *objectification*. In particular, clarifying the distinct significance of alienation involves elucidating phenomena that distinguish it, namely *domination, oppression,* and *exploitation*.

After exploring these concepts, the last major section of the chapter illustrates what is involved in seeing markets, one of the ubiquitous features of modern societies, as always potentially alienated. I relate market phenomena to the main elements of my conception of alienation: social action, objectification, domination, and oppression. I explore a contemporary case of market activity helping sustain exploitive social relations, with sometimes shocking consequences. And I investigate how identifying markets as a potential site of alienation is—and is not—different from another time-honored approach to market critique, one focusing on particular intrusions of market practices in realms where they arguably do not belong.

On Action, as a Step toward Theorizing Alienation

It is not surprising that understanding alienation and democracy requires some reckoning with the problem of agency, the problem of the human capacity to act.[4] Democratic theory has long been, in part, a quarrel about agency: about whether, for example, ordinary people could live up to certain purported standards of democratic agency and about what phase, aspect, or kind of action should be understood as the true heart of democracy. A caustic dismissal of popular agency is really the centerpiece of both Lippmann's critique of the public and Schumpeter's well-known rejection of "classical" democracy.[5] Much participatory theory has been centered on attempts to challenge these skeptical portrayals of ordinary people's agency, as well as, of course, to argue for a more active conception of democratic citizenship. Jeffrey Edward Green's recent work advancing an "ocular" theory of democracy (2010a) also turns crucially on questions of agency. In fact, he distinguishes two kinds of political agents, those who have voice and decide and those who are merely spectators. And although Green aims to dampen expectations of what citizens, the spectators, can do, even their "gaze," in his telling, intervenes significantly in political events: it disciplines politicians, "achieves surveillance," and "functions as the chief organ of popular empowerment" (9–10).

Deliberative theory, for all of its surprising affinities with elite theory,[6] also challenges the elite assumption that ordinary people's political capacities and inclinations constitute a fixed impediment to robust democratic politics. Yet at the same time, it does this from the standpoint of a rather particular, arguably narrow, vision of political agency. Deliberation may be understood as joint, normatively guided communicative action directed toward making decisions. Since deliberation, so understood, is just one of many possible kinds or modes of political action, focusing on it tends to deemphasize or even derogate other modes, like voting, marching, and building political organizations. (I return to this in Chapter 4.) And if decision, the heart of deliberative interest, is (as I shall argue in this chapter) never more than a moment or phase in the ongoing process of social action, generally, deliberative theory may tend to neglect the other phases. Deliberative democracy has much to say about facilitating more ideal discussion but not much about the questions of agency central to this chapter: the powers and capacities that enable and constrain practical political intervention; the possibility that some consequences of common action may return to ordinary people in a form that undermines their agency, and in a shape they do not fully recognize as their own work; and the ambition to make ordinary people's active intervention in politics more fruitful and effective in the future.

Structuration: Reconciling Agency and Structure

Debate about agency in social science, broadly, has tended to play out a little differently than in democratic theory, more specifically. Social theorists have often aligned themselves with approaches that hold either human agency or social structure to be primary, asserting, at one extreme, that society can be understood as reducible to individuals and their voluntary acts or, at the other, that society is really a network of "hidden structures" that make individuals their unwitting instruments (Giddens 1979, 40). But inquiry into the possibilities of democratic life can only be fully compelling in terms of some sort of nonreductive, dialectical understanding of agency and structure.[7] Refusal to derogate either agency or structure—to reduce structure to agency or agency to structure—will prove important to how I portray democracy and its challenges. If society can always be reduced to individuals and their acts, without remainder, then democracy would seem to face only the challenges deriving directly from the proclivities or limitations of agents themselves. Democracy might seem entirely unproblematic, according to one such account, or it might seem prone only to the pathologies resulting from people's motivations or their limited rationality, as elite theorists seem to suggest. In this case, calls for democratization would often seem to lack either critical edge or credibility. On the other hand, if society can be reduced to structure, if action is merely epiphenomenal, then calls for democratization would seem to be pointless and democracy itself a sham. One could only scoff at the ambition of citizens to manage their social worlds on equal and free terms.

People who are not social scientists or philosophers do not routinely refer to "agency," to "action" abstractly, or to "social structure." Yet they constantly use lay understandings of agency, to begin with, and scholarly concepts of agency are just reworkings of these basic ideas. In day-to-day life, we recurrently make judgments, both practical and ethical, for example, about what agents can and cannot do—something we do with the help of at least tentative notions of agency and its limits, as Giddens argues (1993, 78). Such notions are at work when we assign blame or praise, contend that someone should have acted a certain way, claim that someone could have behaved differently, or judge that someone performed well or poorly. Any assessment of Sheila Ramos's story, for example, will necessarily involve such judgments, ones about what actions were open to her and what possibilities were closed off. It is the same with standard political judgments, ones about the doings of parties, movements, and elected officials.

Just as fundamental as a layperson's experience of agency is her experience of confronting patterned aspects of the social world that she has not, on her own, created—features such as languages and social institutions. In Ramos's case, these included the economy, in general, and the banking system, in particular. These structural features of society may limit what a person can do—making it impossible to accomplish certain things or restricting how she can express herself. But they may also enable a person to act, providing her with resources, capacities, and more or less established repertoires for getting things done. At the heart of Ramos's story are the severe constraints the economy finally placed on her, forcing her to choose, for instance, between keeping her grandchildren and staying in Florida. But all along, the banking system also made it possible for her to do certain things, as well: to buy a home, start a business, or just pay for groceries with an ATM card.

As developed by both Giddens and Pierre Bourdieu, structuration theories make it possible to think nonexclusively and nonreductively about agency and structure. For Giddens, "structuration" insists on the "duality of structure." It recognizes "the mutual dependence of structure and agency," the fact that "the structural properties of social systems are both the medium and the outcome of the practices that constitute those systems" (Giddens 1979, 69).[8] This means that it is action—or participation in shared practices—that maintains structures like states and families, even while, at the same time, agents rely on structures to intervene actively in the world. Structure, Giddens argues, should not be seen purely as an external limit on agency; "structure," rather, "is both enabling and constraining" (69). Bourdieu begins with a different conceptual challenge. He sets out to undermine the pretensions of both "subjectivist" knowledge, which privileges the "primary experience" or self-understandings of agents, and "objectivist" knowledge, which claims to discern structures that are entirely independent of what agents know (1973, 53; 1977, 3). His own alternative emphasizes the "dialectic" between "objective structures" and the know-how of agents.

Aspects of the position I outline concerning agency, structure, objectification, and alienation also draw particularly on critical realism, an approach to social theory most closely associated with Roy Bhaskar. In contrast to empiricism and interpretive science, critical realism insists that social science is centrally concerned with the exploration of social structures and their properties.[9] Structuration arguably entails a critical realist viewpoint, a recognition that social structures have causal powers and are, in this sense, real (Shapiro and Wendt 1992, 213).[10]

Structuration helps make it possible to avoid a "Promethean" view of agency; and it sets the stage, as we shall see, for an understanding of one way agency can misfire. Agency is real enough, from the standpoint of structuration, but it does not stand on its own, so to speak. Social structure enables action or shapes the capacities that are necessary for action (Giddens 1979, 53, 69; Bhaskar 1998, 212–218). Basic examples might include the way in which a language constituted by speakers makes it possible to write a poem, express an unconventional opinion, or just order dinner—or the way a banking system makes it possible to write a check or borrow to buy a house. Bourdieu insists that such action-enabling structures are not merely external to human beings but are inculcated in them as "habitus," a set of dispositions or "strategy-generating principle[s]" (1977, 72). This insight that structure enables and constrains action is, again, just one side of structuration theory. Under the heading of "objectification," I shall return soon to the other: the view that structures only exist in virtue of ongoing action.

Action, Reflexive and Social

Another doubt about any vision of human agency as continually innovative, potent, and self-sufficient is that people rarely even enact fully formed, a priori plans and intentions, let alone unprecedented ones. Much of social and political life flows onward without most people seriously, systematically reflecting on it, let alone authorizing by conscious decision what happens or how it comes to be. Compared to how frequently we act—or how much, how continuously, we engage in activity—true, explicit decision is a rarity.

Yet political theory—and democratic theory in particular—is often quite focused on decisions, as I have suggested. This may, to many people, seem hardly worth noting. But in fact we should ask what assumptions could justify the singular emphasis on decision. Two candidates seem apparent. One is *separability*. To justify isolating decisions, we must assume that decision making can be understood as something unto itself, with its own distinct domain. The other is *primacy*. We must assume that decision making does, can, or should shape the rest of social or political life in a way that social and political life do not, cannot, or should not shape decision making. There must be no cost to seeing decision making as distinct, temporally prior to, and causally effective over social and political action. There are a number of ways to call such assumptions into question. I have already suggested that they do not seem to capture very well the experience of movements. And a fully reflexive theory of action also provides a framework that shows why such assumptions should be put aside.

The key is understanding action not as a series of discrete, preplanned, predecided "acts," but as a process, one in which thinking, reflecting, and deciding are thoroughly entwined in the ongoing progress of events.[11] For Dewey, we have seen, such an outlook was related to his determination to puncture philosophical claims for the autonomy of detached, contemplative reason. Dewey argued that philosophers should stop extracting thought from its place in the continuous, active, process of "experience," and instead learn from its inevitable entwinement with "action and undergoing." Experience was, for all agents, thoroughly situated in time, in an "ongoing, unfinished and ambiguously potential world" ([1929] 1958, 53). It consisted of a continuous stream rather than a set of discrete points, a never-ending movement combining "desiring, striving, thinking, feeling" (76). Such experience was ever directed at modifying or transforming the world's tendencies and events—and refining one's capacities, understandings, and goals—all in the name of richer and better-regulated experience in the future. From this temporal standpoint, Dewey argued, it was clear that "conscious intent" emerged not before action, as its autonomous author, but in the midst of action—over time and in response to continual experiences of "resistance and conflict" ([1934] 1980, 35).

Giddens arrives at similar conclusions about time and reflexive action by a different route. He is concerned with undermining the philosophical antinomy of agency and structure, and one way to do this, in his view, is to show the importance of time—time as duration—for agency and, by extension, for structure. Much like Dewey, Giddens portrays action not as "a series of discrete acts combined together," but as *a continuous flow of conduct,*" or "a stream of actual or contemplated causal interventions of corporeal beings in the ongoing process of events-in-the-world" (1979, 55). He argues that human agents do not, by and large, formulate distinct intentions in advance of a series of discrete acts. For

Giddens, "only in the reflexive act of attention are intentions consciously articulated" (40). This "reflexive monitoring of conduct" is a "chronic feature of the enactment of social life," he argues (39). The fact that people do not usually act according to preformed decision does not mean they are thoughtless or incompetent. Although agents are continuously engaged in a flow of action, when asked for an account of what they are doing, they often can provide one. They can make their practical knowledge an object of discursive consciousness, putting into words what they knew before only practically and tacitly. This may involve isolating and explaining a particular phase of action. So in this sense, for Giddens, discrete acts and singular intentions do not exist in themselves, so to speak. They are really the artificial product of thought or reflection, of the mental abstraction of action from the flow of time. And since, for Giddens, there can be no structure without agency, and since action is thoroughly situated in time, structure, too, cannot be understood outside of time. Without continual reenactment, structures could not exist.

For Giddens and Dewey, again, the fact that intentions emerge in the midst of ongoing action does not mean that ordinary agents should be understood as dopes. In fact, for Dewey, Giddens, and Bourdieu, in different ways, day-to-day action is a kind of knowledgeable, skillful enactment. Giddens insists that "every competent member of every society knows a great deal about the institutions of that society" and that "such knowledge is not *incidental* to the operation of society, but is necessarily involved in it" (1979, 71). Bourdieu is in a way even more insistent about this. Rather than understanding social agents as rule followers, he argues we should see them as improvisers who exhibit a kind of "tact, dexterity, [and] savoir-faire" (1977, 10) that cannot be reduced to rules. "Agents," he argues, use a "small batch of schemes" to "generate an infinity of practices adapted to endlessly changing situations, without those schemes ever being constituted as explicit principles" (16).[12]

Since I am very concerned with the way that common action can reproduce very troubling institutions and forces, it is important to say, however, that there is a distinction between the savoir faire needed to function ably within existing society and the greater insight required to grasp how one's acts help reproduce society—and thus the knowledge needed to change the shape and tendencies of that society. We can see this in Dewey's argument in *The Public and Its Problems* ([1927] 1954) that in modern societies people have a difficult time tracing the consequences of their common activities. A little thought about this problem

98

can lead us to the next major topic, objectification. This is because the idea of action's "consequences" is arguably somewhat ambiguous. As I suggested in Chapter 2, Dewey sometimes seems to have thought of consequences in terms of chains of events, some more proximate, some more remote. But in tracing the consequences of action, we should keep in mind two distinctions: an individual versus a social standpoint, and an event-centered versus a more structural standpoint.[13] The first is the distinction between a single person acting and a large number of people doing something similar, engaging, that is, in a shared social practice. The second is the difference between one act causing an event (and then another and another) and a widespread practice generating social forces and structures. Many problems that arise for democracy, I shall argue, can be understood in terms of large numbers of people acting, the social forces and structures their common activities generate, and the need to counteract, look after, or ameliorate them.

It is possible to rethink and amplify on a weakness of elite theory with this insight about reflexivity in mind. Elite theories are preoccupied with the limits of popular reasoning, but too often they think of this reasoning as decision making that must be completed before action is begun. The scandal of democracy, for Schumpeter, is that ordinary citizens lack rational plans of political action, fully articulated political values, and completely adequate political knowledge in advance of their occasional interventions in politics. But the subtlest proponents of representative democracy have offered the right corrective to Schumpeter's critique: that uninformed opinions and incomplete information can improve, recursively, in ongoing experience, and that limited control of political affairs is enhanced by the fact that voters' interventions—elections—are not singular but repeated over time (Mackie 2009, 137, 144).

Objectification

The next step toward alienation is objectification (another correlative term), which I use to refer to the active production or reproduction of entities that humans often experience as given and distinct from themselves. It is apparent to anyone that through labor, a specific form of action, it is possible to produce things from shoes to smartphones— objects that are distinct, separate from their makers. But it is not just labor that that can be *objectified,* and not just material things that ought to count as *objectified action.* The whole of the social world, including

99

social relations, structures, and forces can be understood as objectified action, too—existing only because they are produced and reproduced through ongoing action. Schools could not exist without students and teachers acting out their parts, nor could banks exist without depositors, accountants, and borrowers doing the same. A school without teachers teaching and students learning is, at best, just a building. This is a face of the structurationist conception I have outlined, though so far I have stressed the other face: the dependence of action on structure.[14]

It is often said the reproduction of social structures—their renewal through ongoing activity—is an unintended consequence of action. Certainly reproduction need not be an intended consequence, and quite often it is not. Other, more proximate ends frequently loom larger. Shapiro and Wendt give the example of "participants in a wedding ceremony" who are "self-consciously committing themselves to one another through the marriage contract" while at the same time "reproducing the structure of the nuclear family even if they are utterly unaware of this fact" (1992, 206).[15] But there is no need to insist that actors never intend, or are always entirely unaware, of reproduction. It is useful to keep in mind that the same activity may help reproduce several forces and structures, related and unrelated. Accordingly, the actual degree of unintentionality and unawareness may depend on a few factors. One, obviously, is how closely related is the acknowledged purpose of a practice or activity to the structure it helps reproduce. Someone's intention in donating money to a church or club is likely to include sustaining the organization and even the broader network of organizations to which it belongs. On the other hand, buying one's child a soccer ball with the swipe of a credit card likely has little intended relation to the purchase's tendency to help sustain the international system of payments. Another factor may be the degree to which a broader institution or large-scale force has some local, smaller-scale, relational component of which participants are more conscious. A restaurant manager and a new cashier may not have given much thought to the way, through their agreement to hire and be hired, they are reproducing particular widespread employment practices. But they are likely pretty aware of initiating their own particular employment relationship. Of course, this awareness does not make the local reproduction necessarily benign. Historically, at least, one party to both marriage and employment contracts has promised future obedience to the other, while at the same time helping to reproduce the social structure and the broader practices through which that obedience may be secured. These are not ordinary, voluntary, passing, momentary exchanges, but acts that create a subordinate social relation, as Carole Pateman shows (1985; 1988). They require special scrutiny from the standpoint of democracy, as I shall emphasize again later in this chapter. Finally, movements, artists, civic associations, writers, and political organizations may succeed in making people more aware of the way in which an act whose impact seems negligible for society, broadly, actually sustains a wider institution, or a wider system of exclusion—as has happened at times during the campaign for same-sex marriage, when heterosexual sympathizers have chosen civil unions rather than sustaining marriage as it still exists in many places. The nuanced question of awareness of reproduction, then, has considerable political significance.

Hegel recognized objectification when he referred to "the [social] world" as both the "work of self-consciousness" and as a "reality" that is "already present and given" ([1807] 1977, 294). The most important features of social life are the products or consequences of human action, intended and unintended. And yet this does not mean they are simply transparent and malleable to any of the human agents who help sustain them. Individual consumers and workers may through their activity constitute the economy, but for most purposes they must also regard the present array of products, their prices, the supply and nature of jobs, recurrent waves of expansion and destruction, and so on as already established or already at work, and beyond their ordinary ability to alter. Insofar as social action becomes objectified, much of the social world appears opaque and feels resistant and object-like, not simply like a familiar and pliant extension of ourselves and our doings.

I have referred both to the *structures* that common activities reproduce, and the *forces* many people acting in the same way generate. I mean *objectification* to refer to both. And while analytically distinct, these structures and forces are connected in an important way. It might seem that social forces, such as surging unemployment, could be understood simply as the "sum" of many different people's acts—in this case, the sum of multitudes of employers individually firing or refusing to hire employees. If so, we might understand this force as just the known consequence of a single person's act, multiplied by the number of people engaging in the same activity. But to speak of a social force is to posit not just this multiplier effect but also the structures and the structural properties that shape and direct those forces. It is impossible to understand how myriad separate acts could "add up" to a particular social force, a particular effect, without taking account of the social structures that are also reproduced by activities, indeed by many of the same activities.

Objectification is ubiquitous and, unlike alienation, not intrinsically harmful. We constantly encounter structures and forces that we help reproduce even though we regard them as distinct from us. And yet this is not inherently threatening. And many of these seemingly thing-like structures empower us or help us to accomplish our aims. This point is important for the overall shape of a theory of alienation and democracy. Democratic action may attempt to counteract or resist alienation, but it certainly cannot eliminate objectification.

Alienation: The Roles of Domination, Oppression, and Exploitation

Now we have the background to return to the definition of *alienation* I have offered: the condition that exists when their common action returns to people in the form of social forces, relations, or institutions that dominate some or all of them and enable some people to oppress or exploit others. The previous discussion of objectification explains precisely what it means to say that social action returns to people. It means people's shared practices produce or reproduce social structures and forces that then confront them as both potent and distinct from them. At the same time, the definition of *alienation* underscores that not all objectified social action is alienated. Particular ills distinguish alienation from the more widespread phenomenon of objectification. Institutions, social relations, and forces in general may be regarded as objectified social action, but only those social forms that dominate people, while enabling oppression and exploitation, are alienated.

Domination

Domination, oppression, and exploitation may be regarded as different relations or manifestations of power, where power is defined as "those capacities to act possessed by social agents in virtue of the enduring relations in which they participate" (Isaac 1987b, 80). I begin by exploring, at some length, relations of domination. But while it is important to spend some time on domination, a particular agent's full situation is unlikely to be explicable in terms of domination alone, without considering oppression and exploitation, too—without reflecting on the complex social patterns of power, enablement, and constraint that affect people so differently. This whole picture will not be clear until we thoroughly explore those issues. And this is important to keep in mind because democratic action plays out on a complex social terrain characterized by all three of these kinds of power relations.

Domination describes a situation in which an agent, group, social force, or social structure overshadows or overwhelms some people's capacities to act; imposes necessities on them; or systematically resists their attempts to regulate important spheres of their lives. (See table below.) Domination, so characterized, is a profoundly disproportionate relation of power, not necessarily an exercise of power. (In contrast, oppression and exploitation, discussed below, necessarily entail such an exercise.) We can look at domination from the standpoints of at least two sorts of agents involved. One standpoint is that of agents whose capacities to act are overwhelmed by other agents' power or by a social structure or force—agents whose lives are disrupted or constricted as a result. Another is that of agents who are positioned, because of dominating relations, to wield extremely disproportionate power compared with those with whom they interact. The critical democratic conditions that face movements—the sort of conditions I discussed in Chapter 1—include many examples of domination. These range from the Gilded Age economy to the caste system of the pre–Civil Rights South. Likewise, at the turn of the millennium, the financial system, and particular institutions in it, also overwhelmed the agency of people like Sheila Ramos. So has what many call the "Walmart economy."[16] The combination of older gender and caste relations with more modern state powers is an example of a dominating structure, one that I discuss in Chapter 5. And so is the contemporary security state, the subject of the epilogue.

My understanding of "domination" bears an initial resemblance to Phillip Pettit's (1997; 2001). Pettit calls his theory of freedom "freedom as non-domination," and he defines domination in this way: "Someone has a dominating power over another . . . to the extent that . . . they have the *capacity* to interfere . . . on an arbitrary basis . . . in certain choices that the other is in a position to make" (1997, 52; italics added). Like Pettit, I claim that domination involves capacities or powers that do not necessarily need to be exercised in order for them to be significant. Domination integrally involves power, but it is not necessarily an exercise of power. Domination may affect many people, limit or shape their conduct, for long periods of time without specific acts or exercises of power being directed toward them. It is important to have a name for this phenomenon.

Pettit is right that domination is a crucial problem of freedom. But his discussion of domination focuses too much on individual agents, their traits and acts, with too little attention to social structures and their properties.[17] "I shall often speak as if there are just two individual persons implicated in cases of domination," Pettit writes in his influential book, *Republicanism* (1997, 52). And his language often suggests, as well, that he views the "capacity to interfere" largely as personal. For example, his only clarification of such a "capacity" in *Republicanism* likens it to the individual ability to play the piano (54).

Slavery, "the relationship of master to slave or master to servant" is, for Pettit, the exemplary case of domination is (1997, 22). But he enumerates "many forms" of domination, including those experienced by "the wife of the occasionally violent husband," "the employee whose security requires keeping the boss or manager sweet," and "the immigrant or indigenous person whose standing is vulnerable to the whims that rule politics and talk-back radio" (2001, 137). In each of these cases, we may presume, there is a capacity for interference that is like that involved in the slave-master relationship. But how does this capacity arise? Pettit's personal, agent-centered grammar does not enable him to answer effectively or to show what is similar or different in the capacity for interference when that capacity is exercised vis-à-vis slaves versus the other agents he enumerates, the wife, the employee, and the immigrant.

As soon as we contemplate a historical instance of slavery it becomes clear that it is impossible to explain or theorize the persistent capacities of masters as if they belonged simply to one agent rather than pertaining to a pervasive system of social subordination, including laws, customary institutions, and the beliefs and practices produced and reproduced by many differentiated agents. In antebellum America, for example, the power of a "kindly and non-interfering" slaveholder, to use Pettit's phrase (1997, 22), would have been founded not on some trait of the slaveholder but on social forms or structures, like a legal system that upheld white supremacy by defining slaves as social nonpersons and by decriminalizing violence against them (Burns 1998; Kennedy 1997). A slaveholder's capacities, whether exercised or not, would also have rested on the perpetuation, by many disparate agents, of shared ideologies justifying slavery and racial subordination and on the ongoing, expected cooperation of numerous neighbors and vigilantes in returning escaped slaves. These are features of social life that can be assimilated neither to

104

Alienation and its component phenomena

Phenomenon	Description	Examples
Alienation	Their common action returns to people in the form of social forces, relations, or institutions that dominate some or all of them and enable some people to oppress or exploit others.	Borrowers, consumers, and bankers reproduce through their activities a financial system characterized by the wrongs and ills described below.
Domination	An agent, group, social force, or social structure overshadows or overwhelms some people's capacities to act; imposes necessities on them; or systematically resists their attempts to regulate important spheres of their lives.	People like Sheila Ramos have their lives upended by waves of foreclosures and mass unemployment, or people find that their capacities to act are deeply overshadowed by those of big banks, their lawyers, and their lobbyists.
Oppression	One person or group exercises power over other people harshly, cruelly, unjustly, or in a way that severely restricts or infringes upon their free range of action.	Creditors or loan servicers treat borrowers unfairly or disrespectfully.
Exploitation	One person or group takes advantage of another's vulnerable situation in a way that is contrary to the latter's needs or interests.	Mortgage brokers encourage borrowers to take out loans they cannot afford, or financial institutions take advantage of crisis to obtain favorable bailouts.

traits of individual agents, on the one hand, nor, on the other, lightly dismissed as "a system or network or whatever" (Pettit 1997, 52).

Pettit's analysis of dominating, slavery-like relationships seems crafted to point in almost every example away from such social forms and toward some personal trait that would allow dominating power to persist during the intervals between acts of interference. Thus the dominant husband is "occasionally violent" and the dominant boss may interfere if not kept "sweet" (2001, 137). In fact, there may be rare limiting cases in which domination is attributable solely to the individual traits of the dominator. But in most cases—certainly the cases Pettit names—the capacities to dominate cannot be attributed to such traits alone, any more than can the dominating capacities of slaveholders.

Oppression and Exploitation

In contrast to domination, *oppression,* in my usage, refers to certain acts or exercises of power. One person or group oppresses another insofar as the first exercises power over other people harshly, cruelly, or unjustly, or in a way that seriously restricts or infringes upon their range of free *action.* (See table.)

Similarly, one person *exploits* another, according to my lexicon, insofar as the first person takes advantage of the second's vulnerable situation in a way that is contrary to the latter's needs or *interests.* (See table.) So exploitation, like oppression, involves an exercise of power, and not just its existence. The dependence of exploitation on power relations indicates that exploitation may be connected—through common institutions and forces—to domination and oppression. That is, all three are likely to be features of a common social terrain—features expressed differently in different locales or for different agents.

Putting Objectification, Domination, Oppression, and Exploitation Together

Domination, oppression, and exploitation are not merely separate, additive parts of a definition. Alienation, as I understand it, always entails domination in some form. On the other hand, alienated social relations and institutions only enable oppression and exploitation. One reason these distinctions are important is that the set of people dominated by an institution or social force may not coincide exactly with the set of people whose potential oppression or exploitation derives from it. Although two agents or groups may *both* find their agency overshadowed in some measure by the same social force or structure—may *both* find that it imposes necessities on them—it is unlikely, if they occupy different positions within a social structure, that they will find their powers, capacities, and interests affected in just the same way.

Alienation is not identical to objectification, as I indicated above. Domination, oppression, and exploitation explain the difference. Similarly, although domination is a crucial aspect of alienation, domination and alienation are not identical either. First, dominating forces or conditions are not alienated unless they originate in social action—unless, that is, they can properly be regarded as objectified social action. To emphasize alienation rather than just domination, then, is to emphasize social, not natural domination—being overwhelmed in the face of a recession or a state bureaucracy, for example, not an earthquake. Alienation represents human social action returning to human agents themselves in a particular uncontrolled and democratically troubling form. Moreover, alienation acknowledges that dominating social structures and relations enable other harms, namely oppression and exploitation. Alienation and domination, we might say, then, may refer to related aspects of the same social phenomena. But alienation is not identical to domination because of what alienation excludes (domination of natural, not social origin), because of what alienation includes (the potential for oppression and exploitation), and because of what alienation emphasizes (the poignancy of human social action itself returning in a form that overwhelms our capacities to act).

I bring democracy comprehensively into the picture in Chapter 4, but even here a preview is possible. Democracy may be regarded as a particular, egalitarian form of the collective management of common life. If so, it is surely of *democratic* concern when their own social action returns to human agents in a form that undermines such common management—or the individual autonomy reciprocally connected with it—or when enduring institutions and social relations overshadow some people's capacities to act, while making oppression or exploitation possible.

A wide range of social, cultural, economic, and political institutions and relations may be alienated in the relevant sense. It is not difficult to see how an authoritarian or a highly bureaucratic state, for example, could overshadow the capacities of many people to act, while providing opportunities for apparatchiks to oppress others. Similarly, a complex economy, especially one in crisis, manifests forces that vastly overpower ordinary actors' capacities, while also allowing a well-positioned few to exercise power over others unjustly. Certain overshadowing racial and gender hierarchies, though reproduced by various widespread practices, put some people in a position to treat others unjustly or cruelly. And economic, political, and racial relations and practices can intertwine in alienated structures, as in colonial (and postcolonial) societies. To refer to such social forms as alienated—and not only as dominating or oppressive—calls attention to the fact that they are not merely wrongs or harms imposed on ordinary people, but rather are conditions reproduced by myriad actors and widely shared practices.

107

Whose Enablement? Whose Constraint?

Once the basic idea of alienation is clear, it is important to acknowledge the political significance of texture, pattern, and particularity in alienated social systems. People in different locations within them almost always experience such systems differently. Why? What are some of the possible differences?

One common criticism of the structurationist approach I have adopted here is that it fails to take sufficient account of the fact that some agents do more structuring, as the point is expressed, while others are more often structured (Bauman 1989, 46).[18] But just because many different people are all taking some role in reproducing dominating or oppressive institutions does not mean their contributions are all the same, or that their relationship to those structures is the same. Consider, again, the case of Sheila Ramos. I said at the outset of this chapter that many different sorts of people were actively involved in the creation of the structures and forces we know as the financial crisis: borrowers like Ramos herself, brokers, bankers, and politicians. But it is essential (and perhaps not too difficult) to recognize that each of these types of actors played a different role in the reproduction and transformation of the relevant economic structures and that each experienced a different degree of enablement and constraint. And these differences can be attributed to manifestations of power, "capacities to act possessed by social agents in virtue of the enduring relations in which they participate" (Isaac 1987b, 80). As crucial as it was to the genesis of the financial crisis that people like Ramos took out mortgages that they ultimately could not afford, such economic actors acted under often severe constraints. By contrast, mortgage brokers were far more enabled by the structure of the banking system to further their own interests, even though they were also ultimately unwitting instruments of economic ruin. And at the other end of the spectrum we would find political leaders and politically connected bankers who obviously played far more essential roles in ruinously transforming the financial system, even though they too only transformed and did not create it. And once the Great Recession got going, even the most powerful were overwhelmed by its force, unable to stop it.

All this is crucial for my argument about alienation and its component concepts. The different relations of agents to the process of structuration, broadly, can be understood more concretely in terms of the varying activities in which they engage and the forms of domination to which they are subject, as well as their ability to oppress or exploit or their vulnerability to oppression and exploitation. Dominating forces and institutions, however widespread, are unlikely to affect everyone in the same way. Given their structure and operations, they are likely to provide opportunities for certain actors to oppress and exploit others. It may be true, as Giddens contends, that "vast areas of social life aren't agent controlled, if that means consciously controlled, by anyone," and this applies especially to the financial system (Giddens and Pierson 1998, 65, 85). Once the crisis of 2007 began to unfold, many agents, not just Ramos, confronted the financial hydra. Richard S. Fuld Jr., once the leader of Lehman Brothers, a titanic presence in the mortgage-backed securities business, was essentially powerless to save his firm from bankruptcy, his capacities to act overwhelmed by the spreading crisis. But other similarly situated figures, like JPMorgan Chase's Jamie Dimon, were able to use the crisis to enhance their political influence and justify large bonuses. And although no one was the master of the financial crisis, the structure that generated it, along with the forces of the meltdown themselves, enabled banks and mortgage servicers to exercise power over ordinary borrowers harshly and unjustly—as well as carelessly and negligently—as the borrowers tried to find their way out of their difficulties. The financial system had already, of course, allowed lenders and brokers to take advantage of the vulnerable situations of people like Ramos in a way that was contrary to their interests.[19]

Another face of the same problem can be grasped in the form of an answer to the question, Why would competent human agents reproduce alienated social forces? This question is crucial for anyone whose ultimate interest is in understanding the position of potential democratic agents. First, some people, on balance, may benefit from alienated social forces, or believe that they do. In this case the most obvious meaning of *oppositional democracy* comes into view: democratizing politics encountering resistance from those who find democratization threatens their interests.

Second, for most people, reproduction is constrained. The social action that returns to people in alienated form always has structural preconditions, and these constrain (as well as enable) agents. The challenge for such agents is never simply to create new social structures from scratch. It is at most to transform social structures while reproducing them. In a limiting case, given a great deal of preparation, agreement, and coordination, agents may be able suddenly to overturn a relatively discrete social form, as motorists in Sweden switched from driving on the left to the right side of the road one morning in 1967. But we cannot imagine everyone affected abandoning an entire social system—exchanging, say, capitalism for feudalism—in the same way. Since agents are always engaged in actively reproducing many interdependent social forms at the same time, and have a variety of needs and interests they must continually advance with the help of such forms, they cannot undertake to replace huge, interconnected ones all at once.

Third, the question why agents would reproduce alienated social forms seems less puzzling when we recognize that different agents engage in quite varied activities that together reproduce the same institutions. For example, the contributions of a southern white police officer and an African American student to reproducing segregated schools in the early 1950s obviously would have been quite different. And the nature and severity of the constraints each experienced while reproducing racist social relations would likewise have varied greatly, as would the consequences for each of reproducing the institutions.

Fourth, agents, especially in complex societies, may not always know or reflect upon how their actions help reproduce social forms. This is not just a matter of knowing "facts," but also of employing ideologies that variously illuminate and obscure aspects of the social world. In sum, then, the agents we might expect to refuse to reproduce alienated structures may lack either the alternatives to doing so or the capacities, the knowledge, and the understanding to make use of such alternatives. And each of these points to a different democratic challenge, a point I will pursue in Chapter 4.

Sometimes present political struggle seems to be a struggle against the past as much as it is a struggle against any contemporaries: struggle against old regimes, traditional forms of subordination that somehow persist, atavistic practices, or fateful choices institutionalized long ago. Can the structurationist approach, which tends to emphasize ongoing reproduction of dominating institutions, make sense of this? There are many examples of such living relics, such active vestiges of an earlier epoch. Marx, we saw in Chapter 2, argued that the state of the Second French Empire had been shaped into an entity capable of dominating society during the whole centuries-long process of defeudalization. Schumpeter contended that the "steel frame" of modern capitalist society was actually the feudal aristocracy, itself shaped much earlier ([1942] 1976, 136). Karen Orren (1991) argues, similarly, that labor relations in the United States continued for decades into the twentieth century to be governed, or *structured,* by feudal master-servant law, enforced by courts. This is a phenomenon of considerable political relevance. The American welfare state, for example, has continued to embody the racial politics of its formative epochs.[20]

Margaret Archer has sharply criticized structuration theory for what she sees as its inability to conceptualize this sort of potent atavism—for its neglect of the importance of long-standing structures and, by extension, the power of "long dead" agents (1998, 363) to shape contemporary society.[21] But must we really choose between structuration theory and recognizing this persistence of old social forms? For Archer, the twin structurationist mottoes, no agency without structure and no structure without agency, tend to conflate structure and agency, to treat them merely as different sides of the same thing. She understands no structure without agency, in particular, to mean that present structures are what they are solely because of the activities of present agents.[22] But Archer argues that structures usually preexist present actors. The most convincing examples, she believes, are ones in which the traces of past action are embodied materially: demographic structures produced by past migration and biological reproduction, or runes carved into stone by past artists, yet enduring into the present. But these cases may not be as telling as she thinks. True, in the ordinary course of things, it may take generations to change a society's demographic makeup. We inherit a society with demographic facts already established.[23] Yet present activity—reproduction in the biological sense—is still necessary to maintain demographic structures, however old. In fact, catastrophic human actions, notably wars, can rather rapidly and dramatically change a society's demographic complexion.[24] In the limiting case, ridiculous though it may seem, all demographic structures would after some years cease to exist if everyone stopped procreating. So while it is wrong to think that present structures in their present form exist solely in virtue of present action, it is equally wrong to think that present action is not needed to maintain them. Archer's emphasis on "dead" or "long dead" agents, in particular, also seems like a red herring. Her claim about the relative feebleness of present action depends only on the enduring importance of the preconditions of action, on *past action,* not necessarily on *dead actors.*

Still, Archer's insistence on the enduring significance of structures inherited from the past is quite important. Bhaskar's version of structuration may emphasize a more profound regard for this problem than

Giddens's—or at least it seems to, because of Giddens's strong denial that structure is fixed and external to agency, and his insistence, at times, that structure exists only "in a virtual way," "as memory traces" (1989, 256). This language may not seem to do justice to the fact that actors confront the economy, for example, as something given and preexisting, even though the continued operation of the economy requires the ongoing joint activity of consumers, workers, entrepreneurs, and so on.[25] In light of such experience, Bhaskar insists that humans find society "always already made" and so "reproduce" and "transform" it by their actions, but do not, properly speaking, "create" it. "Society," he insists, "stands to individuals, then, as something that they never make, but that exists only in virtue of their activity" (1998, 214).

Another way of understanding the endurance of old structures is to note that *no structure without agency,* while apt, is not exactly analogous to *no agency without structure.* No individual can act without drawing on existing structures—communicate without a language, pay a bill without a financial system, and so on. But no one actor's efforts, on their own, are sufficient to reproduce those structures. While structures, broadly, would not exist without the reproductive activity of many people, no specific actor's contribution is necessary (let alone sufficient) for social reproduction.

Master and *Métayer,* Banker and Borrower

Another question about the basic character of alienated institutions and the political struggle that may arise in and around them has to do with the contrast between personal and impersonal. Some power relations are closely managed and experienced intimately. Bourdieu, who had deep experience as an ethnographer in Algeria in the middle of the twentieth century, argues that a landowning "master" in Kabyle society must "work away, day in, day out, with constant care and attention" to maintain his dominance over a *métayer,* or sharecropper (1977, 190).[26] In contrast, though, think of the owner of a portfolio of subprime mortgages, whose interests can be guarded against borrowers' interests at arm's length by market mechanisms, the law and regulatory system, lawyers, court officials, and bureaucrats, along with an army of loan-servicing employees. What should we make of these examples and the contrast between them?

Under the heading "modes of domination," Bourdieu fits these two apparently different relations to two contrasting types of societies. There are more or less modern societies with a "self-regulating market," an "educational system," a "juridical apparatus," and a "state." In such societies, Bourdieu argues, domination "no longer needs to be exerted in a direct, personal way." But in his view there are other societies, like that of the Kabyle, where "relations of domination can be set up and maintained only at the cost of strategies which must be endlessly renewed" (1977, 183). Corey Robin draws on a similar distinction between personal and impersonal, but puts it to different use. He argues that it is the personal character of power relations, and the personal sort of *rebellion*, that is almost always crucial politically: "Behind the riot in the street or debate in Parliament is the maid talking back to her mistress, the worker disobeying her boss. That is why our political arguments—not only about the family but also the welfare state, civil rights, and much else—can be so explosive: they touch upon the most personal relations of power" (2011, 10). Robin and Bourdieu, seemingly, could agree on how to characterize the relationship of the Kabyle master to his *métayer*. But what about the banker and the borrower? Robin suggests that impersonal relations are generally not the stuff of revolution and reaction. In contrast, Bourdieu argues that such power relations pervade modern societies and presumably may animate modern political struggles as well.

Actually, it is possible to recognize, with Bourdieu, that both sorts of relations—ones more personal and more impersonal—are possible and potentially significant in politics, and with Robin, that there may be a crucial intimate aspect to almost any concrete domination, oppression, or exploitation. To make this clear, it helps to introduce one new distinction and reintroduce another. The new distinction is between what explains or enables particular power relations and how they are experienced. Robin's claim about personal power relations, although it bears, for example, a certain resemblance to Pettit's approach to personal traits and domination, is not really identical to it. Pettit's point about the occasionally violent husband, for example, seems to be that personal traits and factors *explain* domination or make it possible. Robin seems to mean something else, namely that the personal side of domination, oppression, or exploitation is *felt* most sharply and is crucial to how such relations become subject to political contestation.[27] He does not deny the possibility of impersonal power relations and dynamics.

The second distinction is one between profoundly disproportionate relations of power and malignant exercises of power. I have argued that domination refers, roughly, to a deep overshadowing of an agent's power, while oppression or exploitation refer to harmful exercises of power. Despite appearances, this distinction does not exactly correspond to *impersonal* versus *personal*. Most dominating structures or relations in modern societies—ones that involve many people's agency being overshadowed—are likely also to be in a sense impersonal: referable to large-scale structures, ones maintained as an unintended consequence of common action by many people who are not personally related to each other. But it is possible to name truly personal forms of domination, especially ones that turn substantially on physical strength or force.

What about Bourdieu and Robin, then? Even faced with Bourdieu's compelling portrayal of the close, personal attention Kabyle landowners must pay to dominating their subordinates, the distinctions I am making encourage us to look for the powers or capacities that they draw on in these efforts, powers that are likely attributable not to individual efforts but to structures reproduced by many, many people. Even where there is no state, or no highly developed market, there are likely structures of caste, or shared cultural norms governing wife and husband, landowner and *métayer*. And these are not maintained by the lone efforts of the master. Something similar goes for Robin's rebellious maid and worker. The abusive boss almost always draws on powers vested in him by corporate structure, law, the broader economy, gender roles, and so on. The spark of politicization may be the personal experience of lopsided power, as Robin argues, but the protest itself must take on the social system that makes the experience possible. By the same token, though, even when considering massive, impersonal, and dominating social forces such as the tidal waves of economic dislocation that nearly drowned Sheila Ramos, we should be attentive to the intimate, sometimes humiliating, micropolitical interactions—with court clerks, bank representatives, and so on—that feed on them.

To acknowledge both Bourdieu's and Robin's insights, then, we have to abandon the idea of characterizing every relation of power as wholly personal or impersonal, every society as characterized solely by personal or impersonal power relations and dynamics. In all but a few rare cases we are likely to see mixtures of personal and impersonal.

The surge in interest in intersectionality—studying the juncture of different identities and social relations and of different forms of marginalization and disempowerment—harmonizes well, I think, with an approach to alienation that is attuned to the interaction of domination, oppression, and exploitation in their different forms; to varying power relations that range from more impersonal to more intimate; and to the distinction between what explains a power relation or dynamic and how it is experienced. Distant states and global markets, for example, can help solidify racial or ethnic oppression that is experienced in a very personal way. Through the middle of the twentieth century, the cotton economy, shaped by international market forces and national political alliances, played an important role in sustaining sharecropping—ties between landowner and tenant—and by extension, racial caste relations in the South (McAdam 1982, 66–67, 73–77). And in Chapter 5 I shall discuss the way that modern welfare states can help shape relations of gender and race in ways that enable more intimate oppression or exploitation within the family or the workplace.

A Typology of Alienation Theories

I understand alienation to involve social reproduction, domination, oppression, and exploitation. Since the leading idea here is the shared activities of agents—or the consequences of those shared activities— escaping the agents' control and then returning to many of them in malign form, I call this conception alienation as the escape and troubling return of common action. I have already shown the notable history of such a conception in political thought, in Hegel and Marx and even— though not by name—in Dewey. But this is certainly not the only way the term *alienation* has been used.

In fact, the word has been used to designate so many disparate phenomena that it is important, before proceeding much further, to distinguish the concept I am deploying here from certain others that have been identically labeled. *Alienation* has also been used to refer to a psychological or social-psychological state: as a dissolution of common feelings, especially those tying individuals to society (Josephson and Josephson 1962, 12–13; Parsons 1951, 27, 32), or a condition in which the individual "does not experience himself as the center of his world, as the creator of his own acts" (Fromm [1955] 1990, 120). I pointed out in Chapter 2 that it is possible to derive from Marx both a social-structural and a psychological understanding of alienation, and that Fromm's theory of alienation rests heavily on a psychological version. But while it is possible that the kind of social-structural alienation that interests me could cause or foster a sort of psychological alienation, the two conditions are by no means identical.[28] Moreover, an effort on the part of one group to remake the social world so that they feel wholly at home in it could be democratically devastating.

Alienation has also sometimes signified the loss of deep, natural, and original harmony, whether communal or cosmic. That this was one of the meanings of the word for Hegel is clearest when we consider the whole career of "Spirit" in his *Phenomenology*. But alienation, as I use the term, does not require belief in such possible harmony. In fact, I shall argue that it leads to recognizing the centrality of opposition for democracy. And like a quest to purge the feeling of psychological alienation, a quest to restore natural harmony in politics could easily threaten vibrant democratic life and the forms of autonomy it reciprocally involves. Another usage, finally, treats alienation as the loss of personal capacities, the result of viewing oneself as a set of fixed traits and completed deeds (Sartre [1943] 1956, 352, 354). But the remedy for alienation, viewed in this way, would most likely be an apolitical, personal "ethic of action and self-commitment" (Sartre [1947] 1977, 44).

Markets and Alienation

The story of the financial crisis that swept up millions of people like Sheila Ramos is at least in part a story about markets. It is a story about myriad people buying and selling things, from things as tangible as houses to others as occult as collateralized debt obligations and credit default swaps. It is also a story about the tendency of markets to expand, imperially—the tendency of producers and bankers to pursue gain by selling things that have never been sold before, or to sell them in ways they have not previously been sold. It is a story about how the many acts of buying and selling altered and reproduced social relations—like relations between borrowers and lenders—and combined into large-scale social forces, especially the ones we would identify most closely with the crisis itself, like waves of foreclosures and firings. And it is a story about how those market relations and forces ultimately overpowered ordinary people, like swimmers caught in a riptide, swept further and further from safety.

That housing and lending markets turned against many ordinary people after 2007 is not to deny that markets sometimes work well and serve valid purposes. Markets are useful means for exchanging information about what people want and can provide others.[29] They can allow firms and consumers to cooperate, at a distance, to satisfy human needs—or at least, those backed by buying power. At its best, the price mechanism at work in markets encourages producers to make just as much of a product as consumers will buy. The particular sort of exchanges

116

that underlie market behavior can allow people, without central direction, to find a kind of "ideal" distribution of goods and services—one in
which no one could be made better off without someone else becoming
worse off.[30] And according to some accounts, markets elicit or at least
reward innovation.[31]

But as the financial crisis showed, the birth and life of markets can
disturb profoundly. It is a very old story. In early modern England, the
growth of a market for wool prompted enclosure—the expropriation and
privatization of common peasant land rights.[32] And enclosure, in snatching
away the traditional means of self-support for most rural people, in turn
created something that we often forget had not existed before: the market
for labor, on which a new class became dependent. Sidney and Beatrice
Webb describe the experience of the "men and women of Lancashire and
Yorkshire" with enclosure and industrialization in language that resonates with the vocabulary of alienation: "[They] felt of this new power
that it was inhuman, that it disregarded all their instincts and sensibili-
ties, that it brought into their lives an inexorable force, destroying and
scattering their customs, their traditions, their freedom, their ties of
family and home" (quoted in Piven and Cloward 1993, 26).[33]

Reproducing Exploitation: An Illustration

Instances of market alienation are varied—and yet often connected to
each other. Since the global economy is, in a sense, an interrelated whole,
to identify a case of market alienation is to select certain market practices and trace some of their troubling consequences. Markets for home
loans and complex financial derivatives, discussed earlier in this chapter,
are different in many ways from markets for cheap consumer goods, like
bicycles and towels, explored briefly at the very beginning of the book.
And the alienated structures and forces they may generate are distinctive, as well. The Great Recession and what people call the "Walmart
economy" are just two faces of a single, many-sided evolving economic
system. And yet to be swept along by economic forces leading to foreclosure on one's home is not the same as the experience of moving from job
to job with low pay, little security, and few rights at work. And for a few
pages, I want to look some of the same practices of buying and selling
consumer goods discussed before—in this case, cutthroat markets for
sweaters and smartphones and televisions—but connect them to a distinct set of alienated structures experienced most vividly thousands of
miles away. I want, in particular, to focus on the way that consumer

goods markets in the United States and Europe help sustain the shape and powers of the massive corporate retailers that acquire goods, mostly in the developing world, through complex supply chains connecting buyers, however distantly, to manufacturing shop floors they rarely bother to imagine.[34] And I want to consider some of the forms of exploitation this buying and selling—these supply chains—can foster, sometimes with consequences too shocking for most of us to ignore.

The Children's Place, whose website promises "Big Fashion, Little Prices," operates about 1,100 stores across the United States (Greenhouse 2013b). Relationships in global manufacturing are constantly changing, but during an eight-month period spanning the end of 2012 and the beginning of 2013, about 120,000 pounds of clothes flowed through U.S. Customs to The Children's Place from a manufacturer called New Wave, located in an industrial suburb of Dhaka, Bangladesh (Greenhouse 2013b). In fact, many large retailers, including Gap and Walmart, also acquire clothes in Bangladesh, the second-largest apparel exporter in the world, where the minimum wage is about $37 per month, unions are almost nonexistent, and workers must often endure appalling conditions (Manik, Greenhouse, and Yardley 2013).

In April 2013, the building housing the New Wave factory, the Rana Plaza, collapsed, killing over 1,100 workers. It was a new disaster, staggering in scope, one of the worst of its kind in history—but also part of a very old story. Since the birth of a global garment trade, manufacturing has moved from place to place and country to country in search of rock-bottom wages. No matter the particular place or time, those wages have often been paid to displaced farmers with few alternatives, like the ones pushed into labor markets by early modern enclosure in Europe (Davidson 2013). And these phenomena have made possible, with some regularity, horrible events like the Rana Plaza collapse, for example, a similar, if much less deadly, collapse at the Pemberton Mill in Lawrence, Massachusetts, 153 years before Rana Plaza, as well as the Triangle Shirtwaist fire of 1911 (M. Anderson 2013). And these sorts of tendencies and problems are not limited to apparel manufacturing. Pressured by consumer demand for low-priced, constantly improving electronic gadgets (along with the adept transnational corporations that both stoke and respond to the demand), factories in China and elsewhere stop and retool frequently, then work their low-paid labor force long hours in unsafe plants, often seven days a week (Locke 2013; Duhigg and Barboza 2012).[35] In 2011, two explosions at Chinese factories that make Apple iPads killed four workers and injured dozens more (Duhigg and Barboza 2012).

We could explore other aspects of the practices and evils involved here, tracing buying and selling in the United States and Europe to more geographically proximate, domestic forms of domination, or inquire into the ways that political and social practices in places like Bangladesh are also crucially involved in reproducing exploitation there. But this way of looking at the economy brings out a troubling feature of the way the consequences of our common economic practices can spin so far out of our control. The novelist M. T. Anderson aptly sums up the paradox of alienated markets at work here: "The story of manufacturing half a world away is as close as the Lycra-cotton cloth that swaddles us" (2013). Along with the "Walmart economy" and the Great Recession, I want to keep this enigma of intimacy and distance in view as I further explore problems of markets and alienation.

Markets in Context: States and Corporations

To speak of "markets" in an instance like this is, of course, an abstraction of a particular kind. Obviously there are a number of crucial nonmarket institutions involved, including supply chains, manufacturers, government regulators, and retailers. Any political analysis of markets and alienation can ignore this only at the risk of irrelevance. To view the financial crisis or global manufacturing as market phenomena, as I am suggesting we do, is not to exclude such institutions from consideration—they are much too intimately involved—but only to highlight buying and selling as among the most important practices reproducing the relevant forces and structures. Buying and selling do not just create textbook forces of supply and demand; they sustain a host of institutions, as well. To approach this from another direction: contrary to much dogma, the entire world is not organized on market principles—not even the capitalist world. Markets are not natural, as people sometimes assume, universal phenomena uniquely rooted in human nature, but have to be made. Indeed, most concrete markets do not match up with pure market principles. And markets, in fact, cannot persist on their own without support from nonmarket structures. If we sometimes abstract markets mentally from these concrete conditions, we must at least not forget about them.

Hegel's *Philosophy of Right* (1991, part 1) includes a brilliant demonstration of the view that a world consisting of nothing more than myriad free and equal agents pursuing their private interests according to their

119

own lights—the heart of what we could call the market vision—would soon rip apart in paroxysms of disagreement, aggression, and uncontrolled retribution. His conclusion: the very idea of a working market implies a moral, or at least a legal world, outside of market values and pressures. Indeed, the logic of the market itself rests necessarily on definite limits to its scope (Goodin 1988, 160–173). For markets to work, there must be secure property rights, legal decisions and trust must not be for sale to the highest bidder, and agents must be autonomous in the ways assumed by market theory. Markets themselves guarantee none of this, but states can. So it is generally states that create markets, not only in the ongoing legal sense just mentioned, but in an important historical, original sense discussed earlier. We have already seen that the early modern labor market in England had to be created—and it was the English state, through enclosure acts by Parliament, that created it. A similar process of labor-market creation is going on today in China, as the state forces millions of peasants into cities and the manufacturing economy.

Similarly, corporations, the most powerful of market actors, in order to *be* market actors, are organized internally as command and control organizations, not as markets. Employees of corporations do not sell each unit of labor to the highest-bidding manager or department, hour by hour. And whenever possible, corporations structure markets to their benefit, or even evade pure market relationships entirely. It is impossible to understand global retail empires strictly in market terms. Walmart's innovations have all aimed at making use of cheap labor, in the United States and abroad, taking control of what were once more like arm's-length market relations with suppliers, and gaining close control of the supply chain. It has done this substantially by analyzing massive amounts of data—not, however, information readily available through market processes, but information churned out by a massive proprietary system of computers linked by satellite communication (Lichtenstein 2009). All this explains why the preeminent neoclassical theorist of the firm wrote: "The distinguishing mark of the firm is *the supersession of the price mechanism*" (Coase 1937, 389; italics added).

Labor hierarchies are reproduced, in part, through buying and selling labor, through employment contracts. But employment contracts are not ideal market exchanges; they are not spot sales of some natural commodity. Selling someone my labor is not like selling them an apple or my used desk. Employment contracts create a concrete social relation characterized by nonmarket norms and practices, as I pointed out earlier in this chapter.[36] Or, to put it a different way, labor is a fictitious commodity, as theorists since Karl Polanyi ([1944] 2001, ch. 6) have with good reason argued. For the seller of labor does not merely hand some separable thing over to the buyer, for cash. Instead, to make good on the sale of labor, she enters a subordinating relationship with the buyer, in which she agrees to obey orders (Pateman 1988, 148). This subordination was obviously of fateful importance to the workers at Rana Plaza, who were ordered to continue working even after cracks opened up in the factory building—and who were afraid to disobey.

The conclusion to draw from markets' necessary entanglement with states and corporations is this: to assess markets as prone to alienation is by no means to neglect these other reproduced structures as sites of overshadowed common agency or potential oppression and exploitation.

Corrupting Markets, Noxious Markets

In the next section, I relate the features of my market narratives, point by point, to the conception of alienation I have advanced, focusing on buying and selling, the institutions and forces they help reproduce, and the domination and other ills those social forms make possible. But since the lineaments of that argument are already visible, it may be helpful to explore how it compares to other, possibly more familiar, critiques of markets, especially ones that identify certain markets, or the sale of certain goods, as degrading or "noxious" (Satz 2010, 9).

These critiques have begun, in a sense, with the way that the market mindset—pursuing self-interest while relating to the world as a collection of things that can be bought or sold—can invade areas of life where it arguably does not belong. The section of Marx's *Economic and Philosophic Manuscripts* on money, the medium of market exchange, casts it as "the universal confounding and overturning of things" ([1844] 1964, 167).[37] Of course, this is just one aspect of Marx's critique. But it is one that Michael Walzer, in *Spheres of Justice* (1983), revives, arguing that money has its proper social place, but that it can invade and dominate spheres where it does not belong, creating injustice. This idea that money and markets ought to be confined to a proper region of social life is more or less also the initial thought developed recently by Michael Sandel (2012) and by Debra Satz (2010). The focal point of Sandel's analysis, in particular, is the idea that some human goods are degraded when they are treated as things to be bought and sold. For the most part, what interests him are what he sees as newly commodified goods trampling on established communal values and understandings—"the growing reach of money and markets into spheres of life once governed by nonmarket norms" (2012, 28).

Like Sandel, Satz is concerned to identify the proper limits of buying and selling, but her argument is not based on explicating and defending the present social meanings of goods. In fact, she is quite critical of this approach. She notes, to begin with, that "there are rival views of the meaning of many particular goods" (2010, 81). Her objection is not that controversial judgments about goods must be avoided, but rather that such judgments must always be explicitly defined and defended. In any case, she notes, "There is only a tenuous connection in most cases between the meaning we give to a good and its distribution by a market" (81). For example, one can buy a Bible and still believe its worth is not merely monetary.

An alienation-centered approach is also not premised on Sandel's idea that trouble arises because some services or goods are degraded by being commodified.[38] Neither houses nor clothes nor financial instruments are exactly *degraded* by being sold. But financial markets and the global garment industry, as we have seen, are structured in such a way as to make forms of domination possible and to foster oppression and exploitation. The fact that so many people actively reproduce those structures through their market activity, yet do not organize themselves to manage those troubling consequences, adds a layer of concern. Sandel acknowledges worries about market choices that are not really made freely (2012, 45, 135) or that foster or magnify economic inequality (27–28, 32, 65), but he seems to see these issues as ethically quite distinct from any concerns that are truly intrinsic to buying and selling. For Sandel, the nub of the issue is that markets can have a "corrosive" effect, corrupting "the good things in life" and cultivating "bad attitudes" (9, 15, 34). This is why so much of his analysis turns on discerning and paying respect to the social meanings of goods, which meanings Sandel often seems to take as already given.

Satz rests her case not on the given social meaning of goods but on a set of criteria for identifying and evaluating particularly troublesome markets. Satz's criteria concern both the consequences of certain markets and the "underlying condition" of "market agents" who buy and sell (2010, 94, 96). The relevant consequences of interest may be for individuals or for society as a whole. They include, especially, the risk that certain markets "undermine the framework needed for a society of equals" (9) or promote "servility and dependence" (98). The goal here, for Satz, is especially to avoid "extreme harms" (98). Concern for the "underlying condition" of "market agents," on the other hand, points to the possibility that some market agents exhibit only "weak" agency—they possess limited capacities to act or decide—or are vulnerable because of poverty or desperate need for a good (98). While these two standards may seem disparate, they are linked by an egalitarian "animating vision" of "a society of equals" (6, 100–104). Markets that violate these ethical standards are, in Satz's terminology, "noxious."

Satz's choice and explication of her criteria position her argument much closer to one focused on alienation. Domination, oppression, and exploitation—my key indicators of alienation—could be understood as examples of what is "noxious," and are indeed integrally related to some of Satz's animating concerns, such as inequality, weak agency, and servility. In fact, Satz makes exploitation crucial to her view of noxiousness. Moreover, although an inquiry into market alienation would not have to center on particular "noxious" markets—a point I shall return to in a moment—such uniquely troubling markets could, in some cases, be examples of the phenomenon of our common market activities escaping our control and ultimately dominating us. That is, the noxiousness, the affront to crucial human values or purposes, could be understood as an indication of that loss of collective control. The tendency of market practices to expand imperially in this way might be seen as evidence, in itself, that markets can hinder our attempts to regulate important spheres of our lives in a human way.

Satz is careful to explain that her aim is not to assess the "market system" as a whole (2010, 91). Rather than assessing markets abstractly, or in general, she is concerned to distinguish between particular markets. She sets out to show how some intuitions that certain markets are particularly troublesome may be borne out by rigorous analysis (3, 115). Some markets, she writes, are demonstrably "noxious," for reasons elucidated above, because of the conditions structuring them or because of their consequences (3, 91–112).[39] But an exploration of markets guided by a concern about alienation—a concern about domination, oppression, and exploitation—need not be occupied primarily with identifying particular noxious markets. For the most part, distinguishing one market from another means for Satz distinguishing the goods sold. The troubling features of alienated markets, however, may or may not arise because of the particular characteristics of the service or good sold.[40] And they may or may not be related to a market most people would recognize as particularly "noxious." Take, for example, the buying and selling of labor, generally. Most people take this practice for granted. And it is unlikely that a wholesale alternative to labor markets can be found in the near future. But the buying and selling of any labor—not just child labor, for example—reproduces hierarchical employment relations, structures that may readily foster oppression. And anticipating parts of my next chapter, it is worth saying here that the particular kinds alienation that are possible in labor relations always warrant some sort of democratic response, from unions to workplace democracy, regardless of whether the particular type of labor—the type of human activity sold—is distinctive. My discussion is intended mainly to illustrate what it means to speak of markets as potentially alienated, to elaborate on the ways in which markets can overshadow ordinary people's agency, as well as foster oppression and exploitation. The alienation in question could result not only from the good itself, so to speak, but also from how or to whom it is sold. It could result from forces created through buying and selling. Or it could follow from the structure of factories and corporations, which shape and are shaped by relevant markets. Since I would propose exploring all the ways that market exchanges may help reproduce troubling structures and forces—not just on the most proximate results of the exchanges themselves—my approach necessarily considers how, say, buying and selling clothes in the United States could contribute to the maintenance of structures and practices far away.

Another point of contrast stems from this: neoclassical economics in its original form was built on a number of assumptions whose refutation has consumed generations of scholars. Notably, these assumptions include perfect information and lack of externalities.[41] The first of these assumptions holds that the relevant market agents have all the information they need to make beneficial, rational choices. The second signifies that all the costs and benefits associated with a product or service are borne by the direct parties to its exchange, and so incorporated in its price. When these assumptions do not hold—as often they do not—markets cannot be assumed to be efficient. The paradigmatic case of an externality is pollution, such as air pollution, which imposes costs on people other than those buying or selling a product, such as steel. Sandel and Satz, in varying measure, are concerned to distinguish their evaluations from these standard economic analyses. In Sandel's case, this is because, from the economist's point of view, both imperfect information and externalities lead to inefficiency and decreased utility, and Sandel does not consider these to be properly ethical concerns (2012, 28–32). Satz's deemphasizing of externalities is different. In fact, she assumes that worry about externalities actually "feeds off of moral theory" (2010, 32). For her, the problem is that almost any exchange has some externalities, some costs or benefits to third parties. So the key for her is to specify which ones matter.

It is much less important to my analysis of alienation to draw a sharp distinction between my central concerns—domination, oppression, and exploitation—and imperfect information or externalities. This is, first, because it is possible to see market failure as implicated in the troubling component phenomena of alienation. For example, imperfect information in the mortgage business—what borrowers did not know about home loans and investors did not know about both mortgages and borrowers—has a great deal to do with how financial markets produced forces that overwhelmed the agency of ordinary people. I am also less concerned to distinguish my approach from economic analyses of market failure because the hegemony of certain economic ideologies (call them neoliberalism or market fundamentalism) is also crucially implicated in the financial crisis and similar alienated phenomena. Economists may generally know that most markets depart significantly from neoclassical assumptions, but politics and culture are infused with simplistic characterizations of markets and their advantages. And the resulting blindnesses are part of how people lose effective control over their common actions in the market, reproducing forces that may dominate them.

Alienated Markets

Now it is possible to gather the various strands and sum up what it means to consider markets as potentially alienated, and to look at the financial crisis and global garment production as examples of market alienation. My perspective on alienation, I have said, derives from an understanding of social action, structuration, objectification, domination, oppression, and exploitation. To view contemporary market phenomena as examples of alienation, then, begins with the widespread social activities at the center of markets—with buying and selling and their significance. From the viewpoint that stresses alienation (and ultimately democratic struggle against it), it is essential to remember that the market troubles at hand feature many people engaged in shared economic practices. At the heart of the financial crisis were tens of millions of people buying houses with subprime mortgages. (Just as important, though, were smaller numbers of people buying and selling securities created from those mortgages.) Part of the poignancy—ultimately, the democratic poignancy—of the mortgage meltdown is the fact that so many people's social activities were crucial to engendering runaway forces that ultimately turned on them and harmed them. An alienation-centered approach would also stress the way in which tens of millions of Western consumers, in buying and selling pants and tee-shirts, in seeking out the best bargains and the newest smartphones and tablets, help reproduce the structures of global manufacturing and so contribute to conditions that enable exploitation, along with horrifying industrial accidents and widespread pollution in Bangladesh and China. Of course, mass consumer behavior is just one example—one perspective on the market activities that contribute to the possibility of these evils. One could begin with the buying and selling of labor itself in developing countries, including the constraints under which workers must operate in seeking jobs.[42]

There is a reasonable response to this focus on consumers, of course: it is misplaced, in a certain sense, to "blame" home borrowers for the financial crisis, or buyers of sweaters for appalling labor conditions on shop floors thousands of miles away. We ought to blame corrupt politicians, overconfident bankers, heartless factory owners, and the like. There are actually two sets of issues involved in this objection and a response to it.

One set of questions has to do with focus. My approach in general points away from questions of punishing wrongdoers—which might be more central, for example, to an exploration of markets, ethical conduct, and injustice. I am concerned in the first instance with the way that markets evade democratic control and foster oppression, rather than with deciding which actors' parts in this are most blameworthy. Similarly, my focus in this chapter, in particular, is on buying and selling practices and the institutions and market forces they produce. I have said that such a market focus is to some degree artificial, since buying and selling only take place in particular institutional contexts, ones established by states and corporations. A related line of inquiry concerns the state as an alienated or potentially alienated structure, and its role in economic crises and suffering.[43] The tethering of states to alien agendas certainly explains something about why so few bankers and financiers paid a price for their destructive acts.

There is more than a measure of truth to the idea that we should not, in the ordinary sense, "blame" consumers for financial crises, the "Walmart economy," or the cruelties of global production. But we should attend carefully to the sorts of consequences of common action that are important in the generation of alienation. The issue is not what we often think of as a "consequence": an event causally linked to a previous one. Clothes buyers did not cause the Rana Plaza collapse in the sense that a swerving driver might cause an accident. What is important is the way common activities produce and reproduce social structures and forces, which in turn set the stage for harms like recessions and industrial accidents. These are generally unintended, but on reflection, knowable, consequences of common activities like the buying and selling that make markets. (In fact, antisweatshop activism is partly directed toward making people more aware of these consequences.) This particular discussion of markets simply stresses the way widespread consumer activities, in particular, help generate not just the forces most familiar to undergraduate economics students, such as shifting demand, but also reproduce banks and manufacturers and supply chains.

The other crucial face of market alienation, then, is the way these structures produce domination while enabling oppression and exploitation. Domination pervades the market narratives I have discussed. This includes, first, the way that so many people have been overwhelmed by market forces of foreclosure and unemployment, the way those who have faced foreclosure have felt—have known—their powers to be meager, insufficient to contend with a sprawling network of banks, loan servicers, and call centers. Low-wage workers in our economy are also overwhelmed by labor-market forces and overshadowed by their bosses' power in the workplace. In a different sense, there is also the domination of market logic itself, the ideas and tendencies and incentives that cause commodification to spread almost unchecked. This sort of ideological imperialism connects the pushing of farmers into labor markets to the forces that were behind the financial crisis—the tearing down of regulatory walls and the creation of new investments. And there is a form of ideological domination by markets as well, the unbowed persistence of what Stiglitz calls "market fundamentalism," a set of doctrines that have not weakened despite being deeply implicated in so many recent disasters.

This leads us back to the question of blame. Without doubt, managers like those of the factories in the Rana Plaza could say—they have said—that they are dominated by economic forces, too. They can cite "the pressure on them from U.S. and European retailers to deliver their goods on time" (Manik, Greenhouse, and Yardley 2013) as a reason they could not make working conditions safer or heed the signs of an impending tragedy. But the very fact that there is some truth to this notion—that manufacturers in Bangladesh are subject to necessities beyond their control—points to the need to recognize, as I have suggested, that even dominating market forces do not affect everyone the same way. In addition to recognizing degrees of domination, one of the best ways to get a grip on this is to draw on conceptions of oppression and exploitation. The factory owners may be dominated by global economic forces, but they also exercise power over their employees harshly and unjustly. And in hiring them, paying them, and maintaining labor discipline—in ordering them to work even after inspectors found cracks that prompted shops in the building to close—they took advantage of the workers' vulnerable situation in a way that was deeply contrary to their interests. In comparison, the oppression and exploitation homeowners have faced at the hands of banks and brokers may seem less consequential. But the important thing is that it is quite real. The very structure of finance, the very market forces borrowers helped reproduce, gave various people the power to take advantage of them or push them around unjustly.[44] It remains to be seen how it may be possible to respond democratically to such phenomena.

4

OPPOSITIONAL DEMOCRACY

—————————————→ ←—————————————

A great part of Europe's population helped sustain war from 1914 to 1918. Sixty million volunteered or were conscripted into armed forces. The economies of all the major belligerents were reorganized, making industrial workers very much active participants in the war effort. Familiar archival photographs show crowds lining up at recruiting centers and clambering onto trucks and rail cars early on with ominously naive signs reading *"Nach Paris"* and *"à Berlin."*[1] Other citizens were postered, propagandized, and prodded to buy war bonds. And far from the front, police and courts worked to quash dissent. Despite the broad mobilization and the early delusions of a quick military resolution, though, not all compliance or cooperation should be interpreted as uniform eagerness to go to war. Just as some diplomats felt the European treaty structure impelled them to war, many ordinary people surely felt that they had little choice but to fight, produce, buy, and forego for their countries. That so many millions of people participated in the waging of war does not mean that they did so happily or without being subject to serious constraint.

Even so, the fruit of all their war activity, willing and unwilling, was soon exceedingly bitter. They helped create a war machine, and that war machine ground up their lives and their world. The apparatuses of immobility—the machine gun, poison gas, and trenches—soon overwhelmed the futile but deadly human wave attacks launched against them, and they turned the war into stalemate. Tsarist Russia sent a massive but ill-equipped and poorly provisioned army into war against Germany, and lost two million soldiers to death, injury, and capture in 1915 alone. On all sides combined, almost ten million combatants were killed in four years. States and workplaces became increasingly authoritarian. Towns and villages were destroyed, and economies were ruined.

In late 1918, as armistice negotiations began, a few top German admirals, obsessed with avoiding a humiliating surrender, planned to order the battle fleet to sail from Kiel for one last attack on the British.[2] When enlisted sailors got wind of the plans, they resisted. Their resistance was partially suppressed, which only turned it into open rebellion. Soon, elected sailors' "councils" had formed to direct the uprising in both Kiel and Germany's largest naval base, and contingents of soldiers, sailors, and workers had taken over police headquarters and city halls across the north. Impressed with these successes, soldiers and workers elected councils of differing kinds and compositions across Germany and Austria-Hungary. The basic goals of the spreading movement were radically democratic: "democratization of the army, the civil service and the economy" (Kolb 1988, 15). It is surely no coincidence that this is the very trio of interrelated dominating structures and forces that had been central to the war, and which, up to then, soldiers, sailors, and workers had been reproducing. Dewey's discussion, a decade later, of alienation, democracy, and the Great War reads like a proclamation for the council cause. The war, he said, had seemed to many people to confront them like "the movement of an uncontrolled natural catastrophe," but it was in fact their own activities, transmitted through global "connections and ties" that had produced it ([1927] 1954, 128). "The existing constitution of the political state," Dewey observed, was incapable of coping with the wide-ranging belligerent consequences of such common action, so previously "nonpolitical forces" had to "organize themselves to transform existing political structures" (128–129).

There is nothing arbitrary about calling attention, briefly, to the council movement. Prominent figures in the history of political thought, including Vladimir Ilyich Lenin, Joseph Schumpeter, and Hannah Arendt, have seen the movement as crucial to understanding modern politics, to grasping the meaning of democracy and the alternatives to it.[3] And several things make the council movement, in particular, an illustrative case of democratic action to oppose alienation. The movement set out to tame forces and structures over which society had lost control, with shocking consequences. It aimed its efforts at democratizing the most hierarchical, the most dominating institutions of Central European society: the military, the bureaucracy, and the factory. Its means and ends were both democratic. The councils' participants engaged in a wide variety of political activities—not just forming the councils, electing members to them, and debating about principle and strategy, but also, more mundanely, taking and restarting paralyzed factories, planning military demobilization, and finding and distributing food. Yet for all the diverse functions the councils took on, they did not see themselves as replacements for parliaments or indeed other government organs. Lenin, expediently, and other intellectuals, more sincerely, at times advocated council-states. But the movement's own vision of democracy does not seem to have focused on remaking the political world on the council model, or even on crafting the councils themselves as ideally democratic spaces, but rather on using the councils to oppose, contest, and democratize. On their own, the council movement's lexicon and the electoral and deliberative rules participants improvised do not tell us much about them as a democratic movement. The council upsurge is an illustration—perhaps because of the severity of postwar collapse, a limiting case—showing why it is vital to conceptualize democratic action in the social context in which it perennially arises, namely, one characterized by alienation, as conceptualized in the last chapter. Democratic action continually arises surrounded by collectively reproduced domination and oppression—not necessarily as severe as in 1918, to be sure—and this is why democracy should be seen as an oppositional practice.

In the next section and also the subsequent one, I elaborate on what is entailed in this oppositional view of democracy, including, among other things, what this tells us about the range of activities we should understand as "democratic." This list of democratic activities, I think, should be more extensive than most contemporary approaches allow. The last three sections of the chapter engage with approaches related to the oppositional one I offer: participatory democracy, agonistic democracy, and fugitive democracy. I argue that some of the most interesting intersections of oppositional with participatory theory involve neglected aspects of the latter approach. For example, contrary to some characterizations, participatory democrats have never argued for the perfect realization of democracy in any one institution, but rather for a fruitful democratizing tension between institutional realms, some more and some less democratic, some more and some less alienated. Oppositional democracy shares this interstitial quality. Agonistic democracy, while it certainly emphasizes struggle, differs with my approach both in how it theorizes the origins of the struggle and a democratic response to it. It focuses on the perpetual negotiation of social identity, while saying little about other vital democratic concerns. Finally, I explore Sheldon Wolin's moving portrait of democracy as "fugitive." While Wolin, too, captures something important about the precariousness and strenuousness of democracy, I argue that democratic action is not really fugitive, not really a perfect, momentary attainment in an otherwise fallen world. In fact, given the perennial state of the social world, it is and must be an ongoing struggle, no matter how imperfect.

Democratic Action against Alienation

Europe, in late 1918, was a torrent of common activities and shared practices: millions of soldiers fighting, then demobilizing and beginning to return home; millions more producing food and materiel, and then scrambling for subsistence as the war economy creaked to a stop; suppressed ethnic groups mobilizing politically for nationhood as empires began to collapse. It is in the midst of people contributing to such a turbulent river of ongoing activity that a distinctive form of common action may arise—democratic action, such as that of the council movement.

By democratic action I mean this: action directed toward collectively managing crucial institutions, social relations, and forces in a way that strives for equality of power, while also combating domination and reducing opportunities for oppression and exploitation. Democratic action, so described or defined, is explicitly concerned with a particular kind or face of equality: equality in the power or capacity to intervene in ongoing political contention, equality in collectively managing social forces and relations. This sort of equality should not be regarded as a distant standard of perfection toward which democratic action can only aim hopefully, but rather as what Dewey called an "end-in-view," a good discerned in the present, though imperfectly, uncertainly, and inconsistently—one sought more surely, lastingly, and completely for the future. Although the word *freedom* is not explicitly included in this characterization of democratic action, freedom is part of the ambition expressed here, bound up with many of the definitional terms themselves. Democratic action, more specifically, is concerned both with negative and positive freedom, insofar as it is concerned with resisting domination and oppression, as well as with enhancing people's capacity for "collectively managing" crucial institutions, social relations, and social forces.[4] Democratic action, along with alienation, constitutes one of the interrelated conceptual poles of an oppositional democratic theory. Just highlighting democracy as action incorporates within democratic theory what was said before about action, generally—especially action's imperfection, the fact that it is better seen as intervening than initiating, its reflexiveness, and its dependence on, vulnerability to, and challenging of preexisting structural conditions. Emphasizing democracy as action also responds to the problems of viewing democracy primarily as a regime.

Much as we might hope to experience democratic action as a series of legislative foundings—autonomous, sovereign moments—it is more plausible to envision it as preceded, surrounded, and conditioned by many other kinds of action. The "spirit of the new," the "exhilarating awareness of the human capacity of beginning," to use Arendt's words (1963, 225)— this is what political action might seem to be all about, according to one way of thinking. But at the moment a person or group acts, politically or otherwise, myriad others are always already acting in many disparate and distinct ways. Democratic action never does more than intervene, however dramatically, in that onward rush. And the significance of the intervention, furthermore, cannot be self-contained, inward looking or self-referential, but has everything to do with the flow of action that it enters or attempts to channel. So there can be, for this reason, no immaculate conception for democratic action. It comes into being in a world already set in motion by these many existing activities and practices. And these forms of action, crucially, also reproduce a social world that is always already structured, often undemocratically, by families, armies, corporations, bureaucracies, racial castes, states, corporations, and transnational organizations. Those engaged in democratic action cannot simply direct themselves toward abstract democratic values, nor even exclusively toward others they hope to engage as democratic citizens, nor to the decisions they may make together. They face a definite structural context they cannot escape and that gives meaning to what they do.

It is not difficult to see that there could be many varieties of common action aligned with the democratic motivations at issue: seeking equal power and fighting domination, for example. Not just voting and deliberating, but organizing, dissenting, marching, mobilizing, debating, negotiating, striking, canvassing, and petitioning ought at times to count as forms of democratic action. (I return to the matter of this variety below.) But if democratic action can take different forms and always arises amid other types of action, what characterizes it and distinguishes it from the other kinds of action? The most apparent answers are named in the definition above—striving for collective regulation of crucial institutions, for equality and freedom, and against domination and oppression. But simply posing the question—what is distinctive about democracy?—helps explicate an argument made by the young Marx, one already encountered in Chapter 2. All social and political institutions—even militaries and corporations—are reproduced by myriad people in different social locations and by the social practices they enact. But in many cases, the social relations and forces actively reproduced this way are hierarchical or resistant to common management, and so unyielding, opaque to many of those who reproduce them. These structures seem almost to deny their popular origins, to confront many of the ordinary people who reproduce them as "already present and given," in Hegel's words ([1807] 1977, 294), as someone else's work, rather than as their own. Democratic practices, the young Marx pointed out, explicitly recognize the popular origins of social and political institutions in a special way, valuing each participant in them equally. This, I have argued, explains why Marx referred cryptically to democracy as "the resolved mystery of all constitutions"—because in democracy, "the constitution appears as what it is, the free product of men" ([1843] 1967, 29–30).[5] Democratic practices and institutions, because they cherish the popular origins of all social structures, and because they value and elicit the free and equal participation of each person in generating them, occupy a unique place among the many forms of common action and the social forms common action reproduces.

Democratic action, then, is *set amid* many other different kinds of action and their objectifications—the social relations, institutions, and tendencies those practices create and sustain. More than this, though, democratic action, because of its animating aims and values, finds itself perennially arrayed against alienation, against those structures and forces that overshadow the agency of ordinary people, impose necessities upon them, and provide opportunities for oppression or exploitation. The contemporary social world as we know it encompasses some realms that are characterized by domination and constraint and others with more scope for free action. When people act democratically against the background of such diversity and disparity, they almost inevitably confront resistance. They necessarily set themselves in opposition to institutions and social forces that would otherwise make them vulnerable to injustice or would escape their common control. This is most apparent in the case of social movements, such as the postwar councils, that rise up to challenge overwhelmingly destructive forces and deeply entrenched opponents. It is also the case, although perhaps less dramatically, when a representative legislature simply seeks to regulate chaotic markets in pursuit of public purposes—to curb destructive waves of foreclosures, for example, or to right an imbalance in power within the workplace or between corporations and consumers.

But, this familiar example notwithstanding, the democratic vehicle need not be a state. In fact, like the German *Kaiserreich,* states themselves have been as often the objects as the tools of democratic action. The sometimes useful fiction of the contractual origin of the representative state obscures a recurrent historical pattern: states have not generally been created democratically, but at best, in varying degrees, have been captured, transformed, or managed by democratic action. Democracy does not necessarily find fulfillment through elections or even through popular attempts at state appropriation. Entrenched old power groupings, such as the German bureaucracy and officer corps—or today, what Egyptians term their "deep state"—may cling tenaciously to power. And too few democratic theorists now notice that even the liberal state itself— when, despite elections, it is captured by narrow interests, when it reflects and reinforces oppressive social relations, or when it embodies in its very being a definite limit to the bounds of democratic action—poses problems of alienation, democratic problems.[6]

So a democratic theory that recognizes alienation grasps as well the continual importance of democratic opposition. The enduringly oppositional character of democratic action is due, most generally, to the fact that democratic impulses, when they arise, do so in situations that are already structured by existing social institutions, relations, and forces, some of which are alienated. Democratic action is a prominent—although not the only possible—response to such phenomena. But democratic action, though continually oppositional, is not for this reason simply arrayed against "external" challenges. Part of what makes alienation poignant for democratic theory is that those most affected by the phenomenon generally take some part in reproducing the structures that cause it. Democratic action, in this sense, is a recapturing or a redirection of our own common powers.

I am not alone in arguing, in broad terms, that democracy is oppositional. Ian Shapiro, for example, has also criticized deliberative theorists for undervaluing opposition to domination as a crucial feature of democracy (2003, 3), and has argued that "opposition must enjoy a more independent and exalted status in a persuasive account of just democratic politics" (1999a, 31).[7] But both the democratic practices Shapiro emphasizes and the kind of power relations they are meant to redress are somewhat different.[8] Recognizing domination and opposition, Shapiro argues, should make us look favorably on Schumpeter's elite theory of democracy, insofar as it can be interpreted as advocating the limitation of power through electoral competition (2003, 55–64).[9] In fact, for the most part, when Shapiro contends that democracy derives its significance from opposing domination, he seems to refer mainly to familiar representative institutions and practices (2010, 20).[10]

So again, democracy, according to the view I am proposing, opposes not just domination, but more broadly, alienation. As I indicated in Chapter 3, to speak of alienation, and not only of domination, oppression, and exploitation, is to emphasize the way that these harms are not just chance injuries inflicted by bad actors. They rest on social structures that are reproduced by large numbers of people, including many who find themselves victims of the ills. Domination, from this standpoint, is not just an incidental challenge to democracy, a merely contingent falling away from democratic ideals. Alienation and democratic action—the interacting poles of an *oppositional* vision of democracy—are integrally, not just externally, related. One is not merely the negation of the other. They share a common ground, and neither can be fully understood without considering the other. One cannot theorize democratic action without positing the prerequisite for it, and so the possibility of alienation—nor can one theorize alienation without the generative conditions of democratic action. Both are rooted in a sober, balanced view of agency, reproduction, objectification, and structure. Insofar as any of us prizes democratic action, we must be troubled by its radical misfiring, the radical loss of common control, the destructive failure of common management inherent in alienation. Or, to put it differently, the poignancy of alienation is clearest from the standpoint of an appreciation for democratic action, action through which people can gain a certain kind of egalitarian common control of the social worlds they reproduce. Yet because both alienation and democracy are rooted in action and its travails, this poignancy necessarily colors our whole understanding of oppositional democracy's value.

It is best to distinguish two aspects of democratic opposition. In the first instance, it is possible to think of democratic action arising in opposition to the alienated effects of nearly a whole society's activities and practices. In the limiting case, then, democratic opposition might appear as a whole society trying to manage the consequences of its own almost universally shared practices—and not immediately as opposition between different social groups and agents. Some attempts to put democratic curbs on markets might resemble this limiting case, insofar as participation in market activities is extremely widespread. In such instances, it is not just a matter of citizens and their representatives channeling the economic activity of certain *other* people, but of a public, as best it can, gaining some democratic control over its own buying and selling, as well as the institutions and forces their market exchanges produce. Similarly, when virtually a whole society feeds war, as in Europe in 1914–1918, democratic attempts to end the war and restructure the institutions that waged it will have something of this quality as well. Less dramatically, it may be that the way that most people in liberal democracies conduct themselves in daily life—their neglect of common goals as employees or as consumers, their often isolating, privatized exurban existence, their anemic participation in public endeavors—undermines effective democratic institutions and practices.[11] And this may, in turn, foster the growth of economic, social, or political structures that overshadow ordinary agents or impose severe necessities on them. Democratic attempts to change these sorts of widespread practices, and the structures they perpetuate, are oppositional in one sense.

But while a wide variety of people may take part in some of the common activities that create such alienated institutions, actors usually do not all take part in the same way or bear the same structural relation to the resulting institutions and forces. Overshadowing and constraint may be experienced in varying ways and degrees by different parties. And certain forms of social action clearly reproduce institutions and relations that foster the oppression of particular agents by others. For this reason, the "opposition" in oppositional democratic action may also—and quite often does—refer to conflict between people or groups engaged in different forms of activity, with different social positions, divergent sources of power, and conflicting interests. It is important to emphasize that these are two faces of opposition, not two different kinds of opposition. Neither likely exists in pure form.

Oppositional Democracy's Vision

Late Arrival

From the standpoint of an oppositional theory, democratic action, however creative it may be, is always late on the scene. This is not due mainly to the public's inattention or laziness—as Walter Lippmann suggests when he describes the public as arriving perennially "in the middle of the third act" ([1927] 1993, 55). The issue is that democratic action always emerges or reappears in a world already structured by states, corporations, militaries, families, and castes. Like all action, it plays out in an unfinished, troubled, and discordant world, a world that is, as Dewey reminds us, perilous, ambiguous, and uncertain. Democratic action is, as soon as it appears, in this sense also encumbered. The councils were a crucial part of the revolution that established a new, albeit fragile, German order. But it is apparent from their experience that even such foundings and forward-looking acts cannot sweep away the past or restart political time. Democratic action is in this sense always intervention; it is never pure, unprecedented creation. It interacts with a world that is already structured as well as already in motion, shifting, seething, and active.

Democratic action is also, from an oppositional standpoint, always surrounded, encircled, hemmed in—by other action, both democratic and nondemocratic, and by resulting social structures, including alienated ones. And the relationship of any democratic intervention to these other practices crucially shapes the intervention's meaning. Whereas the idea that democracy arrives late could be understood as the temporal insight of oppositional democratic theory, this surroundedness is, roughly speaking, the spatial insight. Democratic action is forever surrounded by people active in myriad ways—fighting, playing, suffering, buying, consuming, producing—and never just abstractly, but according to varied, concrete social practices. It faces a world, as well, in which the specific social practices according to which people act constantly reproduce social relations, some very troubling. Democratic action cannot help but have a definite, concrete relationship to these activities and relations; it will necessarily be in accord with some and in conflict with others. And so democratic action is never merely self-referential, never a retreat into ideal relations.

Each in its own distinctive way, the rise of Occupy Wall Street, some electoral campaigns in 2008 and after, and the passage by Congress of financial reform, can all be seen as democratic responses to the alienated economic forces and structures of the mortgage meltdown and the Great Recession. (Of course, none of them—especially the elections—were exclusively responses to the recession, and all—especially the reform— were flawed democratic re-actions, to be sure. But at the moment, such evaluation is not my main concern.) None of these could be understood as merely self-contained, inward-directed celebrations of democratic life, though some members of the Occupy movement seem sometimes to have flirted with such a notion. It is impossible to understand what made these actions democratic in the fullest sense—impossible to gauge their democratic significance—without seeing them against the backdrop of the torrent of nondemocratic activities that produced the financial crisis and its aftermath. And the rather limited ability of these actions to reign in the financial system reveals even more about their surroundedness. To express the point a little differently, we cannot separate what was democratic about these efforts from the "issues" they engaged. Their claim to democratic significance has everything to do with their attempts to intervene in the flow of nondemocratic activities, to curb the power of alienated institutions and forces.

Democratic Activities: Movements and More

In the first chapter, I criticized a number of common concepts in democratic theory—democracy as a refuge or quarantine, for example—from the standpoint of what I termed "critical democratic eras." Taken narrowly, the force of those arguments could be construed this way: certain basic assumptions in elite, deliberative, and other models of democracy do not jibe well with what we know about the experiences, challenges, and practices of democratic movements in such eras. Put like this, an apt response, I admitted, would seem to be that my criticisms only apply to the eras in which those particular movements were active, to periods of democratization, and not to democracy itself, proper. But I countered that there are good reasons to think that democracy and democratization are not really to be distinguished so sharply, that all eras are critical democratic eras—though some more so than others, perhaps. Or, one could say, the term *critical democratic eras* is potentially misleading. We should speak instead, I argued, of *critical democratic conditions*. And I said I would show why critical democratic conditions, to some degree or another, are a perennial challenge. In Chapter 3 I tried to make good on this undertaking. The argument, simply, is that because common action continually reproduces alienated social forces and institutions, democratic action always arises in a context characterized at least partly by such social forms. And the meaning of democracy is inescapably linked to challenging them.

If critical democratic conditions are not limited to particular, discrete eras, then the movements and oppositional tactics we find in them should not be regarded as exceptional—or only as instrumental—but as an integral part of democracy. If structures that dominate and that foster oppression and exploitation are not rarities, but endemic to social life—

to the very conditions of common action—then struggle against such social forms and the people who benefit from them is equally integral. And this realization opens the door to recognizing a variety of oppositional practices as important examples of what it means to engage in democratic action. The building-block concepts of an oppositional approach, in other words, suggest a pluralistic view of the activities that should potentially be valued as democratic. In response to deliberative theory, Michael Walzer asks a rather simple question: "Deliberation, and What Else?" (1999). And he offers a telling list of other democratic activities: political education, organization, mobilization, demonstration, statement, debate, lobbying, campaigning, fundraising, and "scut work" (58–66). The alienation-and-opposition approach suggests a number of related reasons why these and other nondeliberative activities deserve recognition, as well as several perspectives from which to sort democratic activities. The heart of the matter is a broad theorization of action, one emphasizing the importance of action's unintended consequences and the fact that decision, reflection, and communication are only moments of the always-ongoing tide of action. This much I have already brought out in the last chapter through a discussion of Dewey, Giddens, Bourdieu, and Bhaskar.

As I have suggested, the main unifying principle for such diverse kinds of democratic action—what marks any activity as democratic—is orientation toward collectively managing crucial institutions, social relations, and forces in a way that strives for equality of power. This may seem to refer exclusively to the purpose of an activity, but it refers simultaneously to some of its inherent qualities as well. Action, I have already suggested, should not be seen as a series of discrete acts, each preceded by a decision, but as an ongoing process. Agents, finding themselves in the middle of this flow, can only reflect upon it, with an eye to redirecting it in a forward-looking way. Once we recognize this, it is not hard to see that to act democratically is often to act in a way that both exercises egalitarian, collective powers now and aims to increase the richness, power, and scope of democratic management of the social world for the future. This emphasis on enhancing the fruitfulness of action is in a sense familiar. Participatory theories of democracy have often emphasized enhancing efficacy, the ability of agents to act politically.

Against a pluralistic view of what should count as democratic action, many approaches identify a particular sort of activity as the principled essence of democracy and characterize other activities as less valuable, less proximate to the true meaning of democracy. Prominent among these approaches, of course, is deliberative theory. And a wider if less hegemonic family of conceptualizations, while not focused on deliberation, per se, also treat democracy essentially as a form of communication.[12] Other approaches stipulate that some other sort of political activity, such as voting for leaders—or just watching them—is particularly fitting for citizens, perhaps even the only sort of democratic activity to which ordinary people can aspire. Such hierarchies of activities are not characteristic of all models of democracy, however. Some theories emphasize ideal "modes" of democratic activity, as these do, while others emphasize the significance of various "sectors" for participation (Hilmer 2010, 46).

It is common to think of action as something distinct from observation, learning, and reflection—or in politics, to separate implementation from debate and decision. But in politics as in life, as Dewey argues, we learn from doing, and do better by learning. The practice of experimentation epitomizes this point. And some of the sorts of democratic activities mentioned by Walzer can be thought of precisely as "experimental"— that is, as a kind of active inquiry, or as educative intervention in the social world. This may be especially true when it comes to learning about power relations. The famous lunch-counter demonstrations of the civil rights movement were something more than theater, something more than expressive outbursts or revelations of new values. They demonstrated to the world through active intervention how the system of segregation worked, how challenges to it provoked violent repression. More mundanely perhaps, campaign volunteers learn from canvassing how other people think and talk about politics and so how to engage them better in the future. Union activists learn vitally about their workplaces, as well as the business and economic sector it is part of, through trying to organize other workers and through engaging management again and again. In contrast to the idea that political learning should happen primarily through discussion, reflection, or passive observation, experimental action suggests a frequently integral relation between acting and growth of political understanding. Of course, it is not hard to see, either, that action can be expressive, communicative. A march may communicate a message or call attention to an idea. But there is no warrant for arguing that because certain democratic actions communicate that they are only or even mainly to be understood as forms of communication. In democratic politics, it often makes little sense to prioritize reflection or discussion over action—or even to see them as truly distinct.

Just as it often seems to rest, at least implicitly, on an overly sharp distinction between doing and discussing, deliberative theory also distinguishes coercive actions (which can at best be nonideal and instrumental) from communicative, noncoercive (ideal) ones. But an acquaintance with oppositional democratic practice suggests that much of what movements do is simultaneously aimed at coercively changing political discourse and restructuring the social relations in which such discourse is situated.[13] For example, by creating crises of order, the civil rights movement tried to force the federal government to intervene on its behalf during the Freedom Rides and related campaigns. Because parties newly drawn into contention often are bearers of ideas and arguments that previously had little traction or little prestige in a particular arena, such strategies upset existing power relations, alter them nonconsensually, and change discourse all at once.[14] Similarly, the postwar councils did not simply consist of people who met, exchanged ideas, debated, or started voting on issues. In the very course of doing these things within newly created fora, they were also upsetting the institutional order, undermining or usurping other actors' power—forcefully creating new political institutions, new centers of power. In various ways, democratic actors often must threaten other actors' interests—take advantage of relative weaknesses—so as to get them to behave a certain way. Democratic actors must often create a crisis, a public realization that things *cannot* go on the same way. An important example is a crisis of confidence in the government, a sense that its power is no longer legitimate, or no longer unchallengeable, that dissent or resistance are possible, even imperative. Gandhi's "salt march," the mass demonstrations in Eastern Europe in 1989, and protests in the Arab world in 2011 all had these effects, or were intended to do, at least. Democratic actors must sometimes threaten others' discursive capital, as well: they must embarrass others into communicating differently by exposing self-dealing or hypocrisy.

One way to think about and to make sense of the variety of democratic activities this approach potentially sanctions begins with considering the reasons that people may participate in reproducing the alienated social structures democratic action resists—an issue taken up in Chapter 3. Of course, a first, obvious answer is that these social forms enhance certain people's power. This points, in general, to the sorts of democratic movement activities just discussed—some coercive—which may force beneficiaries of undemocratic power relations to act differently, to choose between different interests in a way that serves the goals of the democratic movement. But, as I mentioned in Chapter 3, we can also ask why people who are hurt or dominated by alienated social forms would reproduce them. And there were a range of reasons: often people have little choice but to reproduce these forms, simply because they must make a living, or to avoid violence, harassment, or punishment; or they do not know or have not reflected upon the way their actions reproduce dominating or oppressive institutions. These possibilities suggest other kinds of democratic activities or other ways of identifying democratic activities. Some democratic activities, that is, may be crafted to help people withdraw support from or resist being drawn into alienated institutions. This approach might include the long, arduous process of creating organizations and arrangements that support people in acting autonomously; sustaining churches, schools, and affinity groups that foster association and discussion outside of established hierarchies (Freeman 1975, ch. 4; Morris 1984, chs. 1 and 11; Phillips 1991, ch. 5); forming and managing various "alternative" and mutual-aid institutions, like consumer cooperatives, or in the era of the Populists, agricultural cooperatives (Goodwyn 1978, ch. 3); agitating for and building participatory mechanisms within the workplace and government; building strike funds that compensate workers for wages lost during labor actions; donating and collecting money to bail protestors out of jail; or forming and serving on legal teams that monitor police responses and represent people arrested in civil disobedience.[15] This sort of arduous political work is surely neglected by democratic theory that focuses only on voting, spectating, or on deliberating.

As for the possibility that some people may not know or may not have reflected on the way that they participate in reproducing alienated structures, here the challenge for democratic actors is largely ideological, getting people to see the social world and their place in it differently. Gandhi expressed the point well, referring in particular to how the power of the state is upheld: Most people "do not realize that every citizen silently but nonetheless certainly sustains the Government of the day in ways of which he has no knowledge" (1996, 58).[16] The sorts of ideological work needed are as varied as the forms of reproduction and the structures reproduced. Antisweatshop groups try to educate consumers about the way their buying practices create dangerous and exploitive working conditions thousands of miles away. Others, along with journalists and documentary makers, explain how the financial crisis and recession were generated. Labor organizers try to demonstrate to workers how attempting to go it alone against powerful corporations sustains the potentially oppressive power of employers. Another version of this sort of ideological work is focused on persuading oppressed or dominated people not to internalize the justifications for their condition and to have more confidence in themselves and their ability to act. Martin Luther King Jr., for example, wrote about the process by which southern African Americans developed a "new sense of self-respect and sense of dignity" and how this "undermined the South's negative peace" (1986, 6). This ideological work cannot be reduced to the neutral promotion of free and open discourse across society. First, an oppositional approach insists that it is important to identify which arguments about the social world— especially about mechanisms of domination and oppression—are the most accurate, or in pragmatic terms, the most fruitful for democratic transformation. Moreover, the democratic activity involved is often convincing certain agents to act differently and reconfigure the political world *well before* anyone has convinced a broader public—let alone entrenched opponents—of the validity of any new ideas about society and politics. And in any given instance, what I have called "experimental" action, at once vigorously active and oriented toward learning and teaching, may be the most ideologically effective course.

One theme running through this enumeration and analysis of democratic activities is the need directly to undermine or diminish the power of social groups who benefit from domination or engage in oppression. An oppositional approach shows that this can be a democratic activity. A surprising implication of this is well expressed by Suzanne Dovi, who advances an argument, slyly, in her essay "In Praise of Exclusion" (2009). Democratic theorists, she notes, are quite comfortable—perhaps often too comfortable—advocating the *inclusion* of underrepresented groups in representative institutions. But increasing some people's access, she contends, is not enough. Sometimes it is necessary directly to limit or diminish the access of overrepresented or unduly powerful groups. And so we need, she argues, an "ethics of marginalization" that "aims to provide democratic citizens the requisite guidance by articulating principles that they should use in deciding when and how to marginalize" (1182).[17]

One likely response to the pluralism my approach underwrites would be to deny that many of the practices discussed in the last few pages are in themselves to be prized democratically. They can only be regarded, many would argue, as instrumental, nonideal means to an ideal end. (See

Chapter 1.) But understanding democratic action in reciprocal relation to alienation, understanding alienation as a perennial, inescapable[18] consequence of common action, should have the consequence of effacing, within democratic theory at least, any categorical distinction between ideal and nonideal, between ends and means. The division of democratic theory into ideal and nonideal, the idea that those living in nonideal circumstances should be guided by a distant vision of perfect democratic practice, relies on belief that we can imagine that ideal of perfection in which there is no domination, oppression, or exploitation, and somehow remain connected to it by a sort of golden spiritual thread. But a proper reckoning with alienation suggests that such an ideal is so remote that we should doubt our ability to conceive it, and certainly doubt that we ought to derive democratic theory from such a projection. Snip the golden thread and we are left, not with a degraded, irrevocably nonideal politics, but with the actually experienced political world of ideal and nonideal entwined—or rather, a world that is neither ideal nor nonideal. More concretely, we are left with a world in which democratic action is perennially in dialectic not just with the contingent rise of dominators and oppressors but with the perpetual threat of our common action, our common social productions, turning against us—or, at any rate, against some of us.

There is another way to understand the case against derogating certain democratic activities as mere means. Too many approaches to democracy show scant respect for basic organizational, mobilizing activities crucial not just to movements but to all sorts of democratic organizations, like established unions and good-government groups. A range of theories, notably deliberative approaches, tend to devalue any activity that is not expressive or ideally communicative. But Mary Dietz has rightly vindicated basic organizational work under the banner of "politics as a kind of ongoing, methodical work in the world" (1994, 883).[19] While Dietz largely accepts that such work can be seen as instrumental, though, I would stress that an even deeper respect comes from recognizing that it is never just that, that there is something to admire in such action intrinsically. Each in his own way, Giddens and Bourdieu offer deep appreciations of all day-to-day human action as a kind of skillful enactment. Even the ordinary activities that reproduce society have to be seen as adept improvisation, in Bourdieu's view: the use of a "small batch of schemes enabling agents to generate an infinity of practices adapted to endlessly changing situations, without those schemes ever being constituted as explicit principles" (1977, 16). The wide range of democratically oriented improvisational activities that are involved in building successful democratic movements and institutions that challenge alienation would seem to deserve even more respect. Dewey's emphasis on the constant growth of agency and the constant enrichment of experience is perhaps even more apropos. The background to all of Dewey's writings is an appreciation of the constant effort to act in better, richer, fuller ways. It is in part because he sees this as a constantly ongoing process that Dewey refuses to distinguish means from ends; the seeming end of one phase of action becomes immediately the means to another one. Reflecting and deciding and discussing are not distinctly more valuable than this process but integral moments of it.

Democratic activists generally grasp this. Most grassroots political activities, whether by movements or civic groups, are recognized as at once instrumental and valued in themselves—or rather, neither of these, exclusively. A march or a sit-in may be geared toward some apparently external end, but planning it, organizing it, and carrying it out are often valued in themselves as both an exercise and a development of one's political powers—as a chance to enjoy the experience of one's agency, one's ability to overcome resistance, to intervene in the troubled political world, and to enjoy active cooperation and camaraderie.[20] A recent account based on interviews with participants in Occupy Wall Street (Milkman, Lewis, and Luce 2013) illustrates an appreciation for movement activities that casts them neither as ideals nor as purely instrumental to something else ideal. As if following Dewey, these participants seemed to see their political activities as ongoing and reflexive, so that each of their actions was neither just a fulfillment in itself nor merely a means to some ideal democratic future. The terms of this recognition were largely related to the development of political capacities. These participants celebrated the fact that movement activity "unleash[ed] all these sorts of talents and energies" (196); that it "politicized" people, enhancing their future understanding of their social worlds (196); that it gave them opportunities to "learn the right skills" and become "really good leaders and good organizers" (197); that it engendered pride at having "transformed" the Occupy encampment to make it a better site for democratic activity (196); and that it fostered a "sense of community" (197). There is no reason to think this sort of appreciation is limited to movement activities, either—that phone banking, poll watching, precinct walking and the like, that is, the traditional "scut work" of representative politics, do not or cannot have the same quality of being neither means nor ends exclusively.

Indeed, it is important to stress this point: my argument about alienation does not purport to show that democracy is reducible to movements, that distinctive movement activities are somehow the true core of democracy, or that other, more widely recognized democratic practices that are not associated with movements are somehow diminished by that fact. First, not all movements are democratic.[21] Democratic movements are ones that engage in what I have termed *democratic action:* action directed toward collectively managing crucial institutions, social relations, and forces in a way that strives for equality of power, while also combating domination and reducing opportunities for oppression. The point is that there are a variety of activities that could fit this description—that could be so oriented—including (in some cases) voting and deliberating and the many activities associated with electoral or citizen lobbying campaigns, mentioned just above, such as phone banking. And yet the activities associated with representative institutions are also just one set of democratic activities.

Even in representative systems, state powers and agencies can be alienated if they overshadow ordinary people, stop serving common interests, and foster or protect oppressive exercises of power. But democratic opposition is opposition to that alienation, not toward any structure that can become alienated. Opposition to alienation does not mean permanent hostile disengagement from the state, mere influence from the outside, at arm's length, or a retreat into some favored home terrain of democratic activity. Some appropriately oppositional tactics help democrats redirect state power, or deny others access to it. I shall return to this point in the next chapter, and argue that combating alienation in and out of the state requires struggle both with and against the state.

The Parameters of Democratic Opposition

It may seem that casting democratic action as persistently oppositional and sometimes coercive might open the door to all kinds of objectionable political conduct. Deliberative democrats, especially, may think so, because for them the noncoercive exchange of reasons is the primary way—almost the sole indicator—of respecting others' autonomy.

It is important to emphasize, in response to such worries, that I have contended that democracy is intrinsically oppositional, not that all forms of opposition are intrinsically democratic. Similarly, my claim is that democratic action must often be coercive, not that all kinds of coercion are democratic. In addition, coercion—compelling others to act through

147

force or threats—is not the same as violence, viewed as physical force that is intended to cause injury, death, or psychological harm. In any case, the list of democratic activities discussed above should not provoke very much anxiety to those who care about individual rights and autonomy. It leaves off many modes and practices of conflict, antagonism, and enmity, including violent ones. And these are not ad hoc omissions; they flow from the oppositional-democratic approach itself. No activity or practice should be considered democratic unless it is reasonably oriented toward collectively managing the social world on egalitarian terms. And action that attacks the needed conditions of such collective management should be considered out of bounds.

There is an old line of argument claiming that democracy is likely to undermine individual rights. Chantal Mouffe articulates a contemporary version: democracy and liberalism partake of inherently conflicting "logics" (2000, 2–3). The best responses to this claim are illuminating for the present issue—the limits on democratic opposition—as well. One familiar rebuttal to this old argument is that the practice of democracy requires a robust scheme of individual rights—rights to free expression and association, for example, that comprise the democratic process—a point made by Dahl (1985, 24–25). This is one way of understanding the value of representative institutions. And it is enough to establish that there are individual rights that democrats cannot coherently violate, at least not in the name of democracy (Medearis 2005, 69–70). So this clearly places limits on the kind of opposition or coercion that can be accepted as democratic. Habermas, who equates individual rights with "private autonomy" and democracy with "public autonomy," furthers this line of argument by pointing out, as well, that no individual can feel truly autonomous unless she recognizes herself as an "author" of the rights that constitute her own private autonomy (1998). Having those rights imposed externally undermines autonomy. In light of all we have learned about structuration and alienation, I think it is clear that we should not see agents as "authors" of their social institutions. But Habermas's point, duly modified, is well taken. The individual rights that undergird common democratic action have to be reproduced, kept vibrant, by means of collective democratic action.

This is a point that can be understood, as well, in terms of effacing the distinction between means and ends in democracy. It is not just that actors must not adopt means that are inconsistent with democratic ends. It is, rather, as Dewey could have argued, that democrats are always caught up in a flow of events in the world, in which democratic action is needed now to establish the conditions of richer, fuller, more robust democratic action later. And this, too, sets bounds on the kind of action that ought to be called democratic. It is in the context of interrelated means and ends that we can consider another possible limitation on the range of democratic activities. Andrew Sabl (2001) has argued that the most convincing reason for those who are dominated or oppressed to limit themselves to civil disobedience is that it promotes the conditions of future democratic cooperation. The condition, of course, does not always apply. But Sabl's argument, I think, can be understood as a particular version of the Deweyan idea that democratic action should be pursued so as to enable fuller democratic action later.

Old Refrains: Refuges and Quarantines, Citizen Relations, Institutions, and Decisions

Now it is possible to return to the set of problematic conceptions about democracy discussed in Chapter 1—to review how an oppositional vision responds to them. I pointed out that deliberative theory often treats democracy as a refuge from power and inequality, or a mental projection into an ideal future, while elite theory treats properly constituted democracy as a kind of quarantine, a narrowly circumscribed practice separated from the socially necessary activities of elite politicians. The core of an oppositional approach is the idea that democracy, intrinsically, is not a retreat but a direct engagement with dominating structures, or with that which resists common management of society on terms of equality. And the approach justifies this viewpoint by arguing that democratic efforts always arise in a context that is already structured, already active, one in which alienation is permanently possible and recurrently manifest. Direct engagement with dominating forces, oppression, and exploitation is a nearly ubiquitous feature of democratic activity because it is all but impossible to prevent common action from sometimes reproducing harmful forces and institutions. Democratic movements are the most vivid illustration of this perennial challenge. But oppositional democracy is premised more on the perennial threat of alienation than on the contingent rise of movements.

Both elite and deliberative theories, I argued in Chapter 1, often treat democracy as a special kind of relationship among citizens—elite theory because of its essential indifference to those who are not citizens and deliberative theory because of its single-minded focus on how citizens should discourse with each other. Oppositional democracy shows why it is important not to reduce democratic problems to the way citizens treat each other, not to reduce multisided persons who participate in a variety of social relations—many of them hierarchical or exploitive—to one dimension of their social lives, citizenship. Both a boss and an employee may be citizens, but this does not tell us much about the particular social relationship they inhabit. It is equally important, an oppositional approach says, not to collapse malign problems of power and structure into failure to communicate with other citizens in the right way. Such an approach hardly gets at the democratic problems bound up, say, with the German war machine one hundred years ago. Of course, even after these corrections, citizenship remains a crucial concept for democratic theory, but from the standpoint of oppositional democracy, it is best to understand the pursuit of meaningful citizenship not as an ideal relationship between citizens but as a claim, a struggle against the inegalitarian relations that people continually reproduce through their ongoing practices as consumers, workers, and so on.

An institutional, governmental view of democracy is part of both elite and deliberative theory, as well. Even deliberative theorists have been known to quote Schumpeter's definition of democracy as an "institutional arrangement." But if an oppositional view of democracy is correct, democracy is to be found less in a certain kind of regime, a limited set of institutions, and more in a diverse set of challenging practices. Given the many forms alienation can take, it seems likely that democracy must take many organizational forms. By the same token, states that meet many democratic institutional criteria can be alienated. Overly institutional views of democracy also seem to force us to choose between a simple yes or no in asking whether a polity is democratic. But if alienation is a perennial problem that no polity has ever completely escaped, should we say that democracy has never existed? It seems better to focus on democratic action, broadly understood, and to identify democracy with the ongoing, active struggle to resist dominating social forms, oppression, and exploitation.

The conceptualization of democracy as a way of reaching decisions is also quite pervasive, in deliberative and elite theory. For deliberative theory, democracy is a discursive, inclusive, and noncoercive mode of making decisions, whereas for elite theorists, it is a system that allows voters to accept the leaders who do all the actual deciding. Of course, no democratic theorist should be indifferent to how decisions are made. From a democratic perspective, it is important that decision making be egalitarian and open. But there are at least three potentially significant disadvantages associated with overemphasizing decisions. Taken together, these problems suggest that a democratic theory that focuses too exclusively on decisions—even if it insists that more matters be decided democratically—may be insufficiently ambitious. First, alienation arises not from poor decisions per se but as an often unintended consequence of common action—political, social, and economic. So the decision frame does not give us much of a handle on how dominating forces and structures—or opportunities for oppression and exploitation—actually arise. And these forces and structures are persistent challenges for democracy. The problems of markets, for example, do not necessarily rest on consumers' or businesses' decisions being in some way flawed. Their decisions may in fact be quite sound, at least on their own limited terms. Yet they may generate widespread alienation. Second, given the frequent recurrence of alienation, democracy must often take the form of energetic intervention in a world that is already structured unfavorably to democracy. To be successful—or just to avoid futility—people committed to democracy must often abandon one set of practices that reproduces domination and adopt another set that challenges it. In such cases, it is acting differently, not just talking differently, that matters for democracy. For example, the councils' participants had to stop playing their compliant roles as soldiers and workers, had to engage in dangerous acts of defiance against established authority, in order to advance democracy. In fact, they had to engage in defiant actions simply as a condition of creating space to debate what to do next or to decide on political demands. I do not just mean that the councils' participants had first to engage in various forms of challenging movement action so they could then turn to the serious business of deciding things democratically. Rather, especially given the location of the councils in oppressive factories and barracks, the participants engaged in actions that were simultaneously innovative, transformative, risky, mutinous, coercive, and communicative. When democratic actors are faced with overshadowing structures and forces, their common actions ought to be judged not by the quality of their discussion and their decision process alone, but by the efficacy of what they do, as well. They ought to be judged on whether their actions sustain or transform undemocratic structures. Moreover, the worth of their ideas cannot be determined by cloistered discussion or by contemplation alone because the ideas' significance depends substantially on how they relate to existing social conditions. Do the ideas illuminate or obscure surrounding social structures and forces? How do they orient action toward these conditions? These are among the essential questions. Finally, too pure a focus on decision making can also give short shrift to the importance of learning by doing. First, learning basic democratic activities (like organizing, marching, and persuading) through actually performing them is important. But perhaps even more significant is learning about the world through engaging it actively, even challenging parts of it, rather than just talking about it or reflecting on it. It seems quite unlikely that democratic actors can truly come to grips with alienated social forms without experiencing them actively—or that they can learn to reshape these forms without trying, and sometimes failing. An undue focus on deciding can neglect the rest of the active process in which deciding is always enmeshed. And it can denigrate quotidian political activities that seem less communicative and reflective but that are crucial to comprehending and challenging a partly alienated world.

It is possible to treat the conceptions that are unique to deliberative and elite theories of democracy, respectively—noncoercion and severe doubts about mass agency—in tandem with oppositional democracy's avoidance of the extremes of ideal and nonideal theory. At the core of an oppositional view of democracy is the relationship between democratic action and alienation, each shaping the meaning of the other. An oppositional approach would not assume that the value of democracy is summed up in an ideal model of noncoercive discourse, from which we can judge the worth of contemporary politics as a kind of dim reflection. Nor would it assume that democratic theory has to begin with a "realistic" dismissal of mass capacities, from the standpoint of which democratic ideals are obviously chimerical. It finds the value of democratic action in the only democratic politics we have ever experienced, in which such action is continually engaged in a changing struggle with alienation. And it finds the limits of democratic action not in the permanent failings of most actors, but in the intrinsically challenging nature of action, in the features of action that explain both alienation and the possibility of resistance to it.

Opposition and Participation

There are some obvious external similarities between my oppositional approach and the participatory tradition in democratic theory, although the two approaches are by no means identical in focus, premises, or conclusions. Both criticize elite-centered theories of democracy and embrace a far-reaching, bottom-up style of politics. More significantly, though, it is possible to identify a few less obvious but more revealing commonalities, as well. In fact, comparison of the two approaches helps identify and develop two participatory themes also found, on examination, in oppositional theory: an aspiration to enhance ordinary people's capacity for fruitful, rewarding common action, and alertness to the possibly creative democratic tensions that may play out between distinct institutional realms. A little inquiry and exploration—especially into applied work on participatory democracy—also suggests ways in which oppositional practices may be integral to the life of participatory democracy—and to actually existing deliberative practices as well, for that matter.

Almost everyone agrees on the most general description of participatory theory, that it extols "maximum participation of citizens in their self-governance" (Hilmer 2010, 42). Participatory arguments have a long and rich history, but they flourished especially in the 1960s and 1970s, at a time when much democratic theory had gone stale.[22] According to the mainstream view of the time, meager mass political participation and the attendant domination of politics by elites were both inevitable and in many ways beneficial. Participatory theory upset this consensus, not merely by extolling the value of participation but also by challenging what counts as "realistic"—by poking holes in the accepted view of citizen capacities as well as in the explanation for why existing democracies failed to inspire much involvement.

Participatory theories have long been concerned with the ways in which political participation can foster human flourishing. John Stuart Mill ([1859] 1977) and John Dewey ([1929] 1999), both arguably proponents of participation, advocated what they each termed "individuality," and claimed that hierarchical institutions of all kinds, ones that do not allow people to develop and test their own ideas and abilities, inhibit development of this human potential. For Benjamin Barber, somewhat similarly, the nonparticipatory liberal view of politics entails a self-fulfilling view of human beings as "small, static, inflexible, and above all prosaic" (1984, 23), while participation engenders something like the opposite of each of those qualities. Broad as those claims might seem, at the core of participatory theory's interest in flourishing has generally been not a fixed teleology of human perfection, or a hierarchy of possible pursuits, but a straightforward desire to nurture political agency, the ability to work rewardingly and successfully with others to manage the social world. This is particularly clear in Pateman's analysis of participation and what political psychologists term "efficacy": the feeling that one's "political action does have, or can have, an impact upon the political process" (1970, 46).[23] Strictly speaking, "efficacy," for political psychologists, is a subjective attitude, not an actual capacity. Yet it is clear that for most participatory theorists, a stronger faith in one's efficacy, without a corresponding growth in political agency itself, would be hollow. The participatory model, Pateman notes, is about the actual "development of the social and political capacities of each individual" (43). And this, according to most advocates, is best fostered by restructuring the institutions closest to us to elicit our participation.

Already, it is possible to see that this emphasis on the development of political agency is at least congruent with oppositional theory's broad concern for fostering democratic action, action directed toward collectively managing crucial institutions, social relations, and forces in a way that strives for equality of power. But even so, an interest in enhancing efficacy as a component of human flourishing might seem like something quite different from oppositional theory's strong emphasis on combating domination, oppression, and exploitation. It might appear, that is, that efficacy has to do with personal development, with individual capacities to speak and organize and lead, while domination is an external question of social structure, or even of the powers, abilities, and penchants of other people entirely. From an alienation-and-opposition standpoint, however, it is clear that these are really two intimately connected aspects of common action, its prerequisites, and its consequences. As long as we recognize that, along with others, we are always already actively reproducing our social worlds, we cannot think of ourselves as efficacious agents, of our efforts as fruitful, while this active process reproduces structures that overshadow our capacities to act or that allow others to oppress us. A substantial part of becoming more efficacious, that is, must be managing the consequences of our own shared action, which, when it escapes our common management, can lead to dominating, oppressive social forms. To view this from another perspective, we might recall that alienation is a poignant problem for democrats because it represents a misfiring of collective action, a frustration of the democratic ambition that common action should promote equality and freedom. This suggests that one of the ends-in-view of oppositional theory—one of the ends-in-view in challenging alienation—is also a key value for participatory democracy, namely the development of one's social and political capacities, one's powers to manage, with others, the important social realms through which one moves daily.

From here, it is not hard to see that while an explicitly oppositional aspect may seem at first to be absent from participatory theory, it can be found in the view that participation is simultaneously developmental and a strategy for resisting "subordination" (Pateman 1970, 70)—a means, in Mill's terminology, of challenging, even upending social relations that cast some people as "mere servants" of others ([1848] 1965, 3:766). The oppositional approach I am recommending differs from participatory theory mainly in relying on a particular account of what threatens autonomy, both individual and collective: the tendency to alienation. And because of this account, an oppositional theory insists that opposition must be a persistent feature of democracy. It emphasizes that there is no likelihood of a future polity in which subordinating tendencies have been decisively overcome.

To locate another theme in participatory democracy that has fruitful affinities with an oppositional approach, it helps to consider the common but misguided criticism that participation-centered approaches are too homogenizing, treating all sorts of institutions and social locations as just the same—and all as equally amenable to identical forms of common management.[24] According to this view, participatory theory does not recognize the size and complexity—the differentiation of social locations—in modern societies.[25] A little reflection on the substance of participatory arguments about efficacy and about local or workplace participation suggests this cannot be right. The very heart of participatory arguments concerns the interplay between social domains that are clearly understood to be distinct though mutually conditioning. In particular, these arguments rest on the idea that the distinctive practices and power relations that characterize one institution affect the way people take part in other, different ones. Mill does not claim that a large nation-state can be run exactly like a borough, but he does argue that participation in local government and the workplace might train people to participate better and more deeply in national politics. Pateman seeks an explanation for this in the psychology of "efficacy," positing that confidence in one's ability to have a political impact, developed in day-to-day institutions like the workplace, could carry over to politics, more broadly. The very terms of this argument make no sense without a recognition of the *differences* between workplace and state, local government and national polity. Nor can these arguments cohere without foregrounding the relationship, the interplay between institutional realms, rather than treating each such realm as one whose democratization constitutes just another instance of the same repeated task. The interplay in question, it is important to add, is both congruent and oppositional—congruent in that increasing participation in one sphere is said to increase participation in another, oppositional in that the effort to increase efficacy and participation tends to meet resistance, especially from subordinating social relations. An oppositional approach to democracy, it seems to me, could learn something from this. Participatory practices do not oppose more distant institutions like the state only externally, or at a distance, so to speak. Nor do they seek to eliminate the state or to foster participation only locally so as to allow citizens to withdraw entirely from political realms that are less hospitable to their taking part. Rather, they seek to transform local, familiar institutions and in so doing to transform more remote ones both from within and from without. Likewise, democratic opposition to alienation need not mean permanent hostile disengagement from the state or any other institutional realm prone to alienation. There is a sense in which a Leninist refusal to take part in parliamentary institutions, for example—to withhold support and attack them from the outside—could be termed "oppositional." But not in the broad sense I mean by the term. Opposition can engage with and change alienated institutions while at the same time trying to take part in them and redirect their powers. And the approach I favor could only justify this general sort of engaged opposition.[26]

The most active contemporary branch of participatory scholarship, the growing literature on participatory innovations around the world, especially in Porto Alegre, Brazil, provides further evidence of the way opposition may frequently be intrinsic to participatory politics—as well as show how oppositional politics may be necessary to establish participatory institutions in the first place. In place for more than two decades, Porto Alegre's participatory budgeting process, Orçaento Participativo (OP) is essentially pyramidal. At the base are popular assemblies in which any citizen may take part, and in which many—especially the poor, women, and Afro-Brazilians—do.[27] The assemblies elect representatives to budget forums, which in turn choose representatives to a municipal budget council. The participatory process allocates 10 to 20 percent of the city's budget—not the whole. But 10 percent or more of adults in Porto Alegre, a city of well over a million, have taken part in OP at some time (Baiocchi 2006).

It is possible to approach the experience of OP from this direction: if participation challenges existing, subordinating, social relations, how can more participation be attained while those hierarchical relations persist? Presumably, the answer is not by waiting for states and other institutions to reform themselves. What, then, might a political account of the rise of participatory institutions look like? And if participation can be considered an oppositional practice, what is its relation to the other democratic practices and activities?

The first key point about opposition and participation in Porto Alegre is that OP, as Gianpaolo Baiocchi describes it in his book *Militants and Citizens,* "has its origins in social movement demands" (2005, 18). It came to be, in particular, through interaction between movements and state reformers with movement backgrounds. Participatory democracy, as idea and practice, has deep roots within Brazil's left and animated many, even during the era of military rule. As the old regime weakened, "new civic associations and new urban social movements" appeared (Baiocchi 2005, 10). In Porto Alegre, "neighborhood groups began to challenge the clientelist leaders dominating local associations, creating more open and participatory organizations" who used "pressure and protest" rather than working through "personal, closed-door negotiations" (Abers 1998, 515). Around the same time, the Workers' Party (Partido dos Trabalhadores, or PT) was growing in strength. It was itself a party of oppositional movements, radical unions, and activists. Coming to power by surprise in Porto Alegre in 1989, the PT, "inexperienced and besieged" and "in search of legitimacy," reached back to historical participatory visions and began to introduce OP (Baiocchi 2006). Of course, the movement origins of participatory democracy in Brazil should come as no surprise, since participation has movement origins in the United States as well. Participatory democracy's first major appearance was in *The Port Huron Statement,* issued in 1962 by Students for a Democratic Society. Participation is in fact the "central philosophical theme" of the statement (Hayden [1962] 2005, 2). And participation continued to pervade many American and European movements, such as feminism, for several decades (Phillips 1991, ch. 5).

But the fact that movements and movement actions were crucial in establishing participatory institutions in Porto Alegre is not the most interesting part of the story. The evidence simply does not support a partitioning, for example, between merely instrumental oppositional movement activities that were needed to found OP and truly valuable participatory and deliberative activities within the forums, once created. OP, initiated by activists, has at the same time fostered the growth of movements that surround, invigorate, and feed off it. Baiocchi notes that

OP activists "often describe their activities as part of 'the movement' struggling for social justice in Brazil" (2005, 4). These people are both "militants and citizens" who deliberate, vote, organize, and mobilize as part of one connected political process, partly within and partly outside of state organs. Deliberative theory simply "does not capture the full spectrum of political participation in Porto Alegre," Hilmer notes (2010, 56). A similar, interrelated mix of activities and strategies seems to characterize the political participation of many citizens who attend OP sessions, even ones without a long history of activism. Rebecca Abers argues that many such people, for example, have been drawn into electoral campaigning for the PT through their experiences in participatory budgeting (1998, 518). OP in Porto Alegre, then, "calls into question the often-unstated analytic separation between social movement activity and civic engagement" (Baiocchi 2005, 4).

That these forms and locations for democratic practice—participatory and oppositional, deliberative and rebellious, insider and outsider—merge in Porto Alegre probably has much to do with the challenge, the alienated resistance, that participants still face: a historically clientelist state, an "unresponsive, corrupt political system, dominated by patronage" (Baiocchi 2005, 9). With a long twentieth-century history of dictatorship and military rule, the traditional means of incorporating the masses into politics in Brazil have usually involved hierarchical, closed, nonparticipatory relations that channeled demands through personalist leaders (Abers 1998, 513). The movements that favor participation did not simply arise to champion an idea that came from nowhere. They appeared in a context of dominating social and political institutions that gave many, including clientelist leaders, opportunities to oppress and exploit the vulnerable. In this context, one thing that unites the various different practices of Porto Alegre's "militants and citizens" is an effort to uproot clientelism and "curtail the state monopoly on political power" (Hilmer 2010, 56). But they have not done this from the outside only. Through mechanisms like OP, Baiocchi argues, "social movements themselves can come to *change* the state" (2005, 18), even one as historically alienated as the Brazilian one.

Opposition and Agonism

Though it resonates deeply with the preoccupations of much scholarly political theory in the last few decades, the agonistic model of democracy gets somewhat less attention than elite, deliberative, or participatory ones. Like the oppositional approach I favor, agonistic democracy emphasizes conflict and treats it as a recurrent, even ineradicable, feature of politics. Yet its perspective, while crucial for social theory, broadly, cannot supplant a theory of alienation and democracy. Although it has much to recommend it, its underlying theory of the subject is not on its own sufficient for explaining why democracy is oppositional.

At the core of the agonistic approach to politics is a critique of the "subject," the idea of an antecedent, unitary self, the fixed foundation of choosing and acting—and the influence of this idea in politics. Agonists argue, with considerable justification, that humans are not such pre-formed subjects, and in particular that identity is fluid.[28] Neither the subject nor identity are fixed prior to decision and action, according to this view; they rather form with and through activity and reflection.[29] From this perspective, one of the dangers of politics stems from the denial of this fluidity and uncertainty. In particular, the agonistic view holds that too many people—and too many philosophers—cling to the idea of the subject's fixity, while turning against the evidence of plasticity and plurality in others and themselves. So certain strains of identity politics come in for the agonists' particular criticism.

There is no need here to survey agonistic theories, generally. A critical review would entail carefully distinguishing various efforts by theorists such as Bonnie Honig, William E. Connolly, and Judith Butler to root out unwarranted beliefs about identity and the "subject."[30] Since their work is so influential, and the themes they explore so wide-ranging in potential application, agonistic themes have come to pervade political theory. Exploring these lines of influence, addressing the question whether it has been beneficial for so much political theory to focus so heavily on characteristically *epistemological* approaches to challenging identity claims would be a project in itself.[31] So too would assessing the merits of broadly agonistic critiques of Marxism and Rawlsian theory. The question here is simply whether an agonistic understanding of conflict can replace an account of social reproduction, domination, and alienation as the basis for an adequate oppositional theory of democracy.

And that is a question best addressed not by focusing on figures like Honig, Connolly, and Butler, but by critically examining work by Chantal Mouffe, who has most self-consciously developed an agonistic approach to conceptualizing democracy. Surveys of the state of democratic theory often cast Mouffe as the scholar whose work best "exemplifies the model of agonistic democracy" (Gabardi 2001, 553).[32] It is Mouffe, more than anyone else, who has argued that an agonistic approach, in itself, can lay bare the "logics" of democracy (2000, 4, 44). There is a difference, in other words, between arguing that certain problems of identity are pervasive in politics and claiming that they provide not just an element but the raison d'être of the democratic project. A full inquiry into the former claim lies far outside the scope of my project. Exploring the latter gets to the very heart of the matter that concerns me here: different possible accounts of why democracy should be seen as oppositional, and the contrasting political implications of these accounts.

Picking up the theme of hostility toward those who challenge one's exclusive identity, Mouffe contends that the very "criterion of the political is the friend/enemy relation" and writes of "the political" as "the dimension of antagonism that is inherent in human relations" (2000, 101).[33] The "logic" of democracy, she contends, also necessarily involves the "political constitution of 'the people' " in contrast to some other group— the "demos" versus those "outside" it (2000, 4, 44). An oppositional quality to Mouffe's agonistic democracy, then, derives from this irreducible enmity, as well as from the tension between the exclusionary "logic" of democracy and the universalistic "logic" of liberalism (2000, 42–45).

But while much of her attention is devoted to explicating friend/ enemy "antagonism," for Mouffe the point for democrats is not simply to leave this antagonism as it is. It is, after all, based on a basic misunderstanding about identity. So a marked, even surprising, note of reconciliation sounds here. The "political," for Mouffe, is "the dimension of antagonism that is inherent in human relations" (2000, 101). But democratic politics, specifically, transforms this "us/them" opposition (101). Agonists in general counsel people to accept their own—and others'— multiplicity and contingency as a way of moderating their identity-based claims. Mouffe argues, similarly, that democrats should reframe their antagonists as adversaries, people "whose ideas we combat but whose right to defend those ideas we do not put into question" (102). And this for her is not just a counsel of prudence but the very "aim of democratic politics": "to transform *antagonism* into *agonism*," the "struggle between adversaries" (103).

Running through this argument is an important insight: that democracy involves, even grows from, an unavoidable aspect of conflict. Democrats should relinquish "the ideal of a democratic society as the realization of a perfect harmony or transparency" (2000, 100), Mouffe insists. The agonistic understanding of democracy epitomized by Mouffe also has the advantage of evading the dichotomy of ideal versus nonideal theorizing (which I have criticized throughout), because the aim of democracy, for agonists like Mouffe, is mutually conditioned by the problem with which it contends. The difficulty of democracy, as a result, is not envisioned merely as a falling away from a democratic ideal. In much the same way, Mouffe's agonistic approach largely avoids treating democracy as a "refuge" from inequality, power, and coercion. She does not envision a forum free from antagonism—much less the struggle between adversaries—but rather proposes a particular way of both engaging in and managing such conflict.

Mouffe's democratic agonism, however, comes close to venturing a general, comprehensive, and rather particular theory of political conflict, and then deriving democratic politics from this theory. Consider the central claims here, that the "political" refers to "antagonism," which is "inherent in human relations"; that the "friend/enemy relation" is the basic principle of politics; and finally that democracy aims to transform enemies into adversaries. There are basically two steps here: first, Mouffe identifies politics with clashes over identity; and second, she offers a basically derivative claim about the nature of democratic politics. For Mouffe, democracy is politics properly chastened by the right understanding and the right response to identity. The sort of oppositional theory I have outlined offers no general theory of political conflict. Political conflict would seem to be complex, involving differences in structural position, power, resources, interests, ideological orientation, and values, as well as identity. The argument that common action continually produces and reproduces alienated social forms, of course, primarily involves structure, power, resources, and ideology. But it does not deny that identity—or values, for that matter—can be sources of conflict, nor does it attempt to reduce identity, interests, or values to structure, to argue that they can be "read off" of one's structural position in society. An oppositional approach understands alienation, domination, and oppression to be particularly troubling from the standpoint of basic democratic concerns for equality, freedom, and fruitful collective agency. This does not mean, however, that restraining unreasonable demands growing out of identity is not important in democratic politics. Such a goal, though, is surely not uniquely democratic. (Military regimes, monarchies, and one-party states also have to manage sectarian, ethnic, or racial conflict, as well, and presumably not only by brute force.) An oppositional approach highlights the democratic significance of oppression, exploitation, and reproduced structures that overwhelm some people's agency, but it does not insist that they are the exclusive origins of political conflict.

Of the examples of alienation and of oppositional democratic action in this book, the ones that touch most directly on questions of identity arise in the next chapter, which is focused on race, gender, and the alienated state, especially in the United States. But race, for example, would seem from an oppositional viewpoint to be something more than a question of identity. I assume that identities are interpretations—interpretations of who we are and interpretations of who other people are (Warnke 2007, 6). (Such interpretations are enabled and constrained by the cultural categories available, as well as by experience and history.) The plasticity of racial identity in this view, then, is due to the fact that different interpretations, stressing different standards, indices, or attributes, are always possible (Warnke 2007, 49–57). So any one interpretation of identity is probably always partial or provisional (7), as agonists also stress. But when we talk about race in the context of the next chapter, we are not only talking about identity, not only talking about interpretations, even though race is irreducibly a meaningful category, and so subject to interpretation.[34] What makes some racial identities more significant than others for democrats is their relation to power relations, social structure, and resources—in short, to race as a social relation. Take, for example, the modern state, which has among its powers the capacity to structure social relations of race. It plays a crucial role in determining what categories of race are available, as well as the content of race, and how it is experienced. Of course, determining who was free and who was a slave in the antebellum South is a searing example. But the U.S. state, as I will argue in the next chapter, has not stopped, through acts of omission and commission, affording people different sorts of citizenship according to race.[35] Race, to put it differently, makes a great deal of difference in how a person relates to the U.S. welfare state. No doubt there is something deluded and offensive about the sureness, derision, puffing up, obfuscation, and prejudice involved in constructing one's own and others' identities as exclusive. But structural alienation, domination, oppression, and exploitation contribute mightily to what makes such racial attributions and identities malign. In this sense, the concern agonists show for the harms of unreflective identity formation would seem naturally to lead agonistic democracy in the direction of these issues, which are central to the oppositional approach to democracy I offer here.

In common, the agonistic approach to democracy and the oppositional one I outline in this book see conflict as central: both focus on the importance of accepting the ineradicable nature of conflict and on the means of responding to it. But there is an important difference in the forms that response is to take, and the difference stems from the starting point of each approach: a purported logic of identity, in one case, and a theory of social action, alienation, and domination in the other. For Mouffe, steeped in an agonistic understanding of conflict in binary "friend/enemy" terms, the democratic response must largely be conceptual, interpretive, therapeutic—and to a significant degree, conciliatory. Democrats are to reinterpret those whom they have seen as "antagonists" instead as agonistic "adversaries." Democratic relations come into being, Mouffe tells us, when social agents "accept the particularity and the limitations of their claims" (2000, 21). In the case of the bundle of problems surrounding race and the state, this means, presumably, that achieving democratic politics involves persuading people who identify as white, African American, Latino, and so on to understand the partiality and contingency of these claims. Similarly, a radical democratic struggle becomes possible for Mouffe when such a process makes clear the plurality of identity claims. By modifying the identity claims involved so that they are not mutually exclusive—and thereby establishing the "equivalence" between these struggles—democrats can knit together a movement from "the greatest possible number of democratic struggles" (1993, 19, 18). Perhaps this might involve convincing undocumented immigrants and transgender rights advocates to see the partiality of their own struggles and recognize each other's causes as democratic. But Mouffe says little about the kinds of arguments that could successfully establish that there is such common democratic ground, such equivalence, nor much about the shared aims of democratic politics once an adjustment of identities has been accomplished.

In contrast, an oppositional approach has no need to construe the proper form or the challenges of democratic action so narrowly. Democratic agency may face ideological, identity-based problems of the kind Mouffe names, but an oppositional approach neither privileges nor discounts them. From an oppositional standpoint, democratic action aims to overcome real obstacles to the collective regulation of crucial social institutions, on terms of equality and freedom, with an aim of reducing domination and oppression. Confronting a state that helps reproduce dominating and oppressive race relations and unjustly different forms of citizenship could entail a wide array of political practices, from unmasking (the racial dimensions of policies that do present themselves as racialized), deliberating (about both policy remedies and coalitional strategy), to organizing (networks, campaigns, and associations around these issues), and so on, with mobilizing, marching, striking, and petitioning. Rethinking identity may be one of these forms of democratic action, but it is surely not the only one. If agonism's denial of the pre-formed subject is correct—as I think it is—then a reformulation or rethinking of identity, for many people, may actually come about in the process of such democratic activity, rather than as a precondition for it. And if problems stemming from totalistic identities are made significantly worse by differences in structural position, then social structure and its genesis deserve direct attention. But the shape and significance of problems of alienation, structural domination, and exploitation are not deducible from an agonistic approach that conceptualizes conflict largely in terms of a particular logic of identity.

Coda: Must Oppositional Democracy Be Fugitive?

In writings dating back thirty years (1982, 1994, 1996, 2009), Sheldon Wolin has traced the elements of an evocative and arguably oppositional vision of democracy. Like mine, it portrays democracy engaged in struggle, democracy as a way of being that is never assured. It is a non-governmental—really an anti-institutional—view of democracy emphasizing common action. And it is a conception, as well, that draws a great deal from the experience of social movements. This is an impressive list of affinities with oppositional democracy of the sort I favor. Yet there is also a possible and quite crucial difference. Wolin's language and imagery prominently and recurrently stress democracy as thrilling but "fugitive," evanescent, momentary, "conditioned by bitter experience, doomed to succeed only temporarily" (1996, 43). From the oppositional standpoint I propose, however, democracy is not an ideal achievement, a perfect fulfillment rarely, if ever, enjoyed. Instead, the approach I favor portrays democracy as a continual struggle with alienation, neither ideal nor non-ideal—not a mere "moment of experience" (2009, 603) but an always ongoing, incomplete effort.

Interestingly, Wolin sometimes seems to agree with something like this portrayal, as well. At these times, he characterizes democracy as a "continuous," not a fleeting "struggle" (1994, 48), as "standing opposition" (2009, 604). And he contends that democratic toil is "unending" (2009, 604). It would take me far afield to establish, with any confidence, which of these vocabularies is more consonant with Wolin's deepest commitments—the vocabulary of democratic evanescence or of constant democratic effort. So rather than attempt a definitive interpretation, I want to try to learn from Wolin's writings what might underwrite the portrayal of democracy as "fugitive"—and to reemphasize what supports the contrasting view of democracy as an always ongoing struggle.

Wolin's "fugitive democracy" writings consist of a series of historical and contemporary narratives about the attempts by varied thinkers and practitioners to domesticate democracy and thus, inherently, to falsify it. He depicts a struggle between those who episodically practice a transgressive, democratic politics and various figures who try to thwart democracy by building constitutional walls around it. Wolin presents the democratic forces as plural, but they make themselves known in essentially one shape: as the demos, or citizens-as-actors. Their doings are stormy and original: creative, transgressive, disorderly, rebellious, disruptive, unstable, anarchic, and overflowing. Their opponents are multiple. By name, they include Aristotle, the Old Oligarch, and James Madison. They are critics or hostile interpreters of democracy, theorists of constitutionalism, and "faceless representatives of the International Monetary Fund" (Wolin 1994, 30). They place boundaries around democracy and use organization, administration, and manipulation against it. And to this end, especially, they make use of a tried-and-true stratagem: constitutionalizing democracy, converting it into something it can never be, a form of rule or a kind of constitution. They perpetuate "a myth that legitimates the very formations of power which have enfeebled" democracy (2009, 601). "Constitutional democracy," from this standpoint, is "an ideological construct" designed to "repress" real democracy (1994, 32). The nature of the subterfuge is to transform—rhetorically, at least— "political practices into fixed structures or 'arrangements'" (1994, 53).

In all this, what might support the notion of democracy as momentary, transitory? One possibility is that fugitiveness—along with the oppositional quality of democratic action, generally—results from the fact that democracy's enemies are powerful, implacable, only occasionally liable to be defeated, and even then, not for long. For Wolin, Steven Bilakovics notes, "democratic association and action" are so linked to the existence of "a common enemy" as to be "contingent" upon them

(2012, 209). An alienation-and-opposition approach insists, in contrast, on the significance of a particular account of how dominating institutions come to be: widespread social action is constantly reproducing structures, some of which overshadow our abilities to act. So at the most fundamental level, then, the precariousness of democracy, the threat to the democratic effectiveness of the people, is not external to popular agency—a product of its enemies—but something internal to it. Still, alone, even a strong emphasis on enemies would not seem to underwrite democratic fugitiveness. First, the fact that dominating institutions are rooted in common action does not mean that democracy has no enemies—no one, more precisely, with a deep interest, steadfastly pursued, in limiting democracy's reach. In fact, rather obviously, it does have such foes. There is good historical warrant even for Wolin's particular claim that democracy's critics have often proposed various strategies for setting boundaries, building walls around it, without openly opposing it. Elite theorists like Schumpeter fit this description. There is a case to be made that Schumpeter viewed his famous institutional, elite conception of democracy as a blueprint for limiting democracy's transformative power (Medearis 2001). I would just emphasize that those antagonists' strength, their power, derives less from their ideological ingenuity (though this may be considerable), or from obstructions they themselves build (though these may be formidable), but from alienated structures reproduced, in different ways, by large numbers of us. And although Wolin does not elaborate a theory of common action and alienation, he does not undermine its premises, either. In fact, he writes that the Greek demos came to the realization that the "power of the polis," though it might often constrain them, was not something purely external to them; it was, "in large measure, their power" (1994, 46). And this recognition is important to one of Wolin's most evocative lines: "the taking back of one's powers is the crucial move" for democracy (57).

Another possibility is that oppositional democracy, according to Wolin's account, must rest on a certain kind of unstructured, transgressive collective action that cannot possibly be maintained for long. Wolin's sometimes singular concentration on transgressive, disruptive action seems too limiting, from my oppositional perspective. At one point, he defiantly adopts the ancient Greek charge that democracy was anarchic and worse (1994, 37) and adds that it has a general "disrespect for limits" (47). He comes close here to promoting a kind of aesthetic of disruption. Reliance on such an aesthetic, it seems to me, would be misleading for two reasons. First, democratic action, by my account, transgresses mainly to resist alienation, domination, and their train of ills, not out of some subjective disposition or aesthetic preference. Second, oppositional democratic action, as I have stressed, must often be quite organizational in nature. Democratic activists have to engage in a great deal of unglamorous but valuable movement-building work to be effective—a fact, I have suggested, that is underappreciated in deliberative theory. Likewise, democracy should not solely be equated with openly, stylistically rebellious practices; rather, it is important that all genuinely democratic practices, properly speaking, can be oppositional, even the ones that may not at first glance seem so. Ironically, in his derogation of constitutional democracy, Wolin seems actually to underestimate the variety of forms of democratic opposition. He writes, for example: "When democracy is settled into a stable form, such as prescribed by a written constitution, it is also settled down and rendered predictable. Then it becomes the stuff of manipulation: of periodic elections that are managed and controlled, of public opinion that is shaped, cajoled, misled, and then polled" (2009, 602). But even electoral mobilization, the most conventional form of participation in modern liberal, constitutional, representative democracies, can be oppositional, as I stressed earlier in this chapter. In particular, even when it is not seen in exactly this light by voters, it can work to overturn powerful social groups or to redirect the state and prevent it from being entirely captured by powerful interests. Yet just because Wolin valorizes transgressive action and envisions the possibility of co-optation, does not mean we have to read him as being actually disdainful of organizational work. It might, from Wolin's perspective, be entirely possible to recognize democratic work that is organizational but that nevertheless transgresses the particular ideologies and the structures that undermine democratic promise.

There are, however, several leading interpretations of Wolin that do suggest reasons why he might perceive democracy as having ideal qualities that make it virtually impossible to sustain for any length of time. One possibility is that Wolin closely binds fugitive democracy to what he calls the "political." But this concept itself seems as "evanescent" as the accomplishment it describes, as Emily Hauptmann has pointed out (2004, 52). The elusiveness of the idea may lead Wolin to treat the actual phenomena with which he associates it as equally hard to find, as momentary. Relatedly, it may be that Wolin sees fugitiveness as in some sense desirable, ideal in itself. Bilakovics suggests, along these lines, that fugitiveness is a feature, not a bug, of democracy for Wolin. Democracy, according to this view, "must burn out to be true to itself"; it "remains authentic on the condition that it is not enduring" (Bilakovics 2012, 207). If true, this would seem almost the limiting case of ideality, something of value whose uncommonness is its own true claim to value. Another potential explanation is that Wolin is compelled to treat democracy as fugitive because he characterizes it as the rare and complete overturning of "rule," which he understands as "inherently exploitative," "the exercise of power by some over others" (1994, 45). Patchen Markell (2006) points toward this possibility.

None of these approaches would constitute ideal theory in the strict sense discussed in Chapter 1. But to stress any of these themes too strongly would be to flirt with an idea of democracy as something pure and incapable of withstanding much contamination from the "continuous, ceaseless and endless" grind of ordinary politics (Wolin 1996, 31). The aspiration to avoid any such idealizing—to eschew the very positing of ideal and nonideal as really distinguishable modes of theory—is crucial to the oppositional approach I favor. Either pure idealism or pure nonidealism can support a kind of disdain for politics as we know it— aloofness from ordinary agents' ethical failings, or disparagement of their ability to act intelligently. (And binding ideal and nonideal together as supposedly distinct alternatives within a single comprehensive model of democracy can create just paradox and instability, as I suggested in the first chapter.) Aside from any independent plausibility it may derive from rootedness in a sober view of human agency and social structure, a conceptualization of alienation, incorporated at the ground level of democratic theory, can be an effective mechanism for avoiding the ideal/ nonideal division. Such a conception treats alienation and democratic action as rising from the same troubled but valued political ground, rather than as built upon distinct premises, one hopelessly tainted and well known, the other remote, perfect, and pure.

5

CONTESTING THE WELFARE STATE

→ ←

In Zuccotti Park, near Wall Street, and in dozens of similar encampments, members of the Occupy movement sought to nurture a pure, heady form of democracy, while distancing themselves from a state beholden to banks and hostile to their vision of a just society. There is no one answer to why so many of them took this stance toward the state and democracy. Clearly, most believed that the government was in the thrall of finance capital. Many members apparently worried that simply making demands on a corrupt state could lend it undeserved legitimacy, and believed that many unions, political action committees, and parties had settled into just such a relationship. And above all, many Occupiers aspired to experience in their enthusiastic "general assemblies" an inclusive and egalitarian form of decision making quite unlike ordinary state-sanctioned electoral politics.

Occupy's attitude toward state and democracy is not entirely unique. It bears a family resemblance to deliberative theory's impulse to nurture democracy as a refuge. And something even closer to Occupy's dualist democratic vision has been a recurrent theme for a couple of decades. In the wake of nonviolent postcommunist transformations, some thinkers began to urge that the intrinsic logic of state administration is hostile to the "life of democratic associations and unconstrained discussion" and that democrats should make civil society, as they understood it, the "primary locus" of their efforts, eschewing attempts to take or direct state power (Cohen and Arato 1992, viii, x).[1] Other like-minded intellectuals, while critical of this particular view of civil society, have reached a similar conclusion about the state, shunning it as a technocratic behemoth that usurps public initiative, and locating genuine democratic politics in the realm of more local civic self-help projects (Boyte 2004). Still others argue in like fashion that democratic politics should attend mainly to small-scale efforts that disdain centralization—or even political power itself (Wolin 2009, 63; Isaac 2003, 129).

Decades before Occupy, critical theorists developed the most comprehensive and theoretically developed literature on the failures of states to live up to democratic expectations. They lined up behind clashing arguments that, interestingly, shared at least one thing with each other. This was a different dualistic vision that contrasted a state now undemocratically dominated by business and finance to a genuine—in this case, future, postrevolutionary—form of purer democracy. They disagreed about a great deal else, but these critical theorists of the state tended to agree on the possible array of integral solutions to the democratic deficiency of the state. It could be "seized" and then wielded by genuinely democratic forces, or it could be "broken" by dramatically refashioning society so that ordinary people would no longer alienate their own political power. This would allow true democracy to flourish elsewhere or in a completely new institutional form.[2] The ultimate goal, regardless of which of these possibilities was chosen, was a definitive achievement of democracy somewhere far beyond the compass of any contemporary welfare state.

Pervasive democratic suspicion of the liberal welfare state, and the idea that its alienation can and must be overcome in some decisive, singular way, together mark the terrain I explore in this chapter. Occupy's wariness about the state was in a sense well founded. There is ample evidence that at the millennium state power had been harnessed undemocratically to the banks' worldview and interests, rather than to the broader public's. The enthusiastic gutting of New Deal–era banking law in the 1990s reflected an uncritical adoption of the market fundamentalism that had become common wisdom on Wall Street. And when the resulting system self-destructed, politicians and bureaucrats clearly regarded protecting the financial sector's interests—and no one else's— as utterly compulsory. So the bank bailout of 2008 won significant support from both parties, but economic stimulus did not—nor did aid to the auto industry or financial reform. Such reform measures as could pass were exceedingly modest in comparison to the disaster that precipitated them. And few bankers have been held responsible for the widespread suffering their shared practices inflicted.

These stark facts suggest a state whose powers have great potential for alienation. States are structures, that is, produced by all sorts of widely shared activities, like voting, paying taxes, and deference to authority. But despite these popular origins, welfare states can resist democratic management, tower above those who sustain them, have their capacities harnessed to nonpublic agendas, and structure opportunities for the sorts of exploitation experienced by people like Sheila Ramos. The thrust of my argument so far in this book has been that democracy as we know it nearly always faces alienated challenges such as this. As a characterization of the state's democratic deficiencies, at least, this much of my approach has affinities with the democratic thinking of Occupy, as well as with some earlier theorists of the state.

In fact, for much of this chapter, my purpose is actually to extend and elaborate this disturbing vision. Political analysis that is informed by a longer historical view shows that we should always regard the modern state as potentially or partly alienated. In fact, I argue that there are many more ways for state powers to become alienated and to serve undemocratic agendas than the critical theorists of past decades recognized. Some of the most important of these involve how the state covertly shapes relations of race and gender, not only through visible discrimination, but through the pattern by which it intervenes in society or does not, or expands the worth of some people's citizenship and undercuts others'. Welfare states are deeply involved in shaping race and gender—as well as relations of economic inequality—and often that involvement fosters subordination and exploitation.

But my second line of argument in this chapter—one that may surprise readers convinced of the first—is that a full account of state alienation provides no justification for thinking the problem must or can be integrally overcome, no sufficient reason for shunning the state or withdrawing from the struggle to redirect its powers. Because of the many ways things can go wrong—and some ways they can go right—we should be skeptical that the goal of democratic action can be either fully to master the state or finally to supersede it in favor of some perfect democratic forum, some ideal practice elsewhere. The history of the welfare state suggests that we cannot hope to overthrow alienated state powers once and for all, or create a new form of politics that is immune to any form of alienation. There are just too many ways for state powers to escape common control, too many different entrenched groups positioned to take advantage of the vulnerabilities. In any case, state powers can sometimes be redirected toward restructuring dominating social relations, and that is a possibility democratic actors ought not to ignore.

To deepen our understanding of the state and alienation, I turn especially to an intersectional analysis that brings social relations of race and
gender into the theory of the alienated state vis-à-vis the more traditional
focus: economic relations and class. This is one of the best ways to probe
the many potential forms of state alienation. The outlook I shall present
emphasizes the variety of state powers that can be captured or redirected
and the multiplicity of agendas to which these powers can be harnessed.
The critical theorists of the state focused above all on the deployment of
particular regulatory and relief powers and how they were used to further the interests of capitalists and suppress working-class activism. I am
especially concerned in this chapter with a somewhat different set of
powers that involve the state classifying or stratifying people, establishing for them different relationships to the polity, different forms of
citizenship, in the fullest sense, not just according to class but also
according to categories of race and gender.[3] A key issue, then, is the
reciprocal connections, the mutual conditioning, of states and social
relations of race and gender.

If the array of potentially alienated state powers and their malign
uses is so great, why not disdain the state, as so many have argued, or try
to solve the problem by fully capturing or decisively breaking it, transcending its hold? Already my oppositional approach, by emphasizing
that alienation and democratic action share a common ground, an integral relation to each other, casts doubt that any such possibility exists. It
suggests that alienation is a chronic problem rooted in how we act
together, and always lurking throughout our social world. And it suggests that democracy is a perpetual struggle with such alienation, not a
retreat from it. This view of democracy avoids resting on a distinction
between ideal and nonideal theory, and so on any contrast between pure
democratic practice *here* or *now* and deeply tainted politics *over there* or
then. I have argued that democratic action has historically almost always
been oppositional, not perfect and tranquil, perpetually taking the form
of ever-renewed attempts to recapture alienated forces and structures
that we have helped reproduce. And *opposition,* as I have developed the
concept, does not mean permanently standing apart from the state or
any particular institution deemed undemocratic. It is the *phenomenon*
of alienation, the always potential *manifestation* of alienation, that democratic action opposes, not any one permanently alienated structure.
Nor, according to this account of alienation, can democrats ever be fully
confident of their own social ground as the terrain of ideal democratic

relations. All kinds of social relations and practices related to both the state and civil society can become alienated. I have contended that we have no basis in memory or experience for imagining democracy without alienation, democracy that is not crucially oppositional, democracy that is not a constant struggle to reclaim our own common powers. Such a view, then, puts no emphasis on retreating from or decisively defeating alienation. Instead, it insists that democratic action is, in its nature, not a retreat at all but a constant, engaged struggle with forms of alienation that may constantly change.

Recognizing the diversity of state powers that can be alienated, and acknowledging that these powers are crucially involved in maintaining many troubling social relations—not just economic hierarchies but also ones of race and gender—provides an additional set of reasons to think of democracy as a continuous, oppositional effort, sometimes with and sometimes against state powers. First, historical study shows that the potential hierarchy-maintaining powers of states can work both ways. Democratic agents can sometimes force the state to use these powers to restructure dominating social relations, as the U.S. civil rights movement shows. Despite the constant potential for alienation, the state has the very real capacity to democratize aspects of society and the economy. This is just one face of the open-endedness of how state powers are deployed. For there is not just one struggle to use the state—either for democratic or undemocratic purposes. There are many such contests, whose results are contingent. There are multiple groups seeking to use the state to bolster dominating or oppressive social relations: not just various business sectors but also those who want to harness the state to reinforce existing hierarchies of race and gender. And many agents resist these attempts, too. Faced with all of these many state powers, their interpenetration of society, and their potential deployment for both egalitarian and inegalitarian purposes, I argue all the more that democrats have little choice but to struggle to direct these capacities, to democratize both alongside and in resistance to state powers. Because of the extraordinary range of risks and rewards, it is important to adopt an open-ended, flexible view of what democracy may demand. Many of these state powers are too closely involved in shaping undemocratic social relations and institutions to either withdraw and let them operate unhindered or to ignore the need and the possibility of redirecting them. The democratization of the welfare state, the democratic redirection of the state's powers, is too important a prospect to pass up. But it is nearly impossible to imagine accomplishing it in one fell swoop. There are many different welfare state powers up for political contention and many groups and interests with whom to contend. So democratizing the state should be seen as an open-ended, many-sided struggle with no determinate end. It should be identified neither with the attempt to institute, once and for all, an ideal type of unalienated polity, nor as a pure practice to be nurtured far from the possibility of state corruption.

Some important thinkers have advanced an "unproblematic" view of the modern welfare state, one that does not see the state as posing any particular challenges to democracy. In the next section, I review this way of thinking, which despite its clear limitations also contains important insights. Above all, it recognizes that states have the power at times to uproot entrenched undemocratic social relations. But this "unproblematic" view of the state—with its recognition of this democratizing power—is at best a starting point for us. As I review, in subsequent sections, evolving contributions to the study of welfare states and relations of class, race, and gender, I highlight eight additional powers or characteristics of liberal democratic welfare states that are significant, even troubling, from a democratic standpoint. I enumerate these characteristics and powers individually. By *characteristics,* I mean features of how states relate to other social institutions, past and present, and problems that arise in understanding states. By *powers,* I mean simply things states can do. Some of these characteristics and powers were clearly recognized by critical theorists of the state and pertain especially to capitalist market economies. Others are more obviously central to continuity and change in race and gender relations. Together these traits and capacities underscore both the many potential varieties of alienation and the contingency of how the state acts and whom it serves. It is not just business and the labor movement that struggle to direct state powers but also preservers and challengers of the racial status quo. These agents' purposes do not coincide in any fixed, predetermined way. And the outcome of the contest is also not preordained.

For the purposes of this chapter, the state may be understood to be simply an interconnected set of institutions attempting, more or less successfully, to control a given territory and society by making and enforcing collectively binding decisions, monopolizing the legitimate use of force, seeking sovereignty, operating in a distinct public realm, deciding citizenship, and controlling entry.[4] "Liberal democratic" states, in particular, are ones in societies in which there are open, competitive elections

for office and protections for certain civil and political rights.[5] The significance of stressing liberal democratic states is to explore the democratic problems that still remain when these basic or formal conditions
of representative government are met. (Illiberal democracies and authoritarian or totalitarian states present different problems from those I discuss here.) "Welfare" states are those that have the capacity to intervene
effectively to restructure and redirect civil society,[6] especially but not
exclusively its economic relations.

It is important to remember, before proceeding, that attributions of
race have essentially no biological basis and that interpretations of gender
clearly lack the basis in dichotomous and immutable natural difference
so often assumed in everyday discourse. Abundant scholarship has demonstrated the extraordinary mutability of racial and gender categories.
But mutability and social construction, per se, cannot be the sole focus
of critical political inquiry. When we explore historical forms of racial or
gender domination, we face power relations linked to particular understandings of race and gender, such as domination of people understood
as "black." And these racial and gender categories have proved to be
relatively durable over time, so that even though they are socially constructed in the final sense, at any given time, states or social movements
are often only reshaping or reproducing racial categories, not inventing
them anew.[7]

Marshall and State Effectiveness against
Entrenched Undemocratic Relations

T. H. Marshall's lectures, *Citizenship and Social Class* ([1950] 1992),
have remained a classic statement of the ambition that the welfare state
should create conditions for full civil, political, and social citizenship.
Marshall associates each of three dimensions of citizenship with particular
enabling state institutions: civil citizenship with courts, political citizenship with parliament and other elected bodies, and social citizenship with
welfare provision and public schools (8). And he argues that the process
of developing this full, three-part citizenship has been under way, in
stages, since the eighteenth century, culminating with social citizenship
in the middle of the twentieth. Of course, critics have pointed out that
Marshall's sequential narrative really applies only to male workers of European origin. Women in many countries, and African Americans in the
United States, had actually been reached by (inegalitarian or oppressive)

welfare provision well before obtaining full civil and political rights. Moreover, Marshall accepted the premise that full social citizenship could be a reward only for the employed, even though that principle has been used to justify second-tier social citizenship for women. Still, his vision makes a very useful starting point.

Interestingly, Marshall's argument entails a particular juxtaposition of social class—viewed as a system of inequality—and the state as the egalitarian tool for equalizing citizenship and reducing the effects of class ([1950] 1992, 18). So the development of citizenship is not a harmonious process for Marshall, but a "form of conflict between opposing principles" (18). The "impact" of state-fostered citizenship on the system of class inequality, he says, is "bound to be profoundly disturbing, and even destructive" to existing social relations (19). Marshall's vision, then, implies an assessment of the state's power, which in his view must be deployed against real resistance.

Marshall is certainly right, at least in one sense. States have shown themselves capable of challenging and reshaping undemocratic, alienated social institutions. In the United States, enforcement of the National Labor Relations Act (NLRA), passed as a result of intense oppositional political struggle,[8] established for workers the right of collective bargaining. But it did more than this, democratically. It marked an advance in the ability of elected representatives to govern the economy and society, and finally ended the domination of the centuries-old master-servant law that had bolstered workplaces as their masters' minifiefdoms (Orren 1991).[9] It provided some tools, at least, for activist workers partially to democratize their hierarchical work lives. In their long-standing determination to undermine federal labor law enforcement, contemporary business groups still pay ironic testament to these democratizing capacities. But it is not just historic transformations like the tumultuous passage and dramatic court approval of the NLRA that are at issue. The general ability of welfare states to "decommodify" labor and vital services through welfare provision can enhance a person's liberty as much as her resources.[10] It can free people from reliance on overwhelming markets—or again, from oppressive workplace hierarchies. And it can make the provision of labor or health care subject to democratically chosen rules (Esping-Andersen 1990, 18–23). The right sort of welfare provision, for example, can allow a person to quit a job where there are unsafe or unfair work conditions without becoming destitute or losing the ability to see a doctor. Or it can enable a person to forego humbling work in old age.

Relatedly, welfare provision can make people less vulnerable to exploitation of all sorts (Goodin 1988, ch. 5). An unconditional "basic" income from the state, for example, could support autonomy not only from degrading work but also from other dangers (Pateman 2005). Recent vivid examples of exploitation from which well-deployed welfare powers might protect ordinary people include for-profits that send developmentally disabled men to exhausting work in return for housing and feeding them in squalid dormitories—or religious assisted-living homes that take in people with substance abuse and other problems but punish them harshly for not attending services.[11] Direct economic regulation plays a part in this sort of emancipation, too, of course. Proper financial regulation can (although early this century it did not) protect ordinary people from predatory lenders, and housing law can prevent landlords from taking advantage of tenants. Once we broaden the focus to include race and gender, even more examples of the state's ability to democratize social relations become evident. But of course these are by no means the state's only powers, nor the only use to which the relevant state powers can be put. And as the case of the NLRA already suggests, political struggle is very much a part of the story. To put the democratizing power of the state in perspective, it is necessary to probe the decades-old debate between critical theories of the state.

Critical Theories of the State and Democratic Theory

Ralph Miliband's *The State in Capitalist Society* (1969) rejuvenated discussion of the state in political science. The "critical theories of the state" debate that the book helped inaugurate was, in the first instance, a response to pluralism. By banishing any talk of the state as unwarranted metaphysics, and by casting the political system as little more than competition among comparably powerful social groupings, pluralist scholars in the 1950s and 1960s had tended to underestimate the resistance of government to democratic management. In contrast, all of the main critical theories held that welfare states were real entities with real powers, and far from impartial among social groups.

Marxist, neo-Marxist, and post-Marxist theories converged, more or less, on the view that the state tended to pursue a capitalist agenda. In

177

common they also engaged in a kind of unmasking, arguing that often what seemed like benign welfare measures actually benefited business. Where critical theorists differed, mainly, was in explaining the posited tendency to serve these interests. While Miliband's instrumentalist approach contended that at least one crucial factor was overt, often visible, capitalist effort to staff, manage, and direct the state, others tried to show that the state was in some way structurally constrained to pursue capitalist interests. The most lucid alternatives to Miliband's approach, put forward by structuralists like Fred Block and neopluralists like Charles Lindblom, held that such groups may not need actually to colonize the state, because they already occupy a privileged position in society and the economy, their interests regarded as essential to the reproduction of state power. One version of this argument refers to the state's need for tax revenues, another mainly to the need of the state to maintain investment—in either case by bowing to the interests of business and finance. These analyses underestimated the significance of other agendas to which welfare states might be harnessed. But in common they unearthed an important fundamental characteristic of welfare states.

Mutual Structuring of State and Society

That state and society mutually determine and interpenetrate each other may seem obvious, but some familiar approaches to social theory miss the point entirely. Some liberal democratic theories, in their more naive moments, entail the view that the state can be understood *in itself,* so to speak, as a simple agent or an expression of public will, without reference to the structure of society or the economy on which it rests. Economic libertarianism, on the other hand, assumes that economic relations and activity are natural and self-subsistent, and that state regulation and welfare activities are never more than external interference. But state powers reach deep into society and its characteristic relations—and dominant social structures and groups can strongly condition the capacities and propensities of states, quite outside of ordinary electoral channels.

Any of the approaches that show that structural ties (not just public opinion or electoral competition) make the state more responsive to dominant social groups can serve to displace the naive liberal position. Any approach that shows that states are needed to create the conditions for economic market activity—Polanyi's ([1944] 2001) history of the rise of markets for land and labor is one of the most important—rebuts the economic libertarian view. Critical theories essentially all entail the view

178

that states and economic structures are mutually conditioning. Both the structuralist and instrumentalist varieties imply that the particular characteristics and powers of a given state rest on the kind of relations it has with labor, business, and banks. (And wielding such state powers is important, in turn, because the state conditions the structure of the economy.) Critical theorists, in short, agreed that what states are and how they act depends on the characteristics of the social groups and institutions that shape and support them, either because some of those groups have direct access to state positions and power or because the state depends on the continued health of those groups or institutions. Certain critical theories of the state are especially clear in stressing, as well, that the state is in turn crucial in maintaining such groups and institutions—that the state is needed to create markets, to uphold conditions for profitable investment, to make sure a reliable supply of inexpensive labor is available, or to mitigate economic crises.

This mutual structuring is closely connected to at least three of the state powers I discuss further below. The idea that the state has the power to reinforce undemocratic social relations, either by acting or strategically refraining to act, implies, of course, penetration of the state into society. So does the idea that the state stratifies society, assigns members to particular racial or gender categories, and then shapes the experience of being so categorized. And similarly, the idea that the state may be constrained to serve nonpublic agendas—even agendas damaging to common interests—rests on the idea of social relations penetrating the state, conditioning what it is and how it acts.

State Reinforcement of Undemocratic Social Relations

The state can directly reinforce undemocratic social relations, or it can simply decline to intervene in them, thereby establishing and policing the boundaries of democracy. This capacity is, in effect, the mirror image of what I termed above *state effectiveness against entrenched undemocratic relations*. Democracy in liberal capitalism is by and large limited to the representative organs of the state, and does not penetrate many of the "private" institutions of society. And via law and policy the state often both guarantees and is the product of this division. For many Marxist theories of the state and many proponents of economic democracy it is crucial that the workplace and the corporation remain largely undemocratized; indeed, the state may insulate them from democratic pressures. One face of this undemocratic structure is simply that many employees often have no power—or very little—to determine what they do where they spend most of their waking hours. Another is that employees who are not members of unions generally also lack basic democratic rights of free speech and association when at work. They can be and are not infrequently fired for political organization and expression. Under these conditions, more broadly, "common action and democratic potential find no place in civil society" (Thomas 1994, x). A particular state, then, may be characterized as much by the realms of social life it fails to democratize—or protects from democratizing pressure—as by the state institutions that are (at least partially) democratized.

Serving Alien Agendas

The critical theorists also pointed to the potential for business or capitalists to have unique access to state power, to benefit from it exceptionally. Examples already discussed make the point: the responsiveness of the state to banks at the turn of this millennium and the state's policing of the boundaries of democratic life to preserve workplace hierarchy. Insofar as the state serves such particular interests, rather than the common interests of the broader society, it seems clear that there is a problem from the standpoint of democratic theory: an undemocratic mechanism whose operation may subvert the fulfillment of widely shared aims or public goods. But it is not just a matter of particular versus common interests. There is a limitation or frustration of democratic community inherent in this characteristic—an undermining of democratic range and potency. In particular, the same state that draws its legitimacy and some of its power from elections may use those citizen-derived powers to carry out an alien economic agenda that harms them. The state, in these instances, represents the alienated social power of citizens, as well as a kind of remote, detached (and therefore almost illusory) form of common life.

Learning from the Critical Theories Debate:
Contingency and Contestation

The debate between different critical theorists of the state is now ground well tilled by others.[12] Crucial here are the implications of the debate for how we should view relevant problems of democratization. Really to get to the bottom of this, however, it is necessary to explore aspects of the debate with a critical eye. The upshot of such an exploration is that the more compelling contributions to the critical theories debate held that the welfare state's characteristic ways of acting are not predetermined but shaped contingently, making state powers susceptible to political contestation of many kinds.

From the standpoint of a theory emphasizing action and alienation, any account of the state must address at least nine distinguishable features of the problem: (a) the characteristics of states, especially how they relate to other social institutions and structures; (b) the common activities of various groups and agents that reproduce state institutions; (c) the powers or capacities of states, or that states confer on state agents, such as bureaucrats; (d) the weaknesses of states and state agents, and the constraints and necessities they confront; (e) the knowledge and ideology of state agents, who cannot be presumed omniscient; (f) the varying ability or effectiveness of state agents; (g) the knowledge and ideology of nonstate agents, such as businesses; (h) the varying ability or effectiveness of these same nonstate agents; and finally, (i) how the state actually acts and whom it benefits.

At least some of the most charged debates about the state tended to result from collapsing some of these issues into others. Thus Nicos Poulantzas, in his criticisms of Miliband as placing too much emphasis on "a problematic of the subject" instead of the "objective relation" of the bourgeoisie to the state (1969, 70, 73), seemed to believe that in advancing an argument stressing state properties, powers, and constraints (a, c, and d), he could ignore such matters as the knowledge and effectiveness of various agents (e, f, g, and h), and so collapse what the state actually does (i) onto certain of its capacities and constraints (c and d). Broadly, some participants in the debate, then, seemed at times to accord illicit determinacy and certainty to what were best characterized just as powers, enablements, or tendencies of states, ones that could only be realized under certain conditions and with the intervention of agents possessing appropriate knowledge. Theorists like Block—who contended that the state is constrained to act so as to maintain investment levels and business confidence—arguably neglected the various reasons why such outcomes cannot be automatic. Even assuming they are required to promote high levels of capitalist investment, state agents do not simply know, a priori, how to do this, but need experienced research and statistical agencies to make these judgments properly (Barrow 1993, 74). It is crucial, in short, not to veer into teleological thinking, to assume that states inevitably carry out certain functions in the service of capitalism (Isaac 1987b, 169). But at least in the way they expressed themselves, a number of participants in the broader "theories of the state" debate did often blur the line between capital-friendly potentials and capital-friendly outcomes.

181

That would appear to raise the specter of teleology for analysts who claim, for example, that all we need to know about "why relief arrangements exist" can be gleaned from the "functions" that welfare necessarily "serves for the larger economic and political order" (Piven and Cloward 1993, xv).

In short, bound up in these methodological shortcomings was a frequent neglect of the uncertainties and openness of interests, ideology, and effectiveness—that is, a neglect of the historical, empirical variability in how state and nonstate actors understand and make use of the powers at their disposal. Block's contention that state officials know more than capitalists themselves about what is in their interest was far more subtle than positing omniscient class consciousness. But it still rested on a fairly determinate understanding of interests, as well as great confidence in the ability of the state to act rationally to further them. Even economic conservatives differ substantially about what suits business and finance. Moreover, it is quite difficult to explain diversity among welfare states if there exists a fixed set of programs and policies that either capitalists or state elites know they must put in place in the interest of capitalism.[13] It is also hard to explain change over time in welfare state regulation from this standpoint, as well. Some critical theories seemed to hold that most of what the state did, say in regulating banks, benefited capital. But if a regulatory wall between investment and commercial banking benefited U.S. business interests during the sixty relatively prosperous years it was in place, why were such limitations abolished at the behest of both state actors and financial institutions—with such unpredictable and destructive results for the capitalist economy? And if the many gaps in health insurance coverage in the United States benefited business for decades, how do we explain the passage of the Affordable Care Act, let alone the many liberal welfare states that have true universal health care systems? In light of such welfare state variability, Clyde Barrow argues that theorists like Poulantzas and Block "have found it virtually impossible to make a reasonable case that specific institutions or policies are required by the functional needs of particular capitalist societies" (1993, 71).

All this, then, points to much more contingency and openness in the capabilities and activities of welfare states—and so, crucially, to much more room for contestation over what the welfare state is and does. There is no question that U.S. poverty programs have often humbled their recipients and shaped them into a pliant low-wage workforce (Piven

182

and Cloward 1993). But the point is to explain this not as inevitable but as the outcome of political and ideological struggle. There is historical reason to believe that left-leaning coalitions can produce a social-democratic state that promotes a more egalitarian and solidaristic society while protecting people from relentless market forces (Esping-Andersen 1985; 1990). Below I argue that a recognition of a much greater variety of welfare state powers—and a greater number of agendas to which they can be harnessed, especially racial and gender interests—militates even more for a view that welfare states' actions are contingent and subject to meaningful political contestation.

Failure to credit contingency often leads to a rather jaundiced view of welfare states, one that emphasizes only certain of their powers and the constraints affecting them, while paying insufficient attention to political struggle and the differences in knowledge, ideology, and effectiveness of those taking part in it. And such a jaundiced view explains a good deal of why so many critical theories focused on revolution, transition, or crisis. It is not simply that many critical theorists of the state held out some form of democratic socialism as their ethical ideal. For this goal cannot be explained exclusively in normative terms. Their commitment to this goal was inseparable from a view of the welfare state as inevitably subordinate to narrow capitalist interests. And this meant, further, that critical theorists of the state, despite being genuinely concerned with democracy, tended to collapse the question of democracy into questions about transition and revolution and to dismiss as ephemeral or illusory what democratic activity and achievements could be discerned in the political foreground. They seemed susceptible at times to a danger I have pointed out: viewing democratization as a movement toward a definite ideal set of practices or institutions, one facing a single interrelated set of challenges, a process of finite (though not necessarily short) duration, whose outcome, while not assured, could be decisive. Perhaps ironically, exploring the ways in which the state can strengthen racial and gender hierarchies—not just economic ones—raises some of the disquieting questions about this view of democratization and the state.

Race, Gender, and the State

Just as the debate among critical theorists ebbed, other scholars began to show how race relations and gender have shaped and been shaped by welfare states. They have demonstrated serious new exceptions to the hoped-for tendency of the welfare state to emancipate citizens from oppression or keep them from being swept up by overwhelming social forces. And they have shown, troublingly, that hard-won policies proponents thought would be liberating have sometimes turned out to have ironic consequences.

To an extent, work on race, gender, and the welfare state retains and *pluralizes* certain insights of the earlier critical theories. It shows that the characteristics and powers of a given state rest on the kind of structural relations it has with all sorts of social relations in civil society—not just the economy and class structure, but also race and gender relations (and sometimes all these simultaneously). Consider again the fact that any particular state, in its relation to its broader social surroundings, represents a settled limit on the extent of democracy. For many critical theorists, the most important example of this ability has been the failure to democratize the economy, notably the workplace, and to maintain civil society, in general, as a realm in which people pursue mainly private interests without a sense of common purpose. Work on race, gender, and the state identifies more examples of these state-reinforced limitations on the reach of democracy. Beginning in 1876, the U.S. federal government ended Reconstruction and refrained for eighty years or more from further using its powers under the Fourteenth Amendment to challenge the reconsolidation of racial rule in the South. There was nothing natural or inevitable about setting the bounds of democratic life in this way. And soon the federal government even added new segregation legislation to its support of the caste system (McAdam 1982, 72).[14] A similar narrative can be told about the relationship of the state to gender hierarchy, beginning perhaps with coverture laws—which in William Blackstone's words "suspended" the civil existence of a married woman and made her subject to her husband as "lord" (quoted in Pateman 1988, 91). This continued, as I shall soon show, through welfare policies that treated men as autonomous breadwinners and women as subordinate caregivers. So the alien agendas that the state may serve are not at all limited to those that may preserve corporate power, but can include conservative designs to shore up racial hierarchy or the "traditional" structure of the family. When, in more recent times, welfare functions serve such agendas, it is often by virtue of a wide range of powers, especially capacities related to welfare state "stratification" or the operations of the "penal state." The pluralization here involves much more than a numerical multiplication of examples. Dominating or oppressive social relations are not all the same. Their structural differences from each other, their different relations to the polity, and the contrasts in how they are experienced and maintained mean that the state must do different things to support (or undermine) them. The role of commodification and decommodification offers a good illustration of this complexity. Above I presented decommodification as a way of making people less subject to dominating market forces and workplace subordination. But it is not just markets that can be alienated; so too, of course, can race and gender relations. Because a gendered division of labor has been so crucial, historically, to the position of women, opening up labor markets to them and making paid childcare available outside the home has at times strengthened women's autonomy (Borchorst 1994; Bussemaker and van Kersbergen 1994). Such measures, though, could roughly be described as commodifying both women's labor and caregiving. This does not mean, of course, that decommodification, broadly, is somehow bad for women and good for men. The sort of guaranteed income discussed above could make it easier for many women to walk away from abusive relationships.

So without even entertaining more optimistic views of welfare state potential, we can see that the fact that state powers may clearly serve more than one master—and that these services may conflict or at least do not readily harmonize—also suggests the possibility of what I will call below "cross-purposes." The question of whose interests are to be furthered by certain state functions may not ever be permanently settled but may instead always be subject to political contestation. If state powers can be channeled in one direction, it may be possible to channel them in a different one. Powers now harnessed to reinforcing undemocratic relations may be tied to the cause of reforming those relations.

Stratification, Gender-Making, and Race-Making

Welfare state programs have frequently been harnessed since the late nineteenth century to define, demark, and give meaningful content to racial and gender categories.[15] Race, of course, like nationality, has been a "part of the structure of a modern state" for a very long time; and many postcolonial states can be seen to have originated in a "racial contract" from whose terms native peoples were excluded, and racial categorizations and associated "miscegenation" laws were often intended to uphold the status of privileged settlers (Pateman and Mills 2007, 136). Contrary to the most optimistic Marshallian narrative, the provision of welfare benefits, even ones generous to some people, has not always

185

served the interest of equal citizenship. Differences in how states engage with various recipients allow states to produce a kind of social "stratification" that cannot be mitigated solely by more redistribution (Esping-Andersen 1990, 55–78).[16] Welfare states can stratify recipients by according different groups not just unequal levels of cash assistance but also by providing heterogeneous types of benefits and placing people in programs that are structured and thus experienced very differently. Consider the sort of welfare programs that pay little and grudgingly and that subject recipients to constant personal questioning and bureaucratic surveillance, deeply undermining their autonomy. Then consider, by contrast, programs that are often not recognized as welfare at all, arm's-length programs that subsidize home ownership, investments, and health care. The recipients of these latter programs find their capacities to make autonomous choices enhanced by this provision—so much so that in the United States, they often do not see themselves as benefiting from welfare state largesse, which they associate with other people's dependence. But health insurance markets, for example, do not generally arise spontaneously; they must generally be created by the state. In the United States the establishment of such institutions was accomplished through large federal tax subsidies, reinforced by extensive regulation and state-fostered collective bargaining. These latter sorts of programs enhance recipients' security and do not require them to have extensive dealings with inquisitive bureaucrats.

Stratification does not have to rely on explicit race or sex discrimination. Rather, welfare state regimes can tie benefits to employment, for example, and this allows "private" racism and historically gendered employment patterns to operate, often magnified by welfare policies. Or they can award some benefits universally, but others in ways that allow for local authorities to engage in surveillance and to exercise discretion in awarding benefits. The effect of this sort of policy is often to place women or disfavored racial or ethnic groups in the most stigmatized, regulated, and punitive programs. This is not a matter simply of differential treatment of those who fall into independently existing races and genders. If we understand race and gender to be malleable but structured social relations, rather than as natural facts, then it becomes clear that welfare states have not just the capacity to discriminate tacitly based on preexisting race or gender categories but actually to make the particular race and gender relations that characterize a society, to determine the way that race and gender are experienced at a particular place and time.

This clarifies the importance of welfare programs that have often constructed women as uniquely dependent (Fraser and Gordon 1994). In
both Europe and North America social policy was based for at least a
century on a gendered division of labor, according to which, within the
heterosexual family, the man was the breadwinner, working outside the
home, while the woman performed unpaid caregiving (Orloff 2010, 257).
The earliest U.S. welfare programs consisted of two "channels" (Nelson
1990). Women were recognized by the welfare state only when they were
widowed mothers, and they received aid in that capacity only within certain highly discretionary, highly intrusive programs. Meanwhile men, as
workers, benefited from workmen's compensation in routinized programs
that accorded benefits as a matter of right. The "conservative" welfare
states of continental Europe, where the Church and Christian-democratic
parties had formative influence, also emphasized a male-breadwinner
model of provision, but as part of a broader program of "subsidiarity"
meant to ensure that welfare provision would not free women from caregiving or allow people to become independent of traditional family and
church hierarchies.[17] But it is not just the American "liberal" and continental European "conservative" welfare states that have emphasized male
breadwinning. The Dutch welfare state, generally considered to be
"social-democratic," highlights the difference between types of stratification. In the twentieth century, at least, it minimized economic inequalities between households while maintaining sharp differences between the
roles of men and women and their relationship to the welfare provision.

Since the late twentieth century, neoliberal policy has generally
encouraged women to enter the workforce both in the United States and
Europe, even in the "conservative" welfare states (Borchorst 1994, 34).
But that has not always changed the experience of participating in one of
the programs that serve mainly women. In the United States, Temporary
Assistance for Needy Families (TANF), an example of the shift toward
encouraging women to seek paid employment, also closely monitors and
frequently sanctions its overwhelmingly female adult recipients. In effect,
by undermining recipients' autonomy, this practice continues to make a
sort of social reality of the long-standing ideology of women's natural
dependence.

In parallel fashion, the U.S. Social Security Act originally established
different racial tracks (Lieberman 1998, ch. 2; Noble 1997). Old-age
pensions (now simply "Social Security") were set up as a nondiscre-
tionary, nonstigmatizing federal program tied to employment, but the

job categories of most African Americans, such as agricultural and domestic work, were excluded. Meanwhile, while not denying African Americans the benefit of Aid to Dependent Children (ADC), the act devolved its administration, allowing southern states closely to control recipients. This meant that the program's operation would not erode racial hierarchy by giving recipients some autonomy from the agricultural labor market, a key pillar of local power structures. The effects of the racial organization of the U.S. welfare state are still engraved in the social structure. The large socioeconomic gap between African Americans and whites—taken for granted by many people as eternal and almost natural—actually grew substantially during the four decades following the New Deal as the result of welfare programs that built a white middle class, especially through education and housing policies, while denying similar help to blacks (Katznelson 2005).[18] It is not sufficient to characterize this merely as unfair discrimination—though unfair and discriminatory behavior has been involved. The state in this instance shaped the meaning and experience of race and of social citizenship. There are other continuing consequences of this unequal deployment of powers. For example, there is evidence that Americans with the most racially intolerant views disapprove the most strongly of "welfare" programs, which they perceive as serving blacks (Gilens 1999). And this suggests the possibility of a mutual reinforcing pattern in which racist attitudes support systematically biased welfare programs and in which the characteristics of these programs—the way they treat different people—reinforce those same views.

Blood, Brothers: Solidarity and Exclusion

Closely related problems arise with respect to solidarity, one of the ideological faces of welfare state stratification. Ideally, welfare states would be an expression of very broad, equality-favoring solidarity, an expression of a drive toward "full membership of a community" for all (Marshall [1950] 1992, 8). But solidarity building can be a double-edged sword, an invitation to marginalization as well as inclusion. We have already seen that historically the consolidation of welfare states—like the project of state building in general—has been linked to efforts to build solidarity among some people while simultaneously enforcing the exclusion of others. Thus the capacities of modern welfare states and the aspect they show to many citizens are strongly influenced by the nature of these simultaneously solidaristic and exclusionary efforts. British advocates of empire used the welfare state to build working-class support for imperialist policy, distinguishing sharply between white Britons, eligible for incorporation within a growing conception of political and social citizenship, and excluded colonial subjects, especially in Asia and South Asia (Lieberman 2005, 39–48). And this inclusive-exclusive project is obviously integrally linked to race-making, for in Britain, the category of "black" has referred historically to all those living in or emigrating from the colonies.

Similarly, a two-track welfare system has often supported a kind of solidarity among men, conceived of as equal and autonomous earners, especially in contrast to dependent women. It is also possible to understand the Tea Party movement as an expression of a perverse sort of solidarity deeply rooted in perceptions of how different people relate to the welfare state. Many Tea Party activists, predominantly male and overwhelmingly white and older, understand themselves as productive citizens who deserve the generous welfare programs from which they benefit—especially Social Security and Medicare—in contrast with other freeloaders, of whom the most egregious examples are young people and undocumented immigrants (Williamson, Skocpol, and Coggin 2011, 27, 32–33).

Cross-Purposes

The idea that welfare state institutions can have conflicting purposes piggybacks on the idea that states, historically, have served multiple agendas—economic, racial, and gendered. One possible response to some of the foregoing discussion about plural purposes would be to argue that the *true* purpose—the true *function*—of welfare state programs has always been something singular, hidden, and democratically malign. Clearly, in itself, such an argument accepts the idea of contending purposes; it simply insists that one such purpose always rules over the others. This is one version of the "jaundiced" view of the welfare state to which I have referred. For example, it is entailed in this view that the true function of poor relief is to protect business and the wealthy. Even before considering newer scholarship on race, gender, and the welfare state, however, it is worth noting that some strong versions of this sort of argument would have to be regarded with suspicion. Such strong functionalist accounts of the state are suspect when they fail to explain how some posited conservative, systemic "need"—some need of society understood as a self-maintaining, hierarchical system—actually comes to be embodied in a policy or institution.[19] They are also suspect, as discussed above, when they suggest that there can be sure, uncontested knowledge of such systemic needs or interests. (The issue seems acute in the case of claims that the state acts so as to maintain capitalists' profitability, as if capitalists or state managers themselves were in perfect agreement about how to do this—or indeed had reliable ideas about it.) On a similarly abstract level, arguments about the "true" purpose of state actions run afoul of the notorious fact that even individual acts—let alone the doings of states—can be explained, justly, as furthering multiple intentions. "Most institutions," as Barrow remarks, "are multifunctional" (1993, 71).

Suppose we put aside any Marshallian, social-democratic optimism, and accept for the sake of argument that a program such as TANF (what people usually call "'welfare" in the United States) cannot really be attributed to popular demands for equal economic security. Suppose *that* purpose, at least, is fully eclipsed by a project to head off or co-opt protest by the poor, especially during depressions. Even so, it still remains clear, on the basis of more recent scholarship, that TANF and its predecessors historically have reflected a distinct racial purpose, as well: to structure aid so as to stigmatize the more vulnerable recipients of state largesse and to provide discretionary tools that allowed U.S. southern elites to grant and deny aid in order to maintain racial power (Lieberman 1998, ch. 2; Noble 1997). In general, although both of these purposes involve maintaining social order, they point in different directions. In the first case, order is to be achieved, at least in times of recession, by providing benefits and staving off need and protest. In the second, racial order is ostensibly to be secured by either by making benefits insecure or by denying them entirely—in either case with the aim of reinforcing dependence on local power structures.

At this point, though, it is important to readmit the idea that the welfare state can be successful in undermining undemocratic social relations. First of all, it was precisely out of fear of this democratizing potential—fear that benefits would enhance the autonomy of African Americans—that southern white members of Congress resisted aspects of the Social Security Act, and then insisted that it be structured in ways favorable to them. Old-age pensions were crafted to decommodify: to allow many elderly people to enjoy income without entering the labor market. At the same time, the system was crafted to leave out the jobs held by most southern African Americans and so to reinforce the caste system. The initial program, then, was an unstable compromise between democratic and antidemocratic purposes. And the contestation continued with antidemocratic exclusions eventually eroding.

"Coins That Do Not Readily Melt": Durability and Asynchrony

Generally, but not exclusively, the critical theorists of the state I have discussed sought to explain the characteristics and powers of states according to contemporaneous social relations and forces.[20] This was not always true of Marx himself, who argued that the Bonapartist-era state enjoyed powers forged in the monarchical past. "Social structures . . . are coins that do not readily melt," as Schumpeter points out; "once they are formed, they persist, possibly for centuries" ([1942] 1976, 12). As I pointed out in Chapter 3, this idea is not inconsistent with the view that social structures only exist insofar as they are reproduced by present action. It only means that the social forms so reproduced, perhaps unwittingly, can often be quite old and embody old purposes and old conflicts. And this is a source of deep, recurrent historical irony. It raises the possibility that present agents, in going about their everyday activities, may unintentionally (or at least unwillingly) be preserving structures that harm them or foil some of their purposes. It also means, relatedly, that a social structure or institution may be founded at one point by people with one set of problems, beliefs, and concerns, then later be reproduced by people with very different, perhaps contrasting aims— and indeed serve the interests or be subject to exploitation by yet another social group.

The existence of durable, asynchronous state institutions makes it even more likely that there will be plural agendas and conflicting purposes associated with welfare provision. For decades, state institutions can continue to reflect political power relations present at their birth, even when new power relations have taken their place. So there can be a disjunction, a lack of synchrony, between existing institutions and existing beliefs, social activities, and power relations.[21] Schumpeter claimed that capitalist civilization was sustained in part by inegalitarian feudal holdovers in politics and in the structure of labor. And he had a general name for such a condition: "transitional states of society" ([1948] 1991). Consistent with this kind of argument, scholars of the U.S. welfare state have shown that in ways we have already seen, the racial hierarchy of the South had a deep formative influence on the Social Security Act, really the foundation of the modern American welfare state (Lieberman

1998; Noble 1997). This influence was conducted, as it were, through southern Democratic members of Congress without whose support the act could not have passed. But the system of exclusions and discretionary powers they created, intended to ensure that the welfare measures did not upset the old racial order, lived on years after their unique position in Congress lapsed. The need to appease the same southern politicians, first during the New Deal and then in the civil rights era, led to bifurcated state institutions dealing separately with issues of labor-union rights and racial employment discrimination. These separate bureaucracies actually undermined each other's goals in deeply troubling ways, labor law often turning a blind eye to discrimination, and attempts to eradicate discrimination carried out in a way that hobbled unions (Frymer 2008). Years later, when some people—especially those who have come to see state intervention in the economy or in race relations as simply emancipatory—have forgotten the nature of the foundational pressures, a program's furthering of an apparently ulterior, nondemocratic purpose may seem surprising—a peculiar unintended consequence of continued support for and activity within the program.

The Penal State

"Special bodies of armed men having prisons, etc. at their command"—this was one of Lenin's most pungent formulations for describing state power ([1917] 1975, 316). A half century after his death, some critical theorists again discussed the state's police and military apparatus. But their explorations of the state's coercive powers now seem somewhat restricted in scope. Poulantzas's main interest in addressing the coercive apparatus was to shed light on military dictatorships, such as the one that arose in his native Greece in the late 1960s. And Miliband argued simply that modern militaries, despite a pretense of being apolitical, tend to be conservative in outlook and closely tied to business.

But the "penal state"—the state apparatus with the power to punish and imprison—has emerged in recent years as an important political concern. The interest centers not primarily on crime and criminal justice, per se, but on the penal state's close connection to welfare policy and its constitutive role in shaping citizenship and race relations. Much of the attention centers on the United States, its extraordinarily high rate of incarceration, and its soaring prisons spending. But while the United States is a pronounced outlier in these matters, it is one that vividly demonstrates the powers of the penal state.

One way of understanding the close relationship between the penal state and more traditionally recognized aspects of welfare is simply to point to the practical, historical trade-off between spending on prisons and spending on more liberating social welfare efforts. As prison and jail expenditures rose eightfold in the United States from 1980 to 2000, penal state spending more and more crowded out other kinds of domestic expenditure (Wacquant 2008, 58; Holleman et al. 2009). Another aspect of the relationship is that patterns of incarceration in themselves affect labor markets, family welfare, and health (Loury 2008, 15), traditional targets of social welfare spending. And there is some reason to believe that certain people recognize the relationship between the penal and welfare states—at least in an inverted or distorted way. Racial hostility, as we have seen, is closely linked to opposition to programs perceived as "welfare" (Gilens 1999). And at the same time, public views about "welfare" and criminal justice also trended together in the United States from the 1960s through the 1990s (Loury 2008, 14–15).

It is really only when race is fully brought into the picture, and when, at the same time, we consider a broad, Marshallian perspective on citizenship as full membership in society, that the significance of police, courts, and prisons for race and the welfare state becomes clear. In the United States, blacks are eight times more likely than whites to be imprisoned (Loury 2008, 22). The big increase in prison populations in the United States is due substantially to drug enforcement, not rates of violent crime, Michelle Alexander notes in her influential study of the subject, *The New Jim Crow: Mass Incarceration in the Age of Colorblindness* (2012, 101). Yet overall, "people of all races use and sell illegal drugs at remarkably similar rates"—in fact, if anything, whites are far more likely to abuse cocaine and heroin than blacks (97).

The disparity in incarceration is not just a "criminal justice" issue, because policing and punishment have a profound effect on what Marshall called "the claim of all . . . to be accepted as full members of the society" ([1950] 1992, 6). Even for those who are not arrested, charged, or locked away, "the police and penal apparatus" can become, as they are in the United States, "the primary contact between adult American black men and the American state" (Loury 2008, 23). This is the heart of renewed concern about "stop and frisk" policing that targets minority neighborhoods in New York and elsewhere. Beyond this, it hardly needs to be said that imprisonment itself is a severe abridgement of a freedom. But what happens after release is equally important to how those caught up in the system experience citizenship (Alexander 2012, 140–177). The most essential needs of those recently released from prison are inexpensive housing and a job, but federal law makes it essentially impossible for these individuals to live in public housing. And there are virtually no limits on the ability of employers to discriminate based on criminal history, regardless of the offense. For those ex–drug felons unable to get work, "welfare" is no help. The law that created TANF generally makes it impossible for them to receive benefits. Moreover, unlike in many other countries (Karlan 2008, 43–44), in the United States, those convicted of crimes—even misdemeanors—can be disenfranchised, stripped of political citizenship, often for life. It is the combination of racial bias in drug enforcement with lifelong punishment and discrimination of these kinds that leads Alexander to refer to mass incarceration as "the New Jim Crow." "It is no longer socially permissible to use race, explicitly, as a justification for discrimination, exclusion, and social contempt," she writes, so "rather than rely on race, we use our criminal justice system to label people of color 'criminals' and then engage in all the practices we supposedly left behind" (2012, 2). So just as the structure of traditional welfare programs can either be emancipatory or can tend, on the other hand, to "make" race a hierarchical relation, "mass incarceration" and its attendant policies can be "a principal vehicle for the reproduction of racial hierarchy" (Loury 2008, 36–37).

Mass incarceration, the war on drugs, and their extremely disproportionate racial impact constitute a complex example of alienation. The domination and oppression involved are already fairly clear. What is more difficult to assess is exactly who is involved in reproducing these alienated structures, and the degree to which this reproduction is intended. It is worth dwelling on these questions a little because the idea—expressed in its bare form—that widespread practices sustain alienated structures can seem to hide very real variation in the activities and levels of consciousness involved.

In the broadest terms, voters and taxpayers of all races and ethnicities help reproduce the penal state, since from the 1980s they have supported or acquiesced to the policies of the "war on drugs" and dragnet policing. Until recently, there was little enough public attention to these policies that possibly the worst one could say about the intentions of such people—at least some of them—was that they had been taken in by anti-drug rhetoric and were in denial about the policies' effects. But the more attention mass incarceration gets, the harder it will be to offer these defenses. Matters are different with respect to certain conservative white voters and the politicians who have represented them. Many of the same politicians who opposed civil rights until the early 1960s soon turned their attention away from an overtly segregationist agenda to one focused on "law and order" (Alexander 2012, 42). Such "law and order" rhetoric, at first focused on race riots—but soon more broadly on crime of all kinds—appealed strongly to working-class whites, especially in the South (43).[22] So certainly, an acutely race-conscious political strategy for mobilizing voter resentment was involved in the "law and order" program. Perhaps only acknowledgement of the fact that political agents cannot have perfect knowledge should caution us against assuming that there was also a well-formed strategy for maintaining racial caste itself in a new guise. In any case, within a few years, "centrist" Democrats supported the war on drugs and the crackdown on felons—as well as welfare "reform"—generally in an attempt to win the same southern white voters back to the party.

Crucial, as well, in the reproduction of the dominating institutions involved, are new practices of policing—in particular, practices that make it possible to arrest and charge African Americans disproportionately on drug-related charges. This includes especially police practices associated with the near abolition of probable cause as a standard for detaining and searching people and with the legal authorization of police to include race as a factor in deciding who to profile for drug enforcement (Alexander 2012, 63–72). These practices have taken shape because of a very conscious campaign of judicial conservatives to make it nearly impossible to challenge systematic racial bias in criminal justice (109). But unintended effects are important, too. Given the extraordinary discretion given police under these legal and judicial policies, even unconscious bias among officers can have an extraordinary effect on policing.

So the activities and practices that have produced and reproduced racially biased mass incarceration are quite varied. And this means that many people are involved in sustaining an especially egregious example of alienated state power serving an antidemocratic agenda, creating unjust social hierarchy, establishing dramatically unequal forms of citizenship, and fostering domination.

Democratization and the Welfare State

Despite welfare states' varied powers and the many modes of their alienation—or actually, in part, because of these problems—democratic agents should not retreat from them or imagine overcoming their deficits integrally. Drawing this conclusion may seem paradoxical. It may seem puzzling that welfare states' many ways of resisting and undermining democratic life should make us want all the more to engage with them— or at least, engage them in a particular, vigorous, and contentious way. But this apparent contradiction is in fact consistent with the direction of oppositional democracy, which avoids both surrender to existing nonideal conditions and escape to imagined ideal alternatives. And reflection on welfare states, stratification, race, and gender supports this approach.

The two faces of this argument—both the recognition of state alienation and the appeal for robust engagement as a response—can come sharply into focus by comparing an oppositional approach to some leading alternatives, at the same time emphasizing how they all apprehend and respond to these problems of welfare states.

Democratic theory, from the oppositional perspective, should attend carefully to the ways that welfare states can escape the public's control and reinforce forms of oppression and subordination. It ought to make this an explicit focus of critical, ethically guided inquiry. When they have failed this challenge, political thinkers have done so, for the most part, in one of two ways. Some have simply assumed that states are more benign, more pliant to popular direction, than they really are. Others have devoted little direct attention to the actual, nonideal workings of any institutions and social relations that resist democracy, preferring instead to elaborate what ideal democratic conduct might look like. The deliberative democracy literature provides examples of both these defects. It can be prone to viewing the liberal welfare state in purely aspirational terms, as "our collective power" (Laden 2001, 104). But more frequently it just neglects the state—its structure, its powers, and its relation to the wider social world—as a self-standing object of critical inquiry, something requiring explicit attention. Promoters of deliberation tend to approach welfare provision mainly in two ways: as a benign means of providing resources that allow people to deliberate or as a set of policies that are an appropriate subject, among many, of ethically guided discourse.[23] Neither way of thinking grasps the need to be alert to the democratic dangers that alienated states so clearly pose.

Jointly, the studies considered in this chapter show that such approaches won't do. They enter a sobering indictment of welfare states, which can fail in so many ways to be "our collective power." They demonstrate that welfare states pursue a variety of undemocratic purposes—in a manner people too often do not notice because of ties and dependencies that fall well outside the standard democratic decision-making channels. But contemporary democratic theory has not had much of substance to say about such issues—either about the privileged political position of banks or about the historical tendency of welfare states to offer political and social citizenship on unequal terms to men and women, whites and blacks, and so to reinforce social hierarchy.

Once these things are pointed out, most democratic theorists would surely recognize them for the democratic deficiencies they are. So why does so much contemporary theory generally pass over these issues? What does it fail to see about welfare states and democracy? One way to frame an answer is to consider what it means to emphasize democratic decisions, a topic discussed in the first chapter. Such an emphasis can make us blind to the significance of the deep structural interdependence of state and society. This mutual dependence and mutual conditioning is important for a number of reasons. Elections may be free and deliberation may be open, but if some of the state's most characteristic ways of acting, its powers and its liabilities, are not due to considered public decisions but to nonelectoral, nondeliberative, structural ties to civil society, then such representative and discursive institutions (however refined) and practices are not enough to establish democracy. And if the state has *already* structured society undemocratically—for example, by shaping people's capacities unequally or assigning them to different forms of citizenship—then it is not enough for the state to respond to the electoral pressures or the articulated demands these people are then able to generate. And this is especially so if many people are generally unaware of these dependencies.

Focusing on contemporaneous decisions, elections, and discourse also distracts from the ways in which present welfare states may have been shaped by discourses, ideologies, and power relations that seem to have receded into the dim past. These sorts of holdovers can be a significant cause of the continued failure to extend full, meaningful citizenship to everyone. And they represent a tendency of state institutions not to track democratic will. Many current deficiencies of the American welfare state reflect in part the racial and gender dynamics of the 1930s and 1960s. On their own, that is, present voting and the bounds of present discourse do not explain them. This asynchrony, as I termed it above, is somewhat different from the phenomena by which present welfare arrangements may serve the interests of small, current elites. But actually

197

the two phenomena may coexist and intertwine, to the detriment of the democratic responsiveness of the state.

In light of this troubling history, then, why not just give up on the welfare state? Most broadly, because despite their serious defects, what welfare states do is not predetermined, but contingent. State action is shaped by political contestation whose outcome is never certain. Neither the older critical theories nor approaches that counsel a withdrawal into civil society adequately account for this openness. Even the idea that states will act to benefit a given social interest, like that of big banks, is much less determinate than it seems. Differences in the ideological orientation and knowledge of both bureaucrats and financiers can affect their ability to defend banking interests—something many structurally minded critical theorists failed to see. And the decades of scholarship on race, gender, and the welfare state add another dimension to this contingency: the multiplicity of possible antidemocratic uses of welfare states. So even putting aside Marshallian ambitions for welfare states to foster egalitarian citizenship, there are so many interests contending to harness states' powers to bolster their own social positions that it can never be certain what form regulation and social provision will take.

Still, of the potential directions welfare states may take, the most obviously unsettling to arguments for abandoning or breaking states is certainly the real and proven possibility that they may democratize social relations. I have already pointed to the dramatic example of the American state partly democratizing the workplace—and abolishing remnants of the feudal order—by compelling employers to recognize unions chosen by their employees. But even the negative instances I explored above, cases of states enforcing sharp limits to the scope of democratic life, are only phases of longer narratives in which states have sometimes pushed those boundaries outward. The federal government reinforced the racial caste system of the South from 1876 through the 1950s, but before and after, during Reconstruction and the civil rights era, it acted in significant ways to dismantle racial hierarchy. Not all the examples are of such swift and singular transformations. Marshall's hope that welfare states would create the conditions for equal social citizenship has at times, or in some measure, been realized by welfare provision that supports people's autonomy and protects them from exploitation or overwhelming market forces.

Of course, achieving such transformation is not a question of states undertaking democratization alone or automatically; often it entails considerable political struggle. The passage of federal legislation creating a right to collective bargaining followed one of the greatest waves of strikes in American history, one that threatened the industrial order and forced the state to act. And the civil rights movement used strategic local campaigns to provoke disorder that the federal government could not ignore without sacrificing democratic legitimacy at home and abroad. Even as it recognizes the democratizing potential of welfare states, an oppositional approach is not complacent but assertive.

It is also worth reemphasizing a finding above: that even while a welfare state action or program democratizes one set of institutions or relations, it can at the same time further some other social interest. The same New Deal programs that provided some people—especially white male workers—the means to resist market forces or seek a measure of democratic autonomy on the job were also crafted so as to support racial and gender hierarchies. The phenomenon of welfare programs embodying such multiple, even conflicting, purposes has a number of implications for democracy. Above all, the possibility of multiple purposes suggests that the characteristic shape and effects of welfare state programs always remain subject to political contestation, pointing them, potentially, in both democratic and undemocratic directions. Those who favor income support or social insurance to foster broad, egalitarian, and meaningful social citizenship have to be always aware of the possibility that such programs can further other, less explicit, inegalitarian purposes as well. But the inverse is true, too, suggesting that there may be no end to democratic contention. This continual, open-ended contention has implications for how activists view their goals. A successful campaign to achieve democracy-enhancing social welfare institutions in the face of opposition might involve utter capitulation by undemocratic opponents. A far more likely scenario, though, is one of a settlement in which different political forces accept the new programs for different reasons without anyone being certain whose purposes will most be fulfilled. And this stage is sure to be followed by more contention. The stakes, then, are too high to abstain from oppositional democratic action, both when welfare state programs are inaugurated and long after.

So what of seizing or breaking the welfare state for democratic ends? It might be possible to seize a welfare state, win all but perfect democratic control of it, for all time, if there were a single group or interest from whom it had to be taken (forever), and if, once seized, the welfare state would not be liable to further alienations. Almost everything scholars of race and gender have demonstrated about welfare states since the pinnacle of the debate among critical theories militates against such a possibility. It is not just business interests that have succeeded at harnessing welfare states to their aims. So, too, we have seen, have the southern whites in America and Christian-democratic movements in Europe. And it is quite obvious that the various groups whose full democratic citizenship has been at stake in these conflicts have not always, for ideological reasons, recognized each other's interests—as the social democrats of the not-too-distant past ignored the racial and gendered dimensions of welfare provision. A decisive political victory for any one such group or interest—call it a seizure of the state—would not necessarily constitute an achievement for another.

It seems no more likely that a welfare state can be broken, because of many of the same considerations. Breaking the state has typically meant to proponents of the idea restructuring the whole polity so as to foreclose the possibility that political power can be alienated—allowing true democracy to flourish in a completely new institutional form. For the critical theorists who favored it, breaking the state meant in particular socializing and democratizing the economy, ending the need for a state wedded to maintaining capitalism and returning alienated political power to the public. But the thrust of an oppositional approach is that alienation is a ubiquitous possibility. And scholarship on race, gender, and the state demonstrates, again, that state domination by capitalist interests is not the only form alienation can take. If so, ending such domination, were it possible, still would not foreclose the possibility of alienated political power. Or, to approach the matter from a different direction, neither would dramatically restructuring political power. The struggle to reclaim alienated political power seems from this standpoint, too, to be ongoing, provisional, indeterminate, multisided, and without a foreseeable end. And the oppositional viewpoint holds that this struggle, not its successful conclusion, is democracy as we know it.

The varied philosophies that suggest not seizing or breaking the state, but letting it be and seeking democracy elsewhere, especially in civil society, are no more plausible from the perspective of those who recognize the role of states in shaping relations of race, class, and gender. The power that states have to stratify individuals calls into doubt one version of the argument for seeking democracy elsewhere—for keeping a distance from the state. Civil society, according to many such accounts, is the proper locus of democratic attention.[24] These accounts treat civil society as a realm truly distinct from the state, a self-generated sphere of free association and communication in which people advocate "oppositional interpretations of their identities" and attempt to generate "influence" over other spheres without trying to wield state power (Cohen and Arato 1992, ix, x, 429; Fraser 1990, 67).[25] But the relevant state capacities to categorize, sort, and assign people to different kinds of citizenship represent the state helping to constitute the very structure and composition of the civil society whose members are supposed to identify and organize themselves autonomously. On the one hand, then, civil society seems not really to be self-generated in some rather significant ways. And on the other, challenging racial or gender identities and categories, one of civil society's supposed tasks, would seem to require contesting for control of certain state powers. Unless large-scale structural issues are to be set aside, it is difficult to understand why anyone who seeks to democratize social relations would want to give up on state institutions and powers that have proven effective at this task. Even when the state is quite central to the problem at hand—as is the case with mass incarceration, race, and unequal citizenship—redirecting its powers would seem just as central to the solution.

We have already seen examples of what such struggling both with and against the state might look like. In many of its campaigns, the civil rights movement sought to lure the federal government into conflicts playing out on the terrain of the southern racial caste system. But this strategy did not count on the federal government to combat racial domination automatically or on principle, alone—without the state being coerced itself. The movement forced the federal government's hand by mobilizing demonstrations that provoked repression, and so created crises that threatened state interests. And these openly coercive movement strategies had communicative dimensions and worked in tandem with other, more traditionally recognized democratic activities, like citizen lobbying for civil rights legislation. The example of participatory budgeting in Brazil is somewhat different. Viewed narrowly, Orçaento Participativo (OP) centers on inspiring local participatory forums, such as the popular assemblies. But surprisingly, from the standpoint of those who favor shunning state power, these organs are part of the state. To participate in them is to attempt to wield state power. Moreover, the democratic conquest of these state powers is partly in the service of an oppositional effort to resist state clientelism, the capture of the state by old elites with intertwined political, social, and economic power. And, as we have seen, those who participate in OP see the process not as complacent but as integrally connected to contentious movement activities.

Once understood, the message here may seem at once familiar and disheartening—familiar because, as I have just pointed out, many movements and democratic actors have long adopted such an oppositional approach to the state and alienation—and disheartening because it holds out no hope that democracy can ever find a home in some unalienated institution or social space. The familiarity should not be a concern. A theory of alienation, democracy, and opposition is not meant to provide political activists with an unheard-of set of new strategies and tactics to revolutionize their practice. Instead, in pragmatic fashion, it seeks to uncover the value and the logic of oppositional democratic action as it has long existed. And in this sense, rather than demoralization, it is intended to offer a kind of philosophy of such oppositional action, some reflective reassurance for those struggling to address big democratic questions that the antinomies of their approach to the state are justified.

Yet an oppositional approach to democracy embracing the experience of movements for racial and gender equality does not claim to know there can be nothing better than the particular democratic settlement of today, nothing better to be experienced than the existing dialectic of alien state and movements. It does suggest, however, that even if there is a better democratic world to be enjoyed some day, a richer democratic life, oppositional democratic politics—recapturing alienated social forms—will almost surely still be a part of it. And we are also likely to get to this state of affairs only through the same sort of democratic struggle. This is another version of an argument that resonates throughout this book: rather than setting up democracy as a pure, final ideal of one sort or another, we should recognize its oppositional quality as at once a means and an end.

For Westerners, warfare is surely not what it was when the council movement tried to democratize the militaries, bureaucracies, and workplaces of Central Europe. During the first half of the twentieth century, total war—in which a nation's full arsenal was deployed, along with almost all its manufacturing capacity and human strength—required widespread and direct participation, and citizens had to make sacrifices ranging from the trivial to the unbearable. Many of the consequences and concomitants of war, including the death, the dislocation, and the suppression of dissent, were for that reason inescapable and vivid for the public. It is true that the military, political, and economic phenomena involved were exceedingly complex, making it difficult for ordinary people to comprehend all the ways in which those terrible consequences were partly traceable back to their own activities, and also making it difficult for them to imagine how they might gain some common control over events. Dewey emphasized this very point. But still there was an awful immediacy to war's consequences, and this could provoke democratic action. Widespread war mobilization and the patriotic rhetoric that underwrote it entailed the possibility that total war could eventually provoke popular challenges to the military itself or to other dominating forces or institutions. The councils are far from the only example. Another is the African American soldiers who, following World War II, took seriously the idea that they were fighters for democracy and returned to Mississippi and Louisiana with a rebellious proclivity to challenge racial domination. The Vietnam War, while not precisely "total," also demonstrated that the extreme demands made on citizens in war could backfire on the military.

The institutions of contemporary war—and more broadly, the contemporary security state—still require the active support of millions of people, if not always direct participation in combat or acceptance of personal sacrifice and deprivation. Political and civil action, including voting, deference to authority, and taxpaying, reproduce the state that launches drone attacks and vacuums up electronic data. Both commission and omission by citizens matter; it is the overall pattern of public activity that is key to this enablement. And, as in the early twentieth century, war and the security state, though in many ways now quite different, are still marked by structures and forces that seem overwhelming, unstoppable to most of us, dwarfing the agency of countless ordinary people and enabling the oppression and exploitation of many others, especially abroad. The contemporary security state, in other words, is still arguably an alienated state, just as was the state that organized total war. But that alienation now finds a novel and troubling expression.

That is because, for most people in the developed world, war now makes much less dreadful demands. And with burdens on citizens significantly diminished, the most critical doings and effects of the contemporary security state—results of how it spies, how it kills the reclusive leaders of its enemies, and whom it sends to defend its supply lines and do its menial work—are also less clearly known to them, and felt by them far less directly. From the vantage point of any Western public, the doings of the security state can feel remote. The same family of traits and properties are exhibited over and over, all varieties of separation between different living people and the divergent experiences they undergo. These include geographical, temporal, and social distances; secrecy and invisibility; automation, depersonalization, and, at times, even indifference. There are great chasms today between a Western public's experience and that of the people who live in war zones and have a very different experience of the security state. And that chasm is made up of or widened by other gaps—discontinuities between the experiences of any public that might coalesce around security issues and those even of Western soldiers and pilots, and between Western fighters and the non-Western fighters and civilians whose lives they take or trouble. Dewey would have recognized these contemporary problems as breakdowns in the circuits of a possible public's "experience" and would have understood them as a threat to democratic action. But evident as they were in total war in Dewey's day, such discontinuities are especially obvious when we look at the newest, most significant security institutions and powers: electronic surveillance, drone warfare, and private military contracting. Such experiential gaps have the potential to attenuate public understanding, forestall democratic action to manage war and security, and so allow the security state to grow ever more alien.

This may not be the first trouble that comes to mind when we think of democracy and the contemporary security state. A more apparent problem, for many, is the security state's infringement of democratic rights.[1] These are rights that are required for democratic participation, such as free speech and association, as well as rights whose violation could make these political rights hollow, such as due process, privacy, or the protection of bodily integrity. Since 9/11, much of the talk about the security state and democracy has understandably focused on this nexus of security and democracy. The emphasis on democratic rights has pointed the way to an indispensable mode of inquiry that has revealed much of the detailed knowledge we have about how the post-9/11 security state has developed. In simplest form, the democratic rights paradigm asks at least two questions: Whose democratic rights have been violated by the security state? And who has violated their rights? Such questions, although they have proven difficult to answer sometimes, have motivated a vast outpouring of legal filings, articles, books, and reports written by journalists, lawyers, and human rights activists. As a practical matter, anyone interested in the post-9/11 security state, almost regardless of perspective, is indebted to these writings.[2]

But the ongoing development of the security state suggests that identifying actual violations of democratic rights and those responsible for them is not enough. The U.S. security state has evolved, changing in some ways, becoming more settled in others, and the pattern is suggestive of a distinct threat to democracy, one not identical to worries about the infringement of democratic rights. In addition, the actual, active infringement of democratic rights seems to have varied at least somewhat according to who holds and who challenges executive power. A number of the most controversial detention practices and legal claims of the Bush administration have been nixed by the Supreme Court or otherwise abandoned. The Bush administration retreated from waterboarding, and Barack Obama required interrogators to follow the Army Field Manual. But, for all this, Guantánamo remains open. Electronic surveillance has changed form since "warrantless wiretapping" was revealed, but if anything it has widened in scope. And the reliance on drone warfare has increased, as has its geographic scope.

If much of the focus on the security state and democratic rights has led to identifying oppressive *exercises* of power and the people responsible for them, the persistent growth of the security state suggests we also need to be concerned with the *structures* themselves and the powers they bestow. The crucial issues, as I have suggested, involve the interaction of the contemporary security state with a potential democratic public. And the pertinent questions are these: What is the democratic significance of the new structures, powers, and capacities of the post-9/11 security state? More pointedly, is a state with these capacities and powers compatible with democracy? Can a public exercise its democratic rights effectively to manage such a state?

A survey of the scene suggests very worrisome answers. Difficult as it may have been for a public to manage the U.S. security state in the latter half of the twentieth century, the post-9/11 security state appears to present even greater challenges. And this is because the most significant new institutions and powers of the security state, by design or evolution or both, direct the consequences of combat or surveillance away from any public that could organize to manage them. We can see this, most of all, in contemporary surveillance, drone warfare, and private military contracting.

The Voice of the People, Transcribed

Criticism of the U.S. government's phone and Internet surveillance surged in 2013 with Edward Snowden's leaks, but the contours of the programs had been visible for a decade. Thanks to the state's position and technological prowess, and to the fact that so much of social life is now lived electronically, security agencies have acquired the ability to know with whom people interact, how often, and for how long—and this is true for essentially anyone. The sum of such information about a single person can provide the state with a comprehensive picture of his social ties, political leanings, sexual orientation, and health concerns. And the state can obtain this information invisibly—without getting an individual warrant, interviewing anyone, or infiltrating a mosque or a political gathering. In one sense, comprehensive knowledge like this is not a new ambition of the state but just a metastasis of an old one. The early modern state, too, sought to know society as it had never been known, to make it "legible," to master it through comprehending it (Scott 1998).

The nature of these surveillance capacities is intimately connected to a double ability to insulate the public from feeling their exercise—double because it involves straightforward secrecy, as well as a rhetorical focus on people portrayed as "others." For most people, it is impossible to know (or prove) that even their own communications have been scrutinized. Judges have dismissed lawsuits challenging electronic surveillance programs on the argument that the plaintiffs could not prove they had been surveilled. And when plaintiffs actually provided evidence they were, the government has argued not just that particular relevant information could not be disclosed but that the cases had to be dismissed in toto to prevent disclosure of state secrets. But it is not only *what* the state knows or has been finding out that is secret—or even *how* it may know. Even the limits to what the state could try to find out are unknown, since the special secret courts that oversee surveillance have developed a body of occult common law about what is constitutionally permissible.

There has been much attention to the fact that the public response to such surveillance has been ambivalent—not an endorsement, but not a repudiation, either.[3] But it would be a mistake to argue, on the strength of such evidence, that state surveillance is simply an expression of what the public wants. Beyond the ambivalence itself, it is important to remember that the state has its own distinct interests here, which are entwined with the well-being of citizens, but not reducible to either common interests or public opinion. State actors respond to what some call the "security imperative" (Dryzek and Dunleavy 2009, 29; Skocpol 1979, 30). It is difficult to specify the exact nature of this "imperative," but it is fairly clear that those who staff the state—all the way up to the president—are motivated to keep order, to compete for power with other states and nonstate actors, and to retain legitimacy, especially by avoiding crises.[4] In short, surveillance is driven, significantly, by a state agenda that is not unconnected to public interests—but also not really the public's own. So it makes sense to see the powers and doings of the security state, as oppositional democracy would suggest, as the result of a contest between fitful political attempts to provoke public debate and the resistant tendencies of the security state itself.

A Drone Democracy

Since the first uses of air power a century ago, states have developed greater and greater powers for warfare at a distance. If the Tomahawk cruise missile and the Stealth bomber were the characteristic forms of air power during Bush's invasion of Iraq—the hallmarks of "shock and awe"—the Predator drone has become Obama's emblematic instrument of remote warfare in Afghanistan, Pakistan, Yemen, and sometimes Somalia. His administration's counterterrorism strategy has rested heavily on drones, although official language about their use, especially outside of acknowledged conventional war zones, has remained evasive. The technological organization of drone warfare makes for striking contrasts of intrusion and remoteness, concealment and displays of overwhelming power. A Predator drone can hover at high altitude, out of sight, while its operators watch a potential target—a man on a rooftop or some vans driving along mountain roads—for hours or days before striking with missiles. But the voyeuristic, intimate quality is only part of a picture marked by sharp contradictions. The communications infrastructure that brings observers so close to their targets in one way also makes it possible for Predators to be controlled from tremendous distances and by widely dispersed teams. In fact, the drones' remote operation makes it possible to use them in places where the United States has not sent large numbers of troops and perhaps would not if it could, a fact that leads Jane Mayer (2009) to call their potential use "geographically unbounded."

Long before the introduction of the drone, Michael S. Sherry wrote of the "profound difficulties people faced in comprehending air war even as it unfolded" (1987, ix). But drone warfare is even more prone than past incarnations of air power to discontinuities and chasms between state actions and their effects and between public perception and indirect consequences of things done in the public's name. A related factor is the mechanized form of killing involved—another depersonalization, a discontinuity between state actor and human consequence. Now this mechanization, as well, has always been a feature of air power. With drones, however, a pilot, while far away, can still see in telephoto detail the mayhem he or she is causing, making for a combination of detachment and raw intimacy. Finally, there is involved a gap between U.S. citizens, those ultimately responsible (in principle) for American military force, and the selection of drone targets, which is based on secret risk algorithms, local intelligence that can be colored by poorly understood tribal rivalries, and close collaboration with other countries' militaries. Secrecy worsens all these discontinuities, since no one outside government knows exactly how many drones the United States operates, with how many personnel, or—despite some disclosures—under what actual rules.

But the insulation of an American public from the immediate killing and maiming caused by drone warfare does not mean that either these or more remote consequences are insignificant, even for Americans themselves. Americans are largely shielded from the deadly proximate consequences of the attacks, but in their experience they may also find it difficult to trace some of the indirect consequences, which are themselves potentially profound. Former officials once closely connected to drone operations have expressed concerns that they may turn war zone civilians against the United States. The collaboration on drone attacks with the Pakistani and Yemeni militaries very likely strengthens them in ways that may be detrimental to those countries' politics and finally even to the United States. The logic of expansion of drone warfare—driven by technology and tactics—has also already produced an unannounced and until recently undebated change in official U.S. policy in favor of assassination, and thus a national moral coarsening. Relatedly, drone technology has become, without public participation, untethered from its original advertised use, mainly surveillance. Its use could conceivably be changed or expanded yet again without much public notice.

Alien Legion

The growth of private military contracting is just one extreme example of the movement toward the privatization of government services advocated worldwide by free-marketers since the 1970s. Yet the extraordinary scale of U.S. reliance on mercenary guards and other private contractors in Iraq and Afghanistan was a new departure.[5] The Bush administration turned heavily to contractors because it had badly underestimated the need for troops in postinvasion Iraq. It was unable to get international support and unwilling to accept the political costs of admitting its mistakes or of calling up more regular and reserve forces (Singer 2008, 244–245). As a result, in Iraq and Afghanistan, armed contractors replaced soldiers in escorting supply convoys and diplomats, while unarmed workers took over the driving of supply trucks, worked as translators, refueled vehicles, managed logistics, maintained drones and tanks, and worked in food service. Eventually, private contractors took on these roles in truly vast numbers, often greater numbers even than those of uniformed personnel. And it is a crucial fact, though one often overlooked, that the majority of these contractors have not been from the United States. In fact, many have been recruited from the developing world to fill dangerous and poorly paid jobs that are essential to U.S. security state aims.

Candidate Obama was sharply critical of privatized security in Iraq and Afghanistan, but President Obama's plan for withdrawal from Iraq entailed doubling the number of private security guards there, some of whom do not merely protect diplomats but form "quick reaction forces" (Gordon 2010). And private contractors seem very likely to be a feature of future U.S. military operations.

As with drone warfare and electronic surveillance, the democratic significance of private military contracting concerns both its consequences and discontinuities in the way in which those consequences are experienced by citizens and others. Some of the most dire of the consequences, of course, are the deaths of civilians at the hands of mercenary guards. The killings in Nisour Square in 2007 constitute the most famous example, but leaked military incident reports show that the unjustified killings were far from unique in Iraq (Glanz and Lehren 2010). The shootings and, more broadly, the sense of civilians in Iraq and Afghanistan that they were both endangered and treated contemptuously by mercenaries fueled understandable backlash.

Along with incidents like Nisour, deaths and injuries among contractors themselves must be reckoned among the serious consequences of privatized war. Although there were fewer deaths among civilian contractors in Iraq and Afghanistan than among actual military personnel, the numbers were also in the thousands. And as operations in Iraq and Afghanistan wound down, the rate of civilian contractor deaths at times actually overtook the military death rate (Miller 2010). There were, as well, many times more injuries than deaths, of course—tens of thousands of them. And many of those hurt, especially those from the developing world, have not ended up receiving disability compensation to which they are legally entitled because of the complexities of subcontracting, resistance by employers and insurers, and severe deficiencies in the way the U.S. government regulates the compensation system—all these factors leading to more hidden suffering. Often badly wounded contractors and bereaved families, their situations little known to any responsible public, languish in locales from U.S. nursing homes to Philippine slums.

More indirectly, the heavy reliance on private guards also builds and sustains a network of companies and relationships that are of highly debatable public value. Not least among these are the private security companies, some now infamous, like Blackwater (now Xe). And the search for cheap labor that partly motivates privatization in areas like military food service also pours billions of sustaining dollars, through corporations like KBR and DynCorp, into a network of global labor subcontractors, many quite shady. Such firms were known to lure exploitable workers to U.S. bases in Iraq with false promises of high-paid work in Dubai—or to strand workers in a war zone instead of flying them home when the companies lost contracts (Stillman 2011).

But these effects of the privatized warfare are by no means experienced or understood the same way by all those interested and affected by it. Nothing could be more essential for a public to consider than the human cost of war, an ongoing consequence about which there should be a stream of reliable information if democracy is to function. That war casualties (at least on one's "own" side) have a deep impact on voters' judgments is nearly a political axiom. But the deaths of private contractors are far less likely to register publicly than official military casualties. In part, this may be because, in general, the extent of reliance on private military contractors is still not publicly understood. Compared to the fairly prominent news coverage of the deaths of U.S. soldiers, contractor casualties receive little sustained media attention. Nor have elected officials, including Obama, called attention to private contractors, their role, and their deaths and injuries. They acknowledge uniformed military deaths, but not those among what one former contractor terms, with understandable bitterness, an "invisible, discardable military" (Miller and Smith 2009). And if a U.S. public knows little about its own citizens hurt or killed in the course of private military work, the prospect of a public processing the effects of the deaths and injuries among cooks or bus drivers from Fiji, Goa, the Philippines, and Nepal seems even slighter.

Inconclusion

There is little justification for seeing the democratic dangers of these post-9/11 security state powers as incidental to their true nature. In fact, it seems clear that successive administrations have pursued the powers discussed here, in substantial part, precisely to avoid activating an engaged public. That does not mean the pursuit of these powers reflects a conscious strategy to undermine democracy. Rather, the democracy-evading character of these developments seems to have arisen from the attempt on the part of those in the security state to maintain prerogative and flexibility, to pursue the "security imperative," in the face of potential democratic constraints. But this is almost as troubling as actual anti-democratic conspiracy might be. The fact that these new security state powers have grown up in interaction with potential democratic intervention suggests that they may have reached a fairly enduring and evasive accommodation with it.

It is also worth noting that these newer security state powers and structures are entwined, sometime closely, with older ones that have similar troubling characteristics. The all-volunteer military, for example, results in a "casualty gap" (Kriner and Shen 2010), whereby uniformed deaths and injuries disproportionately strike poorer and less educated communities. And this, like the use of private contractors, makes it difficult for a broad public to comprehend the magnitude of war casualties. This gap "concentrates the human costs of war among the very segment of the citizenry that possesses the fewest resources needed to engage government," while it guarantees that "citizens who have the strongest rates of political participation, also have the least direct exposure to the human costs of war" (154). And disturbingly, lower-income and less educated communities that are disproportionately hit with war casualties suffer declines in civic engagement for years afterward, making democratic mobilization to curb the security state even less likely.

The sharp increase in soldiers returning home to live with devastating injuries also plays a role in hiding the consequences of war from public view. Because of changes in the character of warfare, including the prevalence of improvised explosive devices, and because of improvements in body armor and emergency medical care, the ratio of injured to killed soldiers soared in Iraq and Afghanistan. And many of those hurt have suffered traumatic brain injuries, which can lead in time to unprovoked seizures, dementia, depression, and aggressive behavior. Many veterans and their families will experience these ills, often in anonymity, for years to come—the private return, for some, of war consequences that have been publicly repressed. And the fiscal cost of these injuries is also likely to remain undemocratically obscured. The lifetime health-care costs for Iraq and Afghanistan veterans could eventually run to $717 billion, not much less than the total amount that Congress had appropriated for the wars by the last year of Bush's presidency (Stiglitz and Bilmes 2008, 9, 87). These are costs, human and economic, that were not known to a public when the wars were being debated, but that will be suffered and incurred long after the wars are over.

State-of-the-art electronic surveillance, drone warfare, and private military contracting make collective management of the security state, on equal terms, a constant challenge. The problem is not that citizens are incapable of voting out politicians who grow and exercise these astonishing state powers. And it is not that American citizens have been excluded from public discussion of them, or that the raw information about them is entirely lacking. As I have suggested, investigation in the "democratic rights" mode has generated prodigious amounts of material for robust deliberation. The difficulty is that these crucial security powers operate far from many citizens and make their collective initiative look puny in comparison to the state's. They cry out for an oppositional democratic response. But the particular way they work, diverting knowable effects from the very publics that could curb the powers' exercise, seems to make a mass response unlikely. There is reason to think that at least some citizens have accepted new surveillance powers, drone warfare, and a privatized military—perhaps because they are confident that they are sheltered from their effects. They do not expect to be shot at by a Predator or maimed while preparing fast food at a military base thousands of miles from home. They are confident that no spies will root through their Facebook postings. If so many citizens are indifferent, some might argue, then by definition these are matters of democratic indifference. But the inclination to cede public initiative to a state whose powers are overwhelming and whose actions remain dimly experienced and sporadically understood is not a democratic one. Real popular engagement on these issues may only follow from—not trigger—a restructuring of the security state that aligns its doings more closely with what the public experiences and fully understands. But, troublingly, it is not clear whether there are any tendencies leading toward such a reform.

INTRODUCTION

1. Our Walmart, a union-sponsored organization, filed complaints of retaliation with the National Labor Relations Board. The board said in late 2013 that Walmart had "illegally disciplined and fired employees over strikes and protests" (Harris 2013). For its part, Walmart complained that Our Walmart had exceeded the number of days it is legal to picket while seeking union recognition. In response, the organization and its union affiliate, the United Food and Commercial Workers, pledged for the time being not to try to unionize Walmart employees—even while continuing to advocate for higher wages and an end to company retaliation against workers (Greenhouse 2013a).

2. This is the practice of denying workers pay or breaks they have earned. The practice is more common among textile manufacturers than among retailers such as Walmart, and it is more common among retailers than among residential builders. See Pfeifer (2013) and Bernhardt et al. (2009).

1. THE IRONIC PLACE OF MOVEMENTS IN DEMOCRATIC THEORY

1. I understand movements to be collective challenges to dominant groups, ranks, and structures in society mounted by relatively weak or excluded people. See, e.g., Tarrow (1998, 4–7).

2. For more thorough treatments of Schumpeter's response to movements, see Medearis (2001, chs. 2 and 3) and Medearis (2004, 462–467).

3. See Chapter 4.

4. The deliberative literature is now vast. For some classic statements, see Habermas (1996), Rawls (1996), Bohman (1996), and Gutmann and Thompson (1996). For more recent revisions of the main deliberative themes, see Bohman and Richardson (2009) and Mansbridge et al. (2010).

5. Mansbridge et al. (2010) is a joint article by nine deliberative theorists who argue for some alterations to "classic" deliberative theory, some of which I discuss below.

6. In fact, this is characteristic, as well, of approaches to movements and democracy that are communicative but not specifically deliberative. Nancy Fraser, in emphasizing the problem of inequality for democracy, focuses her attention on "disparities in political voice" (2007, 12), inequalities that affect people's ability to take part in "talk" and "interpretation" (1990, 56–57, 67).

7. See also Mansbridge et al. (2010, 66).

8. So, too, for example, does envisioning social life, broadly, as an association of consumers or taxpayers, since no person is just a consumer or just a taxpayer.

9. Karl Marx had this in mind in criticizing the liberal differentiation between "the rights of man" and "the rights of the citizen." However much one exalts citizenship, this may leave other relations untouched. Even when citizenship, viewed this way, is perfected, Marx argued that "man leads a double life, a heavenly and an earthly one, not only in thought and consciousness, but in reality, in life. He has a life both in the political community, where he is valued as a communal being, and in civil society, where he is active as a private individual, treats other men as means, degrades himself to a means, and becomes the plaything of alien powers . . . Man in the reality that is nearest to him, in civil society, is a profane being" ([1843] 2000, 53).

10. See Pateman (1983).

11. In light of these multiple citizen roles, invoking citizenship would at its best not be a description or even an exhortation. It would be a challenge, a practice that makes sense only in light of other roles and social relations a person occupies. Invoking citizenship questions subordination or marginalization in some other role or relation—or says, for example, "Remember that I am a 'citizen' even though I am also a minimum-wage janitor or a disabled person or poor or a member of an ethnic minority." But those other roles, the structures and forces that characterize them, should be an explicitly theorized part of democratic theory.

12. Supporting this interpretation is Dryzek's regret that most deliberative democrats have reached "an easy accommodation with liberal and constitutional thinking" (2000, v).

13. On this subject, see Chapter 3.

14. For a notable exception, see Green (2010a).

15. See also Gutmann and Thompson (2004, 3) and Bohman and Richardson (2009, 253).

16. See also, inter alia, Mansbridge et al. (2010, 66).

17. For a treatment of deliberative democracy, noncoercion, and movements, written when many proponents were more confident that the fit between movement practices and deliberative values was an easy one, see Medearis (2005).

18. For more on Schumpeter's influence, see Medearis (2009, ch. 3).

19. Thus Rawls argues that a theory of justice can begin with a vision of a "perfectly just society" (1999b, 8).

20. On this separation, for example, see Rawls (1999b, 234).

21. In some cases, it can be difficult to discern the approach a theorist is taking to the ideal/nonideal distinction. Fraser is clearly critical of an idealizing tendency in Habermas's thought. But her focus on "Actually Existing Democracy" (1990) might or might not be intended to challenge the dichotomy.

22. On this strategy, see Medearis (2005).

23. Fung's piece warrants attention because it focuses almost exclusively on the set of issues I am exploring. The article by Mansbridge et al. (2010) addresses a wider range of topics, but is unusually interesting because it represents the shared views of nine prominent proponents of deliberative democracy.

24. For an "all bets are off" admission, see Bohman and Richardson (2009). They describe civility as the core duty of deliberators. But then they remark, without much elaboration: "There are cases—such as when hegemonic, dominating power must be confronted, in which citizens have good reasons to be disrespectful [and this] may override the reasons favoring civility" (268).

25. Mansbridge et al. discuss "power as capacity," "power in general," and power as "the capacity to act" or as "potential"—that is, a capacity a person may possess either because of "occupying" a particular social position or because of "established institutions" and "social settings" that facilitate certain kinds of actions (2010, 80, 80n43, 81).

26. The coauthors refer to the "causing" of "outcomes," as by the "threat of sanction" or "the use of force," the act of "lying," the "use of power," or the "exercise [of] power" (Mansbridge et al. 2010, 80–81, 82).

27. Or more precisely, perhaps, her place in a network of social relations. See, inter alia, Isaac (1987a) and Wartenberg (1992).

28. Mansbridge et al. insist that power involves "causing outcomes" (2010, 80). Despite some nips and tucks, this is substantially the same position as that enunciated over fifty years ago in Dahl (1958).

29. On the whole, the coauthors do not seem to be much concerned with clarifying the distinction between potential and actual. Their main concern is distinguishing three types of power that are all to be identified with actualized capacities, causal outcomes. One type of power involves threats, another force, and another neither of these. So when they come to exploring what it means to "occupy" the "status quo," they interpret this to refer not to capacities inherent in occupying a particular position in a social structure, but, again, to threats and force.

30. The confusion is made worse by their apparent acknowledgment, as well, of Foucault's quite distinct view of power—"every human being is constituted by power relations" (Mansbridge et al. 2010, 80).

31. This involves setting a great deal aside. After all, in a capitalist economy, the status quo—to use a term that will soon come up again—is one in which the owners of capital hire management and through them, labor, not in which labor hires management and capital. Yet in ideal deliberation between labor and management, it seems, that status quo would have no force, no priority. Everything would be on the table, including, presumably, democratic management of industry, or an inversion of relations in which, instead of capital employing labor, labor would hire capital.

32. To be sure, Mansbridge et al. next argue that strikes might also be justified as a matter of "self-defense" when "opposing parties do not meet [deliberative] norms" (2010, 83). But here we largely leave the precincts of deliberative theory—and so for these authors, democratic theory, too.

217

33. In this case, the status quo would depend on an agent devoting "his energies to creating or reinforcing" the relevant values and practices, in Bachrach and Baratz's language (1970, 7).

34. I have more to say about this in Chapter 4.

35. To be sure, Fung (2005) does not characterize these as egregious violations of deliberative norms.

36. This paradox results from making "the creation of an ideal democracy . . . dependent on the existence of a number of 'ideal democratizers' in the much less than ideal present" (Stears 2010, 10–11). Stears credits Honig (2007) for this term.

37. Think of Dewey's critique of the "rugged individualism" that is "praised as the glory of American life": "Such words have little relation to the moving facts of life" ([1929] 1999, 18).

38. For more on Dewey's criticism of the ideal/nonideal distinction, see Chapter 2.

2. EPISODES IN THE HISTORY OF ALIENATION AND DEMOCRATIC THEORY

1. By *agency* I mean simply capacities to act. For more on this, see Chapter 3.

2. In Hegel's and Marx's writings there are at least three German words that are of importance here: *Entfremdung, Entäusserung,* and *Vergegenständlichung.* Some scholars prefer to translate the first as "estrangement" and only the second as "alienation." But I generally use the term *alienation* regardless of which of the first two German words was employed by Marx or Hegel in a particular passage. The third, closely related term is properly translated as "objectification"—and I will say more about it later. Although my reading does not hinge crucially on the distinctions between the first two German terms, I do not wish to diminish their importance. For an introduction to the terminological and translation problems involved, see Milligan and Struik (1964, 57–60), Schacht's (1970) chapter on "The Linguistic and Intellectual Background," and Inwood's article on "Alienation and Estrangement" (1992, 35–38).

3. This unique interweaving of individual, social, and metaphysical levels in a single vision, one that is practical and active in one aspect and spiritual and reflective in another, makes possible quite disparate interpretations of Hegelian alienation. Hegel's communitarian reader, Charles Taylor, writes that "alienation arises when the goals, norms or ends which define the common practices or institutions [of society] begin to seem irrelevant or even monstrous" (1979, 90). Richard Schacht suggests that Hegel used the term to signify both "a separation or discordant relation" and a person's "surrender or sacrifice of particularity and willfulness" (1970, 34). Michael Inwood offers a quite abstract definition: "the stage of disunion which emerges from a simple unity and is subsequently reconciled in a higher, differentiated unity" (1992, 35). In Richard Norman's view, alienation existed for Hegel when individuals experience "the social world"—which is "their own creation"—as "something alien and hostile" (1976, 87–88).

4. Relatively early in the *Phenomenology of Spirit,* Hegel presents alienation largely as an individual matter—as a withdrawn epistemological attitude, an

218

extreme form of isolation in which consciousness does not recognize other like beings, and as a purely contemplative posture, detaching an individual from productive work. His later discussion of the "Unhappy Consciousness" (Hegel 1977, 126–138) illustrates the varied pathologies of an individual self-consciousness that projects too many of its own powers onto priests and a misconceived God, resulting in alienation from its own "faculties and powers," "will," "freedom of decision," and "responsibility." But Hegel's discussion of the concept becomes most relevant for political theory in the later sections of the *Phenomenology* in which he deals not just with the attitudes of an individual consciousness but with different societies and their characteristic problems (C. Taylor 1975, 161, 167, 171; Hegel 1977, 265). Here, in Hegel's view, we confront alienation fully.

5. I take up these and related problems in the conclusion of this chapter, as well as in Chapter 3, in the section titled "A Typology of Alienation Theories."

6. During his time studying in Tübingen (1788–1793) and tutoring in Bern (1793–1796), Hegel demonstrated broad sympathy for the revolution—although not for its Jacobin phase (Avineri 1972, 3, 7–9). Alexandre Kojeve argues that Hegel wrote the *Phenomenology* in an attempt to come to grips with Napoleon's approaching armies and with the expansion of a universalistic French state, which the armies represented for him (1969, 44).

7. Charles Taylor agrees that, despite the fourteen years between the publication of the *Phenomenology* and the *Philosophy of Right*, the emergent (if not fully developed) social world to which Hegel refers at the end of the discussion of the Terror "is the state structure which Hegel delineates for us in the PR" (1979, 121).

8. The passage seems to refer to "The Sorcerer's Apprentice," by Goethe, whom Marx named as one of his favorite poets.

9. Marx's *Economic and Philosophic Manuscripts,* which contain his most sustained discussion of alienation, remained unpublished for eighty-eight years. And although Herbert Marcuse wrote an influential review of the manuscripts much earlier, they were widely discussed in the English-speaking world only after Erich Fromm released *Marx's Concept of Man* in 1961.

10. Although it is fair to describe the main current of Fromm's argument in social-psychological terms, Fromm sometimes describes alienation in social-structural terms. On the distinction between what I term "psychological" alienation theories versus theories of "alienation as the loss of common agencies," see the conclusion of this chapter and Chapter 3, the section titled "A Typology of Alienation Theories."

11. In this, he draws on Rueschemeyer, Stephens, and Stephens (1992).

12. Carver (1998, 119–145) uses the *Demands,* with other evidence, to portray Marx as a fairly straightforward constitutional democrat. In this sense, he may be positioning himself, with Nimtz, as an interpreter of Marxian democracy without alienation.

13. Alan Gilbert's interpretation (1981; 1991) also implies that the chief value of democracy for Marx is that it sets the stage for socialism. But his view and Nimtz's differ, in that Nimtz identifies democracy mainly with working-class self-organization, while Gilbert stresses democratic revolution as characteristically bourgeois revolution.

14. Marx criticizes Feuerbach for focusing on "the object" or on "contemplation," to the detriment of "sensuous human activity, practice" ([1845] 2000, 171). He contends that Feuerbach undervalues agency, emphasizing only that "circumstances" change "men" but not that circumstances are changed by men *(von den Menschen)* or by human action (172). He argues as well that Feuerbach forgets that philosophical reflection cannot provide a view from nowhere, but can only be a reflection on action, soon to be tested in continued action. So he adopts the pragmatic position that "man must prove the truth . . . of his thinking in practice" (171).

15. Marx does not argue, as some people think, that changes in the mode of production determine the course of political and social events. But he does say that it is humans' entire "social being" that "determines their consciousness," not their "consciousness" that "determines their being" ([1859] 2000, 425).

16. For some, Marx's claim that many moral "judgments" amount to little more than a social system being assessed by its own self-generated standards might seem to rule out the possibility of ethical reasoning entirely. And it is quite clear that Marx often casts a very skeptical eye, for example, on claims about justice. But most participants in the extensive debate about Marx and justice agree that Marx recurrently makes critical ethical judgments. Much of the debate concerns whether, in order to support such judgments, Marx distinguishes justice claims, in particular, from other sorts of ethical claims (Wood 1980) or follows some other procedure. What almost everyone agrees is that Marx is comfortable with a variety of different ethically charged concepts—especially critical ones, such as exploitation, misery, powerlessness, servitude, lack of human fulfillment—even though he refuses to provide fully elaborated, supposedly pure ideals of nonexploitation, felicity, and so on. His critical ethical judgments do their work in the indefinite foreground rather than in a faraway ideal that is to be compared to reality. This does not mean, of course, that Marx provides a clear and sufficient justification for this approach. But we can reasonably look for the ways it shapes his conception of democracy. For a lucid first overview of the debate about Marx and justice, Norman Geras's essays (1985; 1992) in *New Left Review* serve admirably. A notable collection devoted to the subject is Cohen, Nagel, and Scanlon (1980).

17. Beginning with Bertell Ollman's (1971) treatment.

18. Marx's critique of Hegelian constitutional monarchy partakes, in a sense, of the same form as Hegel's own evocative passages on the "Unhappy Consciousness" where he describes a state of mind that projects its own faculties, capacities, and qualities as aspects of a distant God. "Just as it is not religion that creates man, but man who creates religion," Marx writes, "so it is not the constitution that creates the people but the people which creates the constitution" ([1843] 1967, 30).

19. As Thomas explains, "This separation signified the disjuncture of citizenship in the modern state, a hollow, formal mode of membership, from the life of the individual in civil society, a life which is irreducibly real, immediate, and rent with divisions" (1994, 27).

20. "The Eighteenth Brumaire" renews Marx's analysis in "On the Jewish Question" of the bifurcation of the modern person into the self-interested,

antagonistic economic agent, on the one hand, and the participant in an unreal, distant realm of notionally equal citizens pursuing the good of society, on the other. Under the monarchies that governed from the defeat of Napoleon until 1848, Marx writes, the state bureaucracy was little more than an instrument of the bourgeoisie, enforcing, through law and policy, the private, competitive, capital-dominated character of the economy, even while it posed as an impartial guardian of the public. In such a situation, "every common interest" of real human beings, Marx argues, "was detached from society and counterposed to it as a higher, general interest, torn away from the independently generated activity of individuals within society and made into an object of governmental administration" ([1852] 1996, 115–116). This alienation of the state and the democratic deficiencies it entailed were only intensified with the rise to power of Louis Napoleon Bonaparte, the nephew of the French emperor. Marx also continues to premise his political theorizing on an analysis of the problematics of action—on agency, constraint, self-defeat, and irony. This is clear from the often quoted opening passage in which Marx describes historical events recurring, "the first time as high tragedy, the second time as low farce" (31). For he adds: "Men make their own history, but they do not make it just as they please in circumstances they choose for themselves; rather they make it in present circumstances, given and inherited" (32). Marx presents this reminder about the "given and inherited circumstances" of action as a prelude to a description of how political figures model themselves on historic precursors, but it could be taken, with justice, as an underlying theme of the whole pamphlet.

21. Or as he puts it memorably, "The independence of the executive comes through clearly when its head no longer needs ingenuity, its army no longer needs glory, and its bureaucracy no longer needs moral authority in order to justify itself" ([1852] 1996, 116).

22. Thomas rightly points out that these are "not treated" by Marx "as categorical postulates, but as open-ended questions" (1994, 92–93).

23. This historical context and purpose could explain, if not mitigate, a weakness of "The Eighteenth Brumaire" noted by Gilbert (1991, 189–190): Marx's failure to discuss the importance of rule of law and judicial independence. Of course, Marx does not stress these issues in *The Civil War,* either, probably in part because he is not describing there an ideal democracy but the democratic practices adopted by the Commune to overcome state alienation.

24. On this near consensus, see, for example Kosnoski (2005a, 654) and Stears (2010, 58).

25. See Knight and Johnson (1994, 277; 1996).

26. "Experience" is perhaps the most important example of Dewey's commitment to dissolving dualisms, to denying the validity, the reality of the sharp analytical distinctions that philosophy often takes for granted.

27. Intelligence is, inter alia, Dewey's alternative to the more familiar concept of reason.

28. See MacGilvray (1999) and Westbrook (1991, 359–360).

29. On this, see Westbrook (1991, 406–412, 471–473) and Putnam and Putnam (1989).

30. Democracy, Dewey writes, is "radical because it requires great change in social institutions" ([1937] 1987, 299).

31. Other scholars who interpret *The Public and Its Problems* in the context of Dewey's theory of experience include Kosnoski (2005b), MacGilvray (1999), and to an extent, Ryan (1995, 217–218).

32. There is a great deal written about *The Public and Its Problems* as a response to Lippmann. For a sampling, see MacGilvray (1999, 554–560), Ryan (1995, 216–220), Stears (2010, 65–68, 88–92), and Westbrook (1991, 293–318).

33. He may also mean to refer to what economists term "externalities" or what Ryan terms "spillovers" (1995, 218): costs or benefits of a voluntary exchange between two parties to others who are not immediately involved. The classic example of an externality is industrial pollution, which imposes costs on those who neither buy nor sell the good whose production causes the pollution. But Dewey's understanding of indirect, unintended consequences goes beyond this. Partly this is because he does not share the view of economic man that underlies economists' accounts of "externalities," a view he sees as intimately related to a denigration of public interests.

34. By contrast, the "government" is just agencies or officials (Dewey [1927] 1993, 27).

35. My primary interest is in the phenomenon of potential publics losing control of the consequences of their own shared activities, a phenomenon Dewey describes in *The Public and Its Problems*. But Dewey's discussion of industry points to a related affinity with some familiar arguments about alienation. In Marx's critique of labor under capitalism, two aspects of alienation are especially relevant to how workers experience production: alienation from the process of labor and alienation from species being. Industrial work, in Marx's view, is stultifying. It does not elicit creativity; indeed, it represses it. Fromm picks up on this critique in his analysis of hierarchical, standardized, Fordist labor ([1955] 1990, 125, 181–182). And Dewey reaches a similar conclusion, which underwrites, in part, his support for workplace democracy: "Subordination of the enterprises to pecuniary profit reacts to make the workers 'hands' only," he writes. "Their hearts and brains are not engaged. They execute plans which they do not form, and of whose meaning and intent they are ignorant—beyond the fact that these plans make a profit for others and secure a wage for themselves . . . [The] multitudes are excluded from occasion for the use of thought and emotion in their daily occupations" ([1929] 1999, 64–65).

36. Suggestively, just a page earlier, Kosnoski summarizes the main problematic of *Individualism Old and New* as "rationalization leading to alienation" (2005b, 197).

37. On Dewey's support of the labor movement, see especially Westbrook (1992).

38. See Norman (1976, 103).

39. If we take Dewey's portrayal of pioneer life mainly as a device for illustrating features of the Great Society, this particular utopian risk is diminished. Consider, also, some of Marx's comments about the primitive unity of labor and nature in *Pre-capitalist Economic Formations*.

40. Hence Schacht's criticism that Fromm seems to describe everything in capitalist society of which he disapproves as a problem of alienation (1970, ch. 4).

41. Beyond critically rethinking and extending Marx's theory of alienation, per se, it is also crucial to investigate further the problem of the alienated state that so interests him. I take up this subject in Chapter 5. But I do not attempt to found the discussion there exclusively or directly on Marx's own reflections on the state, as elucidated in this chapter. Marx is surely in the background in my examination of state alienation and its many forms. But my own discussion responds to more recent debates about the state and democracy, and it explores aspects of state power not taken up at any length by Marx, especially questions concerning the welfare state's role in structuring relations of gender and race.

42. On the limits of Dewey's understanding of structure, see Hildreth (2012).

3. A CONTEMPORARY THEORY OF ALIENATION

1. Ramos's compelling story is told in Kiel (2012).

2. The example is from Kiel (2012).

3. There are many good accounts of the financial practices that precipitated the crisis, but see Posner (2009) and Stiglitz (2009).

4. By *agency*, I mean simply capacities to act, to intervene in the ongoing course of events. For many purposes, then, a theory of agency is also a theory of action, including a reckoning of the limits and frailties of action. The phrase "theory of agency" is often used, however, to indicate a particular sort of theory of agency or action, one holding that action depends upon the prior existence of fully formed a priori intentions as well as a fixed, fully formed subject. As my discussion of Dewey (see Chapter 2) already suggests, I do not hold such a view.

5. I argue elsewhere (Medearis 2001; Medearis 2009) that Schumpeter's dismissal of "classical" democratic theory is a crucial moment, but by no means the whole story, of his engagement with democracy.

6. These are outlined in Chapter 1.

7. It can be surprisingly difficult to pin down the meaning of *structure*. Giddens understands structure to mean "rules" and "resources," and distinguishes between structure, structural properties, and social systems (e.g., Giddens 1979, 66–69). More commonly, theorists such as Bhaskar (1998, 209, 211), Andrew (1992, 92), and Jeffrey Isaac (1987b, 56–63, 79–81) closely link structure to social relations or sets of social relations. Despite this difference, there is wide agreement, seemingly, about the sorts of objects to which *structure* refers: families, the capitalist economy, language, schools or the education system, and so on.

8. See Bhaskar (1998, 215).

9. Although it recognizes that science is a social activity that works necessarily with socially constructed concepts, the basic principle of critical realism, according to Bhaskar, is that "perception gives us access to things and experimental activity access to structures that exist independently of us" (1975, 9). It is based on "the

idea of a law-governed world independent of man" and the contention that such a view "is necessary to understand science" (26).

10. Critical realists such as Bhaskar have embraced versions of structuration, but they are not required to do so on the basis of critical realism's most basic assumptions.

11. I often use the term *social action* rather than just *action*. Social action, however, is not a specific type of action. To speak of "social" action or the social character of action is just to view action in relation to the shared social repertoires, understandings, and enabling capacities it draws on, and in light of the social relationships and forces it helps reproduce.

12. A similar respect for the accomplishments of quotidian *political* action colors my view of democracy, as I explain in Chapter 4.

13. I am referring here only to viewpoints or perspectives for viewing action and its consequences. Most individual acts are referable to widespread practices, and most both trigger events and reproduce social relations and structures.

14. Pierre Bourdieu sometimes uses the same term that I adopt for this second side of the structure-agency dialectic: "objectification" (1977, 72).

15. Bhaskar points out, quite similarly, that "people do not marry to reproduce the nuclear family or work to sustain the capitalist economy" but "it is nevertheless the unintended consequence (and inexorable result) of, as it is a necessary condition for, their activity" (1998, 215).

16. This is, of course, another face of the same economic structures that produced the financial crisis—not an entirely distinct set of economic structures.

17. For a similar critique of Pettit's failure to theorize "structural domination" see Gourevitch (2013). But Gourevitch's view of who reproduces dominating structures seems to differ from mine.

18. See also Tucker (1998, 6).

19. As I have emphasized, though, even for those who get the worst of them, dominating social conditions are not generally just imposed from without. Rather, they are reproduced by human social action, often including the very own actions of those who are themselves subject to these conditions. Indeed, those who experience domination, through their interactions with myriad others and their participation in shared practices, generally take at least some part, however unintended or constrained, in reproducing problematic institutions and forces.

20. I discuss this point in more depth in Chapter 5.

21. Archer also argues that Bhaskar is not really a structuration theorist— that he parts ways with structuration theory with respect to the issues she identifies.

22. The concept of economic equilibrium generally does regard order as the product of present forces in balance.

23. The point is not really changed by recognizing, correctly, that many demographic distinctions are socially produced, conventional.

24. I don't mean, of course, that this should make us in any sense optimistic about agency.

25. In truth, this is not news to Giddens. Asked whether his understanding of the duality of structure precludes his recognizing that unemployment appears to

actors as a powerful external force, he replied: "I wouldn't dispute that at all—it certainly is true for an individual facing the labour market. But I don't think that in any way compromises the logic of the relation between agency and structure. Agency doesn't mean that the world is plastic to the will of the individual" (Giddens and Pierson 1998, 80).

26. Bourdieu does not use the term *domination* exactly as I do. Some of his argument could apply as well to other power relations, such as what I call oppression and exploitation.

27. I suppose this could then be interpreted to mean that while the personal dimension does not explain the relationship itself, the personal dimension does explain political conflict.

28. Schaff distinguishes "subjective" alienation from "objective" alienation (1980, 11, 57–58). But the contrast between "subjective" and "objective" is problematic, since it could be taken to imply that there is no subjective or interpretive dimension to alienated social structures or to the loss of control of common agency.

29. For sober appreciations of the virtues of markets by political thinkers with an acute sensitivity to markets' limits, see Kuttner (1996, 11–16) and Satz (2010, 3, 15–26).

30. This situation is called Pareto efficiency. It describes a kind of stable, equilibrium state, because no trades that would make any two traders better off are possible. But despite this special quality, Rawls rightly points out (1999b, 62) that Pareto efficiency has no positive ethical significance, since any distribution, from radical inequality to perfect equality, could be Pareto efficient.

31. But Schumpeter, the most renowned theorist of innovation, did not see it as a result of ordinary market equilibrium mechanisms or even of the profit motive. See Schumpeter ([1942] 1976, 81–110) and Medearis (2009, 40–52).

32. The seminal analysis of this historical process is that of Karl Polanyi ([1944] 2001).

33. In the early modern period, as these twin processes of marketization and industrialization were getting under way, political economists were developing theories of markets as systems whose order—and disorder—were produced unintentionally by the actions of many people. Both the unplanned order and the large-scale dislocation of markets must have seemed to them to be something profoundly new. And this suggests the possibility of an interesting historical conjunction, the possibility that markets are more than an *example* of alienated social forces and structures. The modern expansion of markets—along with awareness of their properties—may have prompted some of the first modern reflection on alienation itself. Lukács in fact suggests that Hegel's mature theory of alienation emerged in part under the influence of his study of the writings of James Steuart and Adam Smith (1976, 171–172, 319–333). He points intriguingly to "Hegel's conviction that the world of economics which dominates man and which utterly controls the life of the individual, is nevertheless the product of man himself" (333).

34. Actually, more than one sort of market is involved here. In addition to consumer product markets, there are labor markets that are of interest, especially

in places like Haiti, Bangladesh, and China. And there are connections between these types of markets.

35. For a comprehensive and illuminating portrait of Walmart, the company that virtually invented the techniques that make this hyperefficient global manufacturing possible, see Lichtenstein (2009).

36. For a superb exploration of exactly how firms are not spot labor markets, see Kuttner (1996, 68–109).

37. Marx also analyzes money, significantly, as "the alienated ability of mankind" ([1844] 1964, 168). There are intimations of both a psychological and an active conception of alienation here: the idea that people wrongly come to think of money as possessing qualities that in fact only human beings have and the idea that human activities are objectified in money, that money represents the escape and troubling return of common action. In either case, money is seen as a dominating power, whether mental or social.

38. However, I do think the commodification of labor—what it means to make good on the sale of labor—does create the potential for serious problems of oppression and exploitation.

39. Actually one could argue that both Sandel and Satz focus on identifying "noxious" markets. This is Satz's term, but one meaning of *noxious*—"morally harmful, corrupting"—captures Sandel's argument perfectly. This means that both Sandel and Satz are focused on identifying particular goods or services whose purchase and sale is characteristically troubling. Although their examples, judgments, and criteria are different, both Sandel and Satz distinguish the parts of their respective terrains by identifying goods and services whose buying and selling seem especially worrying, from ghostwritten wedding toasts (Sandel 2012, 97–98) to women's reproductive labor (Satz 2010, 115–134).

40. Of course, it is always possible to define a particular product partly according to who sells it, who buys it, how it is bought, and so on. For example, one could say that the problems behind the financial crisis included selling mortgages to particular unqualified borrowers and under certain conditions—namely, in such a way that mortgage investors lacked information about those borrowers. Alternatively, though, one could, in effect, collapse those conditions into one's definition of the product itself and say the problem was a particular kind of product, subprime mortgages.

41. For differing but complementary explorations of these assumptions, their weaknesses, and their steady undermining, see Kuttner (1996, 16–23) and Stiglitz (2009, 239–256).

42. One of the constraints, of course, involves the pressures placed on employers by the demands of Western corporations and consumers. So these issues are by no means separate.

43. I return to this question in Chapter 5.

44. I have stressed a number of times that to talk about markets is, in a sense that must not be forgotten, an abstraction. Markets and market behavior are intrinsically bound up with states and corporations in ways I have already indicated. States, markets, and corporations are pervasive and characteristically modern institutions that are always potentially alienated. But one could just as

well consider relations of race and gender as alienated social structures. And like "markets," "race" and "gender" are in truth also abstractions in the sense that these social relations exist nowhere by themselves, but are always thoroughly entwined with other relations and structures. In early America, for instance, racial and gender hierarchies and their reproduction were inextricably linked, notably in miscegenation laws (Pateman 2007). When I turn in Chapter 5 to the most elaborated discussion of alienation and democracy, I shall endeavor to do justice to the interrelations between state, market, race, class, and gender. In fact, the very point of the discussion will be to show how we can enrich the literature on "theories of the state"—and its lessons for democratic theory—by bringing into the story the way states shape not just class and markets but also race and gender.

4. OPPOSITIONAL DEMOCRACY

1. For nuanced discussions of the evidence for and against popular war enthusiasm, see Gregory (2004), Neiberg (2004), and Strachan (2001), upon which I rely here.

2. The following account of the uprising at Kiel and the subsequent council movement is drawn from Craig (1978), Kolb (1988), and Tobin (1983).

3. For more on the way these figures interpreted and misinterpreted the council movement, see Medearis (2004).

4. It should be clear, then, that I am persuaded by a line of argument dating at least to Gerald MacCallum (1967) that criticizes Isaiah Berlin's (1969) classic distinction between negative and positive freedom, and that holds that freedoms are all complex, requiring both that particular agents be free from certain constraints and that they possess certain capacities to act.

5. For a fuller discussion of this passage, see Chapter 2.

6. This is the subject of Chapter 5.

7. See also Shapiro (2010, 11).

8. One crucial contrast is that Shapiro means something different by "domination," namely "the illegitimate exercise of power" (2003, 4). Domination, for me, refers more broadly to any profoundly disproportionate relation or comparison of power, a dwarfing of some people's capacities to act, an imposition of necessities. Thus, crucially, it is possible to be dominated, in my sense, not just by other people or groups but also by social forces and structures many people reproduce. Some of the most important examples, discussed in Chapters 3 and 5 and in the epilogue, are the deep overshadowing of agency that is always potential in markets, welfare states, and security-state institutions, even when these are found in representative settings. In addition, emphasizing the struggle against alienation—not just domination—means emphasizing that it is common action that reproduces dominating structures. So the ongoing aim of democratic action is not only to resist oppressors (though this is frequently involved) but also to regain collective control of runaway social forms we collectively sustain.

9. In advancing his later elite theory, Schumpeter draws so stark a contrast between elite and mass agency that it is not clear to me he really thinks of electoral competition as limiting the power of elites vis-à-vis ordinary citizens.

10. My approach differs not in discounting electoral activities but in emphasizing a wider set of democratic practices, including some most associated with movements, and having possibly a more skeptical view of whether the representative democratic state can resist alienation. I discuss the first of these issues later in this chapter and the second in Chapter 5.

11. For two rather different versions of such a claim, see Thomas (1994) and Putnam (2000).

12. This includes, for example, Nancy Fraser's work expanding and "rethinking" the idea of the "public sphere," which she defines precisely as the "theater in modern societies in which political participation is enacted through the medium of talk," "hence an institutionalized arena of discursive interaction" (1990, 57). Fraser deftly challenges the idea that there can be a single public, positing the idea of "counterpublics," which function something like movements. But she does this while adopting the basic idea of a "public sphere," a realm of talk, and characterizing it as "indispensable," consequently portraying the role of "counterpublics" in primarily communicative terms. Counterpublics, in her view, contest "the exclusionary norms of the bourgeois public" (61).

13. For a longer discussion, see Medearis (2005).

14. The latter sort of strategy can be quite institutionalized, as when a union convinces a labor relations agency to enter the fray and prevent or redress unfair labor practices. But, even before such institutional channels exist, the very creation of such procedures may come about through a similar process of forcing the state to intervene in widespread conflict. This is essentially the story of how the labor movement contributed to the passage of the National Labor Relations Act in 1935.

15. Roughly speaking, these are all examples or aspects of what social movement scholars sometimes call "mobilizing structures."

16. For Gandhi, of course, this was not only a point about the social world and how it is reproduced, but also about personal responsibility for oppression and therefore about why violent means were to be shunned: "Every citizen therefore renders himself responsible for every act of his Government" (1996, 58).

17. For the most part, in Dovi's treatment, the marginalizing would be the work of citizens voting against outright advocates of racial or ethnic domination and even against those who have benefitted from oppression. One idea here is much like mine: diminishing entrenched power can be a valuable democratic practice. There is also a family likeness to the way we propose to put principled limits on marginalization or strategies to reduce others' power. For Dovi, marginalization is justified when it is directed at "those who oppress" and "those whose privileged status sustains oppression" (2009, 1182). I argue, similarly, that democratic attempts to undermine others' power are justified when they are reasonably aimed at diminishing alienation, domination, oppression, and exploitation, and the structures that enable them. There are some significant contrasts with my oppositional argument, though. Dovi is largely concerned with racial, ethnic, and gender oppression, but my oppositional approach would be just as applicable to resisting the power of corporations and runaway states. Dovi also focuses on representative institutions and principles that citizens should apply, generally in the course of

voting. I would argue that such a manner of voting is just one example of a more varied oppositional-democratic practice that movements, civic groups, and politicians, as well as voters, can adopt. Indeed, it seems unlikely to me that voters will apply any such principle of electoral exclusion in the absence of a broader movement whose attempts to curb illegitimate power are far more wide-ranging.

18. Inescapable in the sense of *impossible to will away* if not in the sense of *fated* or *ubiquitous*.

19. See also Boyte (2011).

20. I shall revisit this issue in discussing participatory democracy below.

21. Certainly this is the case if we understand movements, loosely, as large numbers of people engaged in activities in furtherance of some common political or social goals. I prefer a somewhat narrower definition: collective challenges mounted by relatively weak or excluded people to dominant, groups, ranks, and structures in society. According to this definition, it is possible to question whether, for example, the Tea Party is a movement since, self-image aside, it is composed, demographically, of relatively privileged people, draws considerable support from business elites, and is ideologically focused on defending its members' ground from groups it sees both as unworthy and growing in strength (Williamson, Skocpol, and Coggins 2011). But even according to my preferred definition, it is not hard to identify movements by which relatively weak people have challenged dominant groups through violence, disqualifying themselves from earning the "democratic" label.

22. Some of the most widely cited contributions to the participatory literature include Hayden ([1962] 2005), Pateman (1970), Macpherson (1977), and Barber (1984). Depending on one's view of participatory theory, it is possible to find precedents in the work of Jean-Jacques Rousseau, John Stuart Mill, G. D. H. Cole, and John Dewey.

23. Pateman here quotes Angus Campbell, Gerald Gurin, and Warren E. Miller.

24. For a critical discussion of the argument by many deliberative theorists that participatory democracy fails to credit social complexity, see Hauptmann (2001).

25. See Benhabib (1997), Bohman (1996, 12), Cohen and Arato (1992, 19, 7), and Warren (1996, 242).

26. I shall have more to say about this in the particular context of the welfare state in Chapter 5.

27. For general information about participatory budgeting in Porto Alegre, I draw on Abers (1998), Baiocchi (2005), Baiocchi (2006), Hilmer (2010), and Pateman (2012).

28. Steven Bilakovics (2012, ch. 4) refers to Sheldon Wolin as an agonistic democratic, but since he does not derive his approach from this view of the subject and identity, I prefer to use the phrase *fugitive democracy* to designate his work.

29. For a Deweyan cousin of such a claim, especially concerning reflexive agency, see Chapters 2 and 3.

30. Butler (1990), focusing especially on gender, argues that all identity is performance, so that any idea of distinguishing what is real and what is imitation is

inappropriate when it comes to matters of identity. Honig emphasizes more strongly the contingencies left out of any imposition of a fixed identity. "The self," she contends, is a "creature that is always agonistically engaged and implicated with established identities and subjectivities that never quite succeed in expressing it without remainder" (1993, 9). William E. Connolly critiques what he sees as a politics of "totalistic identities engaged in implacable struggles against those differences that threaten their hegemony or exclusivity" (1995, xxi), a politics in which human plurality is underappreciated and at worst is repressed or criminalized.

31. Joseph Schwartz has criticized contemporary political theory for an "inordinate focus upon epistemological questions of 'identity' at the expense of analyses of the political, ideological, and economic structures that constrain individual and group agency" (2009, ix).

32. See also Hilmer (2010).

33. See also Mouffe (1993, 68). Mouffe notes (2000, 21–22) that some of this analysis dates back many years to *Hegemony and Socialist Strategy,* which she coathored with Ernesto Laclau ([1985] 1993). The guiding thread of that book was a critique of Marxist theorists who treated economics as an autonomous, determining ground for politics, while also accepting that the working class was able to claim that the whole of capitalist society could be understood from their position. This is precisely the sort of mistaken view of one's own identity that Mouffe is concerned to critique in later work. *Hegemony* also contains a critique of certain understandings of the subject. According to Laclau and Mouffe, the subject should be seen not as a unified whole but as an ensemble of subject positions (115).

34. To be sure, the state interprets racial identity—or, perhaps, authorizes certain racial identities. It does this, for example, in laws that define race and in court cases in which parties claim one racial identity or another.

35. Since race is not a given, this could be expressed differently: states contribute to determining the structure of race as a social relation and the content of race as an experience.

5. CONTESTING THE WELFARE STATE

1. See also Dryzek (2000, ch. 5).

2. That is, they tended to portray "seizing" and "breaking" the state as the main choices, even though it is not the case that each critical theorist of the state straightforwardly adopted one of these strategies. See Barrow (1993, 69), Miliband (1977, 188), Offe (1984), Poulantzas (1969, 78), Poulantzas (1978, 19, 23), and Thomas (1994, 16–17).

3. Of course, a similar stratification of citizenship, civil, political, and social, is clearly also in question when the state exercises its powers over migration and when it determines what kinds of families and relationships it will recognize and endow with rights. But the literatures explicitly linking U.S. welfare state development over time to gender and to race are especially well developed. And given the emphasis on critical junctures in this history, especially the New Deal and civil rights era, in which the southern system of racial caste loomed large, these

literatures emphasize stratification between whites and African Americans, with much less emphasis on Latinos or Asian Americans.

4. I borrow here from Dryzek and Dunleavy (2009, 2–3). The consequence of adopting a rather accommodating definition of the state like this one is to treat controversy over the state as debate about the state powers and characteristics and when and how these are exercised, rather than one about the definition of states, per se.

5. For a longer discussion, see Dryzek and Dunleavy (2009, xi).

6. Throughout this chapter, I use the term *civil society* in something closer to a Hegelian sense than the idealistic sense of many contemporary civil society enthusiasts. I use it to mean an actual network of social relations and movements, ones not normally identified as being part of the state but that exist in mutual relation with it. The scope of what is encompassed by the term, then, is not defined by aspiration. In particular, civil society, according to this conception, is not simply a realm of free, uncoerced discourse and voluntarism, although civil society may include such practices. Similarly, the scope of the term, as I understand it, includes markets, corporations, and relations of inequality, but is not limited to these, either. In short, the characteristics of civil society and its ethical value may vary and should be determined not by definition but by critical investigation.

7. Relatedly, when I refer to *class* here I adopt a very commodious conception. I mean only to refer broadly to social relations characterized by economic inequality or by differential economic status, e.g., in labor and employment or market power. Almost every treatment of the welfare state recognizes that it structures and responds to economic inequality, labor markets, and relations of employment. So when speaking of *class* I do not mean a single opposition between capitalists and working class. In addition to acknowledging many caveats about the frequent "failure" of workers to recognize themselves as a class, and the tendency of late capitalism to produce rather complex class distinctions, I am persuaded by this: depending on the problem at hand, it may be useful to conceptualize economic relations of inequality in different ways—bankers versus borrowers, consumers versus corporations, the 99 percent versus the 1 percent, or workers versus bosses and owners.

8. See Goldfield (1989). And for an alternative view, see Skocpol and Finegold (1990).

9. This change in the law was not a complete or a final democratic triumph, though. Although it abolished a remnant of feudalism, it did not mark the end of the ability of courts to govern the workplace. Moreover, the NLRA embodied racist elements, a point to which I shall return. See Frymer (2008).

10. On some complexities of decommodification, see the section on "Race, Gender, and the State" below.

11. There are recent, well-publicized instances of each of these.

12. See Barrow (1993), Carnoy (1984), Isaac (1987b), and Jessop (1982).

13. For one influential typology, see Esping-Andersen (1990).

14. A full explanation of the end of Reconstruction involves not just the election-year political calculations often cited, but also factors quite consistent with traditional critical theories of the state. It was very much in the interest of

Northern industrialists to end the disruption to Southern agriculture caused by Reconstruction and so guarantee a steady supply of cotton for their mills and the export market (McAdam 1982, 66–67). This of course does not justify the conclusion that the racial dimensions to this episode are somehow reducible to class and economic factors.

15. Theories of the social construction of race and gender are now, of course, many and various. But I take the useful term *state "race-making"* from Lieberman (2005). Arguably, the powers in question are rooted in long-recognized capacities of states—indeed, the historical ambitions of state and nation builders. As far back as 1648, the Treaty of Westphalia recognized the right of princes to determine the religious identity of their subjects. Later, in the era of democratic and national revolution, "state interests" came to depend on the loyalty and participation of the "ordinary citizen," and this placed the "citizen's feelings" toward the whole polity—in this case, the constructed nation—"at the top of the political agenda" (Hobsbawm 1990, 83). This points toward questions of producing solidarity: How did states and state builders construct nationality and identity in the nineteenth and twentieth centuries? How did it fit people—shape them—to conform to national and ethnic categories? They did so, it turns out, with many of the most basic tools available to those with access to state power: through education, including the teaching of language and history; through cultural institutions such as museums; through conscription and national military service; and even through the simple designation of persons to convenient racial categories and of places and map borders according to national ambitions (B. Anderson 2006, 163–185; Dryzek and Dunleavy 2009, 191; Weber 1976, 195–374).

16. Critical theorists of the state as different, otherwise, as Miliband (1969), Offe (1984), and Poulantzas (1984) advanced parallel arguments that the state was capable—was needed, in fact—to produce class, or more particularly to guarantee that labor was available as a commodity and to ensure the conditions under which the majority of people would have to sell their labor to survive.

17. See Esping-Andersen (1990, 58), Borchorst (1994, 34), and Palier (2010, 604).

18. To take one example of the effects, while unemployment rates among African Americans and whites were the same in 1930, by 1965 the rate among African Americans was twice as high (Katznelson 2005, 14–15).

19. For a helpful summary of the limits of functional explanation, see Little (1991, 91–102).

20. This is not the same as saying that they attempted to explain these state properties in terms of a simple bourgeoisie versus proletariat dynamic. That would certainly not be true of a slew of Marxist writings, beginning with Marx's own "Eighteenth Brumaire" ([1852] 1996). See Barrow (1993, 53).

21. Of course, this is not quite accurate, because these seemingly atavistic institutions are part of the existing power structure. And far from being alien to present practices, they can continue in force only so long as present action reproduces them.

22. "Among whites, those expressing the highest degree of concern about crime also tend to oppose racial reform, and their punitive attitudes toward

crime are largely unrelated to their likelihood" of being crime victims (Alexander 2012, 54).

23. See Medearis (2008).

24. As indicated above, I think it is better to adopt an open-ended understanding of civil society as a network of social relations whose character has to be investigated, as opposed to defining civil society in such a way that positive claims about it simply become true by definition.

25. Fraser actually challenges the very sharp separation between state and civil society posited originally by Habermas, but mainly in order to defend the idea of "strong publics" that do not limit themselves to influencing the state (1990, 75–76). Her two main examples of "strong publics" are parliaments and self-managing civil society groups.

EPILOGUE

1. For example, see "Democracy Matters" (2004), "Must-Do List" (2007), and "Surveillance: A Threat to Democracy" (2013). Among democratic theorists, Ian Shapiro registers the prevalence of such critiques and notes that "many journalists, scholars and public intellectuals on both sides of the Atlantic are speaking out" on them (2007, xiv). Though her main concern is with the political effects of "neoliberalism," Wendy Brown also seems to have these issues in mind, for example, when she refers to the "ostentatious clear-cutting of democratic institutions" evident in the Patriot Act (2006, 692).

2. The abundance of information made available by people engaged in this mode of inquiry, along with the extent of discussion about it, points to issues of concern to deliberative theory. Interestingly, Gutmann and Thompson (2004, 1–2) argue that something approximating good deliberation took place in the lead-up to the Iraq war, although the deliberation was cut short before it had been exhausted and was marred by the casting of aspersions regarding others' motives. (For a deliberative critique of an exchange about the war's justification between Tony Blair and a British citizen, an account focused on "explicitness" in discourse, see Knops [2006]). I am inclined to agree that debate about the war involved enough of an exchange of reasons partially to meet deliberative standards. But this is yet another reason to question whether deliberative standards tell us all we need to know about democracy. The democratic deficiencies associated with the war simply cannot be reduced to mere discursive failures.

3. See "Poll Shows Complexity of Debate on Trade-Offs in Government Spying Programs" (2013).

4. The "security imperative," whatever it may be, precisely, is not something objectively fixed. State officials cannot know precisely what they need to do to accomplish the aims just mentioned, and their views of this—not to mention their views of what constitutes a danger to security—are inevitably ideologically conditioned.

5. On this subject, I have relied substantially on Miller (2009a), Miller (2009b), Miller and Smith (2009), Singer (2008), and Stillman (2011).

Abers, Rebecca. 1998. "From Clientelism to Cooperation: Local Government, Participatory Policy, and Civic Organizing in Porto Alegre, Brazil." *Politics and Society* 26, no. 4 (December): 511–537.

Ackerman, Bruce, and James Fishkin. 2004. *Deliberation Day.* New Haven, CT: Yale University Press.

Alexander, Michelle. 2012. *The New Jim Crow: Mass Incarceration in the Age of Colorblindness.* Rev. ed. New York: New Press.

Anderson, Benedict. 2006. *Imagined Communities: Reflections on the Origin and Spread of Nationalism.* Rev. ed. London: Verso.

Anderson, M. T. 2013. "Clothed in Misery." *New York Times,* April 29. http://www.nytimes.com/2013/04/30/opinion/bangladeshs-are-only-the-latest-in-textile-factory-disasters.html?pagewanted=all. Accessed June 13, 2013.

Archer, Margaret. 1998. "Realism and Morphogenesis." In *Critical Realism: Essential Readings,* ed. M. Archer, R. Bhaskar, A. Collier, T. Lawson, and A. Norrie, 356–382. London: Routledge.

Arendt, Hannah. 1963. *On Revolution.* New York: Viking.

Avineri, Shlomo. 1972. *Hegel's Theory of the Modern State.* Cambridge: Cambridge University Press.

Bachrach, Peter, and Morton S. Baratz. 1970. *Power and Poverty: Theory and Practice.* New York: Oxford University Press.

Baiocchi, Gianpaolo. 2005. *Militants and Citizens: The Politics of Participatory Democracy in Porto Alegre.* Stanford, CA: Stanford University Press.

———. 2006. The Citizens of Porto Alegre: In Which Marco Borrows Bus Fare and Enters Politics. *Boston Review,* March/April. http://bostonreview.net/gianpaolo-baiocchi-the-citizens-of-porto-alegre. Accessed August 1, 2013.

Ball, Terrence. 1978. "Two Concepts of Coercion." *Theory and Society 5,* no. 1 (January): 97–112.

Barber, Benjamin. 1984. *Strong Democracy: Participatory Democracy for a New Age.* Berkeley: University of California Press.

Barrow, Clyde W. 1993. *Critical Theories of the State: Marxist, Neo-Marxist, Post-Marxist.* Madison: University of Wisconsin Press.

————. 2002. "The Miliband-Poulantzas Debate, an Intellectual History." In *Paradigm Lost: State Theory Reconsidered*, ed. S. Aronowitz and P. Bratsis, 3–52. Minneapolis: University of Minnesota Press.

Bauman, Zygmunt. 1989. "Hermeneutics and Modern Social Theory." In *Social Theory of Modern Societies: Anthony Giddens and His Critics*, ed. D. Held and J. B. Thompson, 34–55. Cambridge: Cambridge University Press.

Benhabib, Seyla. 1997. Review of *Between Facts and Norms*, by Jürgen Habermas. *American Political Science Review* 91, no. 3 (September): 725–726.

Berelson, Bernard, Paul F. Lazarsfeld, and William N. McPhee. 1954. *Voting: A Study of Opinion Formation in a Presidential Campaign*. Chicago: University of Chicago Press.

Berlin, Isaiah. 1969. "Two Concepts of Liberty." In *Four Essays on Liberty*, 118–172. Oxford: Oxford University Press.

Bernhardt, Annette, Ruth Milkman, Nik Theodore, Douglas Heckathorn, Mirabai Auer, James DeFilippis, Ana Luz Gonzalez, Victor Narro, Jason Perelshteyn, Diana Polson, and Michael Spiller. 2009. *Broken Laws, Unprotected Workers: Violations of Employment and Labor Laws in American Cities*. http://www.unprotectedworkers.org/index.php/broken_laws/index. Accessed March 13, 2014.

Bhaskar, Roy. 1975. *A Realist Theory of Science*. Leeds, U.K.: Leeds Books.

————. 1998. "Societies." In *Critical Realism: Essential Readings*, ed. M. Archer, R. Bhaskar, A. Collier, T. Lawson, and A. Norrie, 206–257. London: Routledge.

Bilakovics, Steven. 2012. *Democracy without Politics*. Cambridge, MA: Harvard University Press.

Block, Fred. 1977. "The Ruling Class Does Not Rule," *Socialist Revolution* 3, no. 7 (May–June): 6–28.

Bohman, James. 1996. *Public Deliberation: Pluralism, Complexity, and Democracy*. Cambridge, MA: MIT Press.

Bohman, James, and Henry S. Richardson. 2009. "Liberalism, Deliberative Democracy, and 'Reasons That All Can Accept.'" *Journal of Political Philosophy* 17, no. 3 (September): 253–274.

Borchorst, Annette. 1994. "Welfare State Regimes, Women's Interests, and the EC." In *Gendering Welfare States*, ed. D. Sainsbury, 26–44. London: Sage.

Bourdieu, Pierre. 1973. "The Three Forms of Theoretical Knowledge." *Social Science Information* 12, no. 1 (February): 53–80.

————. 1977. *Outline of a Theory of Practice*. Cambridge: Cambridge University Press.

————. 1979. "Symbolic Power." *Critique of Anthropology* 4, nos. 13–14 (Summer): 77–85.

Boyte, Harry C. 2004. *Everyday Politics: Reconnecting Citizens and Public Life*. Philadelphia: University of Pennsylvania Press.

————. 2011. "Constructive Politics as Public Work: Organizing the Literature." *Political Theory* 39, no. 5 (October): 630–660.

Brown, Wendy. 2006. "American Nightmare: Neoliberalism, Neoconservatism, and De-democratization." *Political Theory* 34, no. 6 (December): 690–714.

Burns, W. Haywood. 1998. "Law and Race in Early America." In *The Politics of the Law: A Progressive Critique,* ed. D. Kairys, 279–284. New York: Basic Books.

Bussemaker, Jet, and Kees van Kersbergen. 1994. "Gender and Welfare States: Some Theoretical Reflections." In *Gendering Welfare States,* ed. D. Sainsbury, 8–25. London: Sage.

Butler, Judith. 1990. *Gender Trouble: Feminism and the Subversion of Identity.* New York: Routledge.

Carnoy, Martin. 1984. *The State and Political Theory.* Princeton, NJ: Princeton University Press.

Carver, Terrell. 1998. *The Postmodern Marx.* University Park: Pennsylvania State University Press.

Coase, R. H. 1937. "The Nature of the Firm." *Economica* 4, no. 16 (November): 386–405.

Cohen, Jean L., and Andrew Arato. 1992. *Civil Society and Political Theory.* Cambridge, MA: MIT Press.

Cohen, Marshall, Thomas Nagel, and Thomas Scanlon, eds. 1980. *Marx, Justice and History.* Princeton, NJ: Princeton University Press.

Connolly, William E. 1995. *The Ethos of Pluralization.* Minneapolis: University of Minnesota Press.

Craig, Gordon A. 1978. *Germany, 1866–1945.* New York: Oxford University Press.

Crouch, Collin. 2011. *The Strange Non-death of Neoliberalism.* Cambridge: Polity Press.

Dahl, Robert A. 1958. "A Critique of the Ruling Elite Model." *American Political Science Review* 52 (June): 463–469.

———. 1985. *A Preface to Economic Democracy.* Berkeley: University of California Press.

Davidson, Adam. 2013. "Economic Recovery, Made in Bangladesh?" *New York Times,* May 14. http://www.nytimes.com/2013/05/19/magazine/economic -recovery-made-in-bangladesh.html?pagewanted=all. Accessed June 13, 2013.

"Democracy Matters." 2004. Editorial. *San Francisco Chronicle,* January 11. D4.

Dewey, John. [1908] 1993. "Intelligence and Morals." In *John Dewey: The Political Writings,* ed. D. Morris and I. Shapiro, 66–76. Indianapolis, IN: Hackett.

———. [1916] 1966. *Democracy and Education: An Introduction to the Philosophy of Education.* New York: Free Press.

———. [1917] 1993. "The Need for a Recovery of Philosophy." In *John Dewey: The Political Writings,* ed. D. Morris and I. Shapiro, 1–9. Indianapolis, IN: Hackett.

———. [1922] 1993. "Individuality, Equality, and Superiority." In *John Dewey: The Political Writings,* ed. D. Morris and I. Shapiro, 77–80. Indianapolis, IN: Hackett.

———. [1927] 1954. *The Public and Its Problems.* Athens, OH: Swallow.

———. [1929] 1958. *Experience and Nature.* New York: Dover.

———. [1929] 1999. *Individualism Old and New.* Amherst, NY: Prometheus Books.

———. [1934] 1980. *Art as Experience.* New York: Perigee Books.

———. [1935] 2000. *Liberalism and Social Action.* Amherst, NY: Prometheus Books.

———. [1935] 1993. "Liberty and Social Control." In *John Dewey: The Political Writings,* ed. D. Morris and I. Shapiro, 158–160. Indianapolis, IN: Hackett.

———. [1937] 1987. "Democracy Is Radical." In *The Later Works, 1925–1953.* Vol. 11, *1935–1937,* ed. J. Boydston, 296–299. Carbondale: Southern Illinois University Press.

———. [1938] 1993. "Means and Ends, Their Interdependence, and Leon Trotsky's Essay, 'Their Morals and Ours.'" In *John Dewey: The Political Writings,* ed. D. Morris and I. Shapiro, 230–233. Indianapolis, IN: Hackett.

———. [1939] 1993. "Creative Democracy—the Task Before Us." *John Dewey: The Political Writings,* ed. D. Morris and I. Shapiro, 240–245. Indianapolis, IN: Hackett.

———. [1939] 1989. *Freedom and Culture.* Amherst, NY: Prometheus Books.

Dietz, Mary G. 1994. "'The Slow Boring of Hard Boards': Methodical Thinking and the Work of Politics. *American Political Science Review* 88, no. 4 (December): 873–886.

Dovi, Suzanne. 2009. "In Praise of Exclusion." *Journal of Politics* 71, no. 3 (July): 1172–1186.

Dreier, Peter, Saqqib Bhatti, Rob Call, Alex Schwartz, and Gregory Squires. 2014. *Underwater America: How the So-Called Housing "Recovery" Is Bypassing Many Communities.* Berkeley, CA: Haas Institute.

Dryzek, John. 2000. *Deliberative Democracy and Beyond: Liberals, Critics, Contestations.* Oxford: Oxford University Press.

Dryzek, John, and Patrick Dunleavy. 2009. *Theories of the Democratic State.* New York: Palgrave Macmillan.

Duhigg, Charles, and David Barboza. 2012. "In China, Human Costs Are Built into an iPad." *New York Times,* January 25. http://www.nytimes.com/2012/01/26/business/ieconomy-apples-ipad-and-the-human-costs-for-workers-in-china.html?pagewanted=all. Accessed June 13, 2013.

Eliel, Carol S. 1989. *The Apocalyptic Landscapes of Ludwig Meidner.* With a contribution by Eberhard Roter. Los Angeles: Museum Associates, Los Angeles County Museum of Art.

Esping-Andersen, Gøsta. 1985. *Politics against Markets: The Social Democratic Road to Power.* Princeton, NJ: Princeton University Press.

———. 1990. *The Three Worlds of Welfare Capitalism.* Princeton, NJ: Princeton University Press.

Fournier, Patrick, Henk van der Kolk, Kenneth Carty, Andre Blais, and Jonathan Rose. 2011. "Should We Let Citizens Decide?" In *When Citizens Decide: Lessons from Citizen Assemblies on Electoral Reform,* ed. P. Fournier, H. van der Kolk, K. Carty, et al., 145–157. Oxford: Oxford University Press.

Fraser, Nancy. 1990. "Rethinking the Public Sphere: A Contribution to the Critique of Actually Existing Democracy." *Social Text,* no. 25/26: 56–80.

———. 2007. "Transnationalizing the Public Sphere: On the Legitimacy and Efficacy of Public Opinion in a Post-Westphalian World." *Theory, Culture and Society* 24, no. 4 (September): 7–30.

Fraser, Nancy, and Linda Gordon. 1994. "A Genealogy of Dependency: Tracing a Keyword of the U.S. Welfare State." *Signs* 19, no. 21: 309–336.

Freeman, Jo. 1975. *The Politics of Women's Liberation: A Case Study of an Emerging Social Movement and Its Relation to the Policy Process.* New York: David McCay.

Fromm, Erich. [1941] 1996. *Escape from Freedom.* New York: Henry Holt.

———. [1955] 1990. *The Sane Society.* New York: Henry Holt.

———. 1961. *Marx's Concept of Man.* With a translation from Marx's *Economic and Philosophical Manuscripts,* trans. T. Bottomore. New York: Frederick Ungar.

Frymer, Paul. 2008. *Black and Blue: African Americans, the Labor Movement, and the Decline of the Democratic Party.* Princeton, NJ: Princeton University Press.

Fung, Archon. 2005. "Deliberation before the Revolution: Toward an Ethics of Deliberation in an Unjust World." *Political Theory* 33, no. 2 (June): 397–419.

Gabardi, Wayne. 2001. "Contemporary Models of Democracy." *Polity* 33, no. 4 (Summer): 547–568.

Gandhi, Mohandas K. 1996. *Selected Political Writings,* ed. D. Dalton. Indianapolis, IN: Hackett.

Geras, Norman. 1985. "The Controversy about Marx and Justice." *New Left Review,* no. I/150 (March–April): 47–85.

———. 1992. "The Controversy about Marx and Justice." *New Left Review,* no. I/195 (September–October): 37–69.

Geuss, Raymond. 2008. *Philosophy and Real Politics.* Princeton, NJ: Princeton University Press.

Giddens, Anthony. 1979. *Central Problems in Social Theory.* Berkeley: University of California Press.

———. 1989. "A Reply to My Critics." In *Social Theory of Modern Societies: Anthony Giddens and His Critics,* ed. D. Held and J. B. Thompson, 249–301. Cambridge: Cambridge University Press.

———. 1993. *New Rules of Sociological Method: A Positive Critique of Interpretive Methodologies.* 2nd ed. Stanford, CA: Stanford University Press.

Giddens, Anthony, and Christopher Pierson. 1998. *Conversations with Anthony Giddens: Making Sense of Modernity.* Stanford, CA: Stanford University Press.

Gilbert, Alan. 1981. *Marx's Politics: Communists and Citizens.* Oxford: Martin Robertson.

———. 1991. "Political Philosophy: Marx and Radical Democracy." In *The Cambridge Companion to Marx,* ed. T. Carver, 168–195. Cambridge: Cambridge University Press.

Gilens, Martin. 1999. *Why Americans Hate Welfare: Race, Media, and the Politics of Antipoverty Policy.* Chicago: University of Chicago Press.

Gittlin, Todd. 2012. *Occupy Nation: The Roots, the Spirit, and the Promise of Occupy Wall Street*. New York: HarperCollins.

Glanz, James, and Andrew W. Lehren. 2010. "Use of Contractors Added to War's Chaos in Iraq." *New York Times*, October 23. http://www.nytimes.com/2010/10/24/world/middleeast/24contractors. Accessed July 12, 2011.

Goldfield, Michael. 1989. "Worker Insurgency, Radical Organization, and New Deal Labor Legislation." *American Political Science Review* 83, no. 4 (December): 1257–1282.

Goodin, Robert E. 1988. *Reasons for Welfare: The Political Theory of the Welfare State*. Princeton, NJ: Princeton University Press.

Goodwyn, Lawrence. 1978. *The Populist Moment: A Short History of the Agrarian Revolt in America*. New York: Oxford University Press.

Gordon, Michael R. 2010. "Civilians to Take U.S. Lead as Military Leaves Iraq." *New York Times*, August 18. http://www.nytimes.com/2010/08/19/world/middleeast/19withdrawal.html?ref=privatemilitarycompanies. Accessed June 14, 2011.

Gourevitch, Alex. 2013. "Labor Republicanism and the Transformation of Work." *Political Theory* 41, no. 4 (August): 591–617.

Gregory, Adrian. 2004. "British 'War Enthusiasm' in 1914: A Reassessment." In *Evidence, History and the Great War: Historians and the Impact of 1914–18*, ed. G. Braybon, 67–85. New York: Berghahn.

Green, Jeffrey Edward. 2010a. *The Eyes of the People: Democracy in an Age of Spectatorship*. Oxford: Oxford University Press.

———. 2010b. "Three Theses on Schumpeter: Response to Mackie." *Political Theory* 38, no. 2 (April): 268–275.

Greenhouse, Steven. 2004. "Workers Assail Night Lock-Ins by Wal-Mart." *New York Times*, January 18. http://www.nytimes.com/2004/01/18/us/workers-assail-night-lock-ins-by-wal-mart.html. Accessed March 13, 2014.

———. 2013a. "Labor Union to Ease Walmart Picketing." *New York Times*, February 1. http://www.nytimes.com/2013/02/01/business/labor-union-agrees-to-stop-picketing-walmart.html?_r=0. Accessed March 13, 2014.

———. 2013b. "Retailers Split on Contrition after Collapse of Factories." *New York Times*, May 1. http://www.nytimes.com/2013/05/01/world/asia/retailers-split-on-bangladesh-factory-collapse.html?ref=benettongroupspa. Accessed June 15, 2013.

Gutmann, Amy, and Dennis Thompson. 1996. *Democracy and Disagreement*. Cambridge, MA: Harvard University Press.

———. 1999. "Reply to the Critics." In *Deliberative Politics: Essays on Democracy and Disagreement*, ed. S. Macedo, 243–279. New York: Oxford University Press.

———. 2004. *Why Deliberative Democracy?* Princeton, NJ: Princeton University Press.

Habermas, Jürgen. 1990. *Moral Consciousness and Communicative Action*. Cambridge, MA: MIT Press.

———. 1996. *Between Facts and Norms: Contributions to a Discourse Theory of Law and Democracy*, trans. W. Rehg. Cambridge, MA: MIT Press.

————. 1998. "On the Internal Relation between the Rule of Law and Democracy." In *The Inclusion of the Other: Studies in Political Theory*, ed. Ciaran Cronin and Pablo de Greiff, 253–264. Cambridge, MA: MIT Press.

Harris, Elizabeth A. 2013. "Labor Panel Finds Illegal Punishments at Walmart." *New York Times,* November 18. http://www.nytimes.com/2013/11/19 /business/labor-panel-finds-illegal-punishments-at-walmart.html?_r=0. Accessed March 12, 2014.

Hauptmann, Emily. 2001. "Can Less Be More? Leftist Deliberative Democrats' Critique of Participatory Democracy." *Polity* 33, no. 3 (Spring): 397–421.

————. 2004. "A Local History of the Political." *Political Theory* 32, no. 1 (February): 34–60.

Hayden, Tom. [1962] 2005. *The Port Huron Statement: The Visionary Call of the 1960s Revolution.* New York: Avalon.

Hayek, Friedrich A. von. 1979. *Law Legislation and Liberty.* Vol. 3, *The Political Order of a Free People.* Chicago: University of Chicago Press.

Hegel, Georg Wilhelm Friedrich. [1807] 1977. *The Phenomenology of Spirit.* Oxford: Oxford University Press.

————. [1821] 1991. *Elements of the Philosophy of Right.* Cambridge: Cambridge University Press.

Held, David. 2006. *Models of Democracy.* Stanford, CA: Stanford University Press.

Hildreth, R. W. 2009. "Reconstructing Dewey on Power." *Political Theory* 39, no. 6 (December): 780–807.

————. 2012. "Word *and* Deed: A Deweyan Integration of Deliberative and Participatory Democracy." *New Political Science* 34, no. 3 (September): 295–320.

Hilmer, Jeffrey D. 2010. "The State of Participatory Democratic Theory." *New Political Science* 32, no. 1 (March): 43–63.

Hobsbawm, E. J. 1990. *Nations and Nationalism since 1780: Programme, Myth, Reality.* Cambridge: Cambridge University Press.

Holleman, Hannah, Robert W. McChesney, John Bellamy Foster, and R. Jamil Jonna. 2009. "The Penal State in an Age of Crisis." *Monthly Review* 61, no. 2. http://monthlyreview.org/2009/06/01/the-penal-state-in-an-age-of-crisis. Accessed June 21, 2012.

Honig, Bonnie. 1991. "Declarations of Independence: Arendt and Derrida on the Problem of Founding a Republic." *American Political Science Review* 85, no. 1 (March): 97–113.

————. 1993. *Political Theory and the Displacement of Politics.* Ithaca, NY: Cornell University Press.

————. 2007. "Between Deliberation and Decision: Political Paradox in Democratic Theory." *American Political Science Review,* no. 101 (February): 1–17.

Huntington, Samuel P. 1975. "The United States." In *The Crisis of Democracy: Report on the Governability of Democracies to the Trilateral Commission,* ed. M. Crozier, S. Huntington, and J. Watanuki, 59–118. New York: New York University Press.

Inwood, Michael. 1992. *A Hegel Dictionary.* Oxford: Blackwell.

Isaac, Jeffrey C. 1987a. "Beyond the Three Faces of Power: A Realist Critique." *Polity* 20, no. 3 (Autumn): 4–31.

———. 1987b. *Power and Marxist Theory: A Realist View.* Ithaca, NY: Cornell University Press.

———. 1992. *Arendt, Camus and Modern Rebellion.* New Haven, CT: Yale University Press.

———. 2003. *The Poverty of Progressivism: The Future of American Democracy in a Time of Liberal Decline.* Lanham, MD: Rowman and Littlefield.

Jessop, Bob. 1982. *The Capitalist State.* New York: New York University Press.

Josephson, Eric, and Mary Josephson. 1962. Introduction to *Man Alone: Alienation in Modern Society,* 9–53. New York: Dell.

Karlan, Pamela S. 2008. Response to Loury. In *Race, Incarceration, and American Values,* by G. C. Loury, 41–56. Cambridge, MA: MIT Press.

Katznelson, Ira. 2005. *When Affirmative Action Was White: An Untold History of Racial Inequality in Twentieth-Century America.* New York: Norton.

Kennedy, Randall. 1997. *Race, Crime, and the Law.* New York: Vintage.

Kiel, Paul. 2012. "The Great American Foreclosure Story: The Struggle for Justice and a Place to Call Home." ProPublica, April 10. http://www.propublica .org/article/the-great-american-foreclosure-story-the-struggle-for-justice -and-a-place-t. Accessed May 15, 2013.

King, Martin Luther, Jr. 1986. *A Testament of Hope: The Essential Writings and Speeches of Martin Luther King, Jr.,* ed. J. Washington. New York: HarperCollins.

Knight, Jack, and James Johnson. 1994. "Aggregation and Deliberation: On the Possibility of Democratic Legitimacy." *Political Theory* 22, no. 2 (May): 277–296.

———. 1996. "Political Consequences of Pragmatism." *Political Theory* 24, no. 1 (February): 68–95.

———. 1997. "What Sort of Equality Does Deliberative Democracy Require?" In *Deliberative Democracy: Essays on Reason and Politics,* ed. J. Bohman and W. Rehg, 279–320. Cambridge, MA: MIT Press.

Knops, Andrew. 2006. "Delivering Deliberation's Emancipatory Potential." *Political Theory* 34, no. 5 (October): 594–623.

Kojeve, Alexandre. 1969. *Introduction to the Reading of Hegel: Lectures on the Phenomenology of Spirit,* trans. J. Nichols, Jr. Ithaca, NY: Cornell University Press.

Kolb, Eberhard. 1988. *The Weimar Republic.* London: Allen and Unwin.

Kosnoski, Jason. 2005a. "Artful Discussion: John Dewey's Classroom Model of Deliberative Association." *Political Theory* 33, no. 5 (October): 654–677.

———. 2005b. "John Dewey's Social Aesthetics." *Polity* 37, no. 2 (April): 193–215.

Kriner, Douglas L., and Francis X. Shen. 2010. *The Casualty Gap: The Causes and Consequences of American Wartime Inequalities.* New York: Oxford University Press.

Kuttner, Robert. 1996. *Everything for Sale: The Virtues and Limits of Markets.* Chicago: University of Chicago Press.

Laclau, Ernesto, and Chantal Mouffe. [1985] 1993. *Hegemony and Socialist Strategy: Towards a Radical Democratic Politics.* London: Verso.

Laden, Anthony Simon. 2001. *Reasonably Radical: Deliberative Liberalism and the Politics of Identity.* Ithaca, NY: Cornell University Press.

Lenin, Vladimir Ilyich. [1917] 1975. "The State and Revolution: The Marxist Theory of the State and the Tasks of the Proletariat in the Revolution." In *The Lenin Anthology,* ed. R. C. Tucker, 311–398. New York: Norton.

Lichtenstein, Nelson. 2009. *The Retail Revolution: How Wal-Mart Created a Brave New World of Business.* New York: Henry Holt.

Lieberman, Robert C. 1998. *Shifting the Color Line: Race and the American Welfare State.* Cambridge, MA: Harvard University Press.

———. 2005. *Shaping Race Policy: The United States in Comparative Perspective.* Princeton, NJ: Princeton University Press.

Lindblom, Charles E. 1977. *Politics and Markets: The World's Political-Economic Systems.* New York: Basic Books.

Lippmann, Walter. [1927] 1993. *The Phantom Public.* New Brunswick, NJ: Transaction.

Little, Daniel. 1991. *Varieties of Social Explanation: An Introduction to the Philosophy of Social Science.* Boulder, CO: Westview.

Locke, Richard M. 2013. "Can Global Brands Create Just Supply Chains? A Forum on Corporate Responsibility for Factory Workers." *Boston Review,* May/June. http://www.bostonreview.net/forum/can-global-brands-create-just-supply-chains-richard-locke? Accessed June 13, 2013.

Loury, Glenn C. 2008. "Race, Incarceration, and American Values." In *Race, Incarceration, and American Values,* 3–37. Cambridge, MA: MIT Press.

Lukács, Georg. 1971. *History and Class Consciousness: Studies in Marxist Dialectics.* Cambridge, MA: MIT Press.

———. 1976. *The Young Hegel: Studies in the Relations between Dialectics and Economics,* trans. Rodney Livingstone. Cambridge, MA: MIT Press.

MacCallum, Gerald, Jr. 1967. "Negative and Positive Freedom." *Philosophical Review* 76, no. 3 (July): 312–334.

MacGilvray, Eric A. 1999. "Experience as Experiment: Some Consequences of Pragmatism for Democratic Theory." *American Journal of Political Science* 43, no. 2 (April): 542–565.

Mackie, Gerry. 2009. "Schumpeter's Leadership Democracy." *Political Theory* 37, no. 1 (February): 128–153.

Macpherson, C. B. 1977. *The Life and Times of Liberal Democracy.* Oxford: Oxford University Press.

Manicas, Peter T. 1987. *A History and Philosophy of the Social Sciences.* London: Basil Blackwell.

Manik, Julfikar Ali, Steven Greenhouse, and Jim Yardley. 2013. "Western Firms Feel Pressure as Toll Rises in Bangladesh." *New York Times,* April 25. http://www.nytimes.com/2013/04/26/world/asia/bangladeshi-collapse-kills-many-garment-workers.html?pagewanted=all. Accessed June 16, 2013.

Mansbridge, Jane, James Bohman, Simone Chambers, David Estlund, Andreas Føllesdayl, Archon Fung, Cristina Lafont, Bernard Manin, and José Luis

Martí. 2010. "The Place of Self-Interest and the Role of Power in Deliberative Democracy." *Journal of Political Philosophy* 18, no. 1 (March): 64–100.

Markell, Patchen. 2006. "The Rule of the People: Arendt, Archê, and Democracy." *American Political Science Review* 100, no. 1 (February): 1–14.

Marshall, Monty G., and Jack Goldstone. 2007. "Global Report on Conflict, Governance and State Fragility 2007." *Foreign Policy Bulletin* 17: 3–21.

Marshall, T. H. [1950] 1992. *Citizenship and Social Class.* London: Pluto.

Marx, Karl. [1843] 1967. *Critique of Hegel's "Philosophy of Right."* Cambridge: Cambridge University Press.

———. [1843] 2000. On the Jewish Question. In *Karl Marx: Selected Writings*, 2nd ed., ed. D. McLellan, 46–70. Oxford: Oxford University Press.

———. [1844] 1964. *Economic and Philosophic Manuscripts of 1844.* New York: International.

———. [1845] 2000. "Theses on Feuerbach." In *Karl Marx: Selected Writings*, 2nd ed., ed. D. McLellan, 171–174. Oxford: Oxford University Press.

———. [1852] 1996. "The Eighteenth Brumaire of Louis Bonaparte." In *Marx: Later Political Writings*, ed. T. Carver, 31–127. Cambridge: Cambridge University Press.

———. [1857–1858] 1964. *Pre-capitalist Economic Formations*, trans. J. Cohen. New York: International.

———. [1859] 2000. "Preface to *A Critique of Political Economy.*" In *Karl Marx: Selected Writings*, 2nd ed., ed. D. McLellan, 424–428. Oxford: Oxford University Press.

———. [1871] 1996. *The Civil War in France.* In *Marx: Later Political Writings*, ed. T. Carver, 163–207. Cambridge: Cambridge University Press.

Marx, Karl, and Friedrich Engels. [1848] 2012. *The Communist Manifesto*, edited and with an introduction by Jeffrey C. Isaac. New Haven, CT: Yale University Press.

Mayer, Jane. 2009. "The Predator War: What Are the Risks of the C.I.A.'s Covert Drone Program?" *New Yorker,* October 26. http://www.newyorker.com /reporting/2009/10/26/091026fa_fact_mayer. Accessed May 13, 11.

McAdam, Doug. 1982. *Political Process and the Development of Black Insurgency, 1930–1970.* Chicago: University of Chicago Press.

McLellan, David. 1969. "Marx's View of the Unalienated Society." *Review of Politics* 31, no. 4 (Fall): 459–465.

Medearis, John. 2001. *Joseph Schumpeter's Two Theories of Democracy.* Cambridge, MA: Harvard University Press.

———. 2004. "Lost or Obscured? How V. I. Lenin, Joseph Schumpeter and Hannah Arendt Misunderstood the Council Movement." *Polity* 36, no. 3 (April): 447–476.

———. 2005. "Social Movements and Deliberative Democratic Theory." *British Journal of Political Science* 35 (April): 53–75.

———. 2008. "Deliberative Democracy, Subordination, and the Welfare State." In *The Illusion of Consent: Engaging with Carole Pateman*, ed. D. I. O'Neill, M. L. Shanley, and I. M. Young, 205–230. University Park: Pennsylvania University Press.

———. 2009. *Joseph A. Schumpeter.* New York: Continuum.

Miliband, Ralph. 1969. *The State in Capitalist Society.* New York: Basic Books.

———. 1977. *Marxism and Politics.* New York: Oxford University Press.

Milkman, Ruth, Penny Lewis, and Stephanie Luce. 2013. "The Genie's Out of the Bottle: Insiders' Perspectives on Occupy Wall Street." *Sociological Quarterly* 54 (Spring): 194–198.

Mill, John Stuart. [1848] 1965. *The Principles of Political Economy, with Some of their Applications to Social Philosophy* (Parts 1 and 2). Vols. 2 and 3 of *Collected Works of John Stuart Mill,* ed. J. M. Robson. Toronto: University of Toronto Press.

———. [1859] 1977. *On Liberty.* In *Essays on Politics and Society* (Part 1). Vol. 18 of *Collected Works of John Stuart Mill,* ed. J. M. Robson, 213–310. Toronto: University of Toronto Press.

———. [1879] 1967. "Chapters on Socialism." In *Essays on Economics and Society* (Part 2). Vol. 5 of *Collected Works of John Stuart Mill,* ed. J. M. Robson, 703–753. Toronto: University of Toronto Press.

Miller, T. Christian. 2009a. "Contractors in Iraq Are Hidden Casualties of War." ProPublica, October 6. http://www.propublica.org/article/kbr-contractor -struggles-after-iraq-injuries-1006. Accessed July 15, 2011.

———. 2009b. "Foreign Workers for U.S. Are Casualties Twice Over." ProPublica, June 19. http://www.propublica.org/article/foreign-workers-for-u.s.-are-casualties -twice-over-619. Accessed July 15, 2011.

———. 2010. "This Year, Contractor Deaths Exceed Military Ones in Iraq and Afghanistan." ProPublica, September 23. http://www.propublica.org/article /this-year-contractor-deaths-exceed-military-ones-in-iraq-and-afgh-100923. Accessed July 14, 2011.

Miller, T. Christian, and Doug Smith. 2009. "Injured War Zone Contractors Fight to Get Care from AIG and Other Insurers." ProPublica, April 16, 2009. http://www.propublica.org/article/injured-war-zone-contractors-fight-to -get-care-from-aig-416. Accessed July 15, 2011.

Milligan, Martin, and Dirk J. Struik. 1964. "Translator's and Editor's Note on Terminology." In *The Economic and Philosophic Manuscripts of 1844,* ed. D. J. Struik, 57–60. New York: International.

Mills, Charles. 2005. " 'Ideal Theory' as Ideology." *Hypatia* 20, no. 3 (Summer): 165–184.

Morris, Aldon D. 1984. *The Origins of the Civil Rights Movement: Black Communities Organizing for Change.* New York: Free Press.

Mouffe, Chantal. 1993. *The Return of the Political.* London: Verso.

———. 2000. *The Democratic Paradox.* London: Verso.

"The Must-Do List." 2007. Editorial. *New York Times,* March 4, A11.

Neiberg, Michael S. 2004. "Revisiting the Myths: New Approaches to the Great War." *Contemporary European History* 13, no. 4 (November): 505–515.

Nelson, Barbara. 1990. "The Origins of the Two-Channel Welfare State: Workmen's Compensation and Mothers' Aid." In *Women, the State, and Welfare,* ed. L. Gordon, 123–151. Madison: University of Wisconsin Press.

Nimtz, August H., Jr. 2000. *Marx and Engels: Their Contribution to the Democratic Breakthrough*. Albany: State University of New York Press.

Noble, Charles. 1997. *Welfare as We Knew It: A Political History of the American Welfare State*. New York: Oxford University Press.

Norman, Richard. 1976. *Hegel's Phenomenology: A Philosophical Introduction*. Brighton: Sussex University Press.

Offe, Claus. 1984. *Contradictions of the Welfare State*, ed. John Keane. Cambridge, MA: MIT Press.

Ollman, Bertell. 1971. *Alienation: Marx's Conception of Man in Capitalist Society*. Cambridge: Cambridge University Press.

Orloff, Ann Shola. 2010. "Gender." In *The Oxford Handbook of the Welfare State*, ed. F. G. Castles, S. Leibfried, J. Lewis, H. Obinger, and C. Pierson, 252–264. New York: Oxford University Press.

Orren, Karen. 1991. *Belated Feudalism: Labor, the Law, and Liberal Development in the United States*. Cambridge: Cambridge University Press.

Palier, Bruno. 2010. "Continental Western Europe." In *The Oxford Handbook of the Welfare State*, ed. F. G. Castles, S. Leibfried, J. Lewis, H. Obinger, and C. Pierson, 601–615. New York: Oxford University Press.

Parsons, Talcott. 1951. *The Social System*. New York: Free Press.

Pateman, Carole. 1970. *Participation and Democratic Theory*. Cambridge: Cambridge University Press.

———. 1983. "Feminism and Democracy." In *Democratic Theory and Practice*, ed. G. Duncan, 204–217. Cambridge: Cambridge University Press.

———. 1985. *The Problem of Political Obligation: A Critique of Liberal Theory*. Berkeley, CA: University of California Press.

———. 1988. *The Sexual Contract*. Stanford, CA: Stanford University Press.

———. 2005. "Another Way Forward: Welfare, Social Reproduction, and a Basic Income." In *Welfare Reform and Political Theory*, ed. L. M. Mead and C. Breem, 34–64. New York: Russell Sage.

———. 2007. "Race, Sex and Indifference." In *Contract and Domination*, ed. C. Pateman and C. Mills, 134–164. Cambridge: Polity Press.

———. 2012. "Participatory Democracy Revisited." *Perspectives on Politics* 10, no. 1 (March): 7–19.

Pateman, Carole, and Charles Mills. 2007. *Contract and Domination*. Cambridge: Polity Press.

Pettit, Philip. 1997. *Republicanism: A Theory of Freedom and Government*. Oxford: Oxford University Press.

———. 2001. *A Theory of Freedom: From the Psychology to the Politics of Agency*. Cambridge: Polity.

Pfeifer, Stuart. 2013. "Wal-Mart Contractor to Pay $4.7 Million to Settle Lawsuit by Workers." *Los Angeles Times*. December 11. http://articles.latimes.com/2013/dec/11/business/la-fi-mo-walmart-contractor-to-pay-47-million-to-allegedly-underpaid-workers-20131211 Accessed March 10, 2014.

Phillips, Anne. 1991. *Engendering Democracy*. University Park: Pennsylvania State University Press.

Piven, Frances Fox, and Richard Cloward. 1993. *Regulating the Poor: The Functions of Public Welfare.* Updated ed. New York: Vintage.

Polanyi, Karl. [1944] 2001. *The Great Transformation: The Political and Economic Origins of Our Times.* Boston: Beacon.

"Poll Shows Complexity of Debate on Trade-Offs in Government Spying Programs." 2013. Editorial. *New York Times.* July 10. http://www.nytimes.com /2013/07/11/us/poll-shows-complexity-of-debate-on-trade-offs-in -government-spying-programs.html?src=xps. Accessed August 15, 2013.

Posner, Richard A. 2009. *A Failure of Capitalism: The Crisis of '08 and the Descent into Depression.* Cambridge, MA: Harvard University Press.

Poulantzas, Nicos. 1969. "The Problem of the Capitalist State." *New Left Review,* no. I/58 (November–December): 67–78.

———. 1973. *Political Power and Social Classes,* trans. Timothy O'Hagan. London: NLB.

———. 1978. "The State and the Transition to Socialism." *Socialist Review,* no. 38 (March–April): 9–36.

Putnam, Hilary, and Ruth Anna Putnam. 1989. "Dewey's Logic: Epistemology as Hypothesis." In *Words and Life,* 198–220. Cambridge, MA: Harvard University Press.

Putnam, Robert. 2000. *Bowling Alone: The Collapse and Revival of American Democracy.* New York: Simon and Schuster.

Rawls, John. 1996. *Political Liberalism.* With a new introduction and "Reply to Habermas." New York: Columbia University Press.

———. 1999a. *The Law of Peoples.* With "The Idea of Public Reason Revisited." Cambridge, MA: Harvard University Press.

———. 1999b. *A Theory of Justice.* Rev. ed. Cambridge, MA: Harvard University Press.

Robin, Corey. 2011. *The Reactionary Mind: Conservatism from Edmund Burke to Sarah Palin.* Oxford: Oxford University Press.

Rueschemeyer, Dietrich, Evelyne Huber Stephens, and John D. Stephens. 1992. *Capitalist Development and Democracy.* Chicago: University of Chicago Press.

Ryan, Alan. 1995. *John Dewey and the High Tide of American Liberalism.* New York: Norton.

Sabl, Andrew. 2001. "Looking Forward to Justice: Rawlsian Civil Disobedience and Its Non-Rawlsian Lessons." *Journal of Political Philosophy* 9, no. 3 (September): 307–330.

Sandel, Michael J. 2009. *Justice: What's the Right Thing to Do?* New York: Farrar, Strauss and Giroux.

———. 2012. *What Money Can't Buy: The Moral Limits of Markets.* New York: Farrar, Strauss and Giroux.

Sartre, Jean-Paul. [1943] 1956. *Being and Nothingness: A Phenomenological Essay on Ontology,* trans. H. E. Barnes. New York: Washington Square.

———. [1947] 1977. *Existentialism and Humanism.* New York: Haskell House.

Satz, Debra. 2010. *Why Some Things Should Not Be for Sale: The Moral Limits of Markets.* Oxford: Oxford University Press.

Sayer, Andrew. 1992. *Method in Social Science: A Realist Approach.* 2nd ed. London: Routledge.

Schacht, Richard. 1970. *Alienation.* Garden City, NJ: Doubleday.

Schaff, Adam. 1980. *Alienation as a Social Phenomenon.* Oxford: Pergamon.

Schumpeter, Joseph. [1918] 1991. "The Crisis of the Tax State." In *The Economics and Sociology of Capitalism,* ed. R. Swedberg, 99–140. Princeton, NJ: Princeton University Press.

———. [1918–1919] 1991. "The Sociology of Imperialisms." In *The Economics and Sociology of Capitalism,* ed. R. Swedberg, 141–219. Princeton, NJ: Princeton University Press.

———. [1928] 1989. "The Instability of Capitalism." In *Essays on Entrepreneurs, Innovations, Business Cycles, and the Evolution of Capitalism,* ed. R. V. Clemece, 47–72. New Brunswick, NJ: Transaction.

———. 1939. *Business Cycles: A Theoretical, Historical and Statistical Analysis of the Capitalist Process.* 2 vols. New York: McGraw-Hill.

———. [1941] 1991. "An Economic Interpretation of Our Time: The Lowell Lectures." In *The Economics and Sociology of Capitalism,* ed. R. Swedberg, 339–400. Princeton, NJ: Princeton University Press.

———. [1942] 1976. *Capitalism, Socialism and Democracy.* New York: Harper and Row.

———. [1948] 1991. "Wage and Tax Policy in Transitional States of Society." In *The Economics and Sociology of Capitalism,* ed. R. Swedberg, 429–437. Princeton, NJ: Princeton University Press.

Schwartz, Joseph M. 2009. *The Future of Democratic Equality: Rebuilding Social Solidarity in a Fragmented America.* New York: Routledge.

Scott, James. 1998. *Seeing like a State: How Certain Schemes to Improve the Human Condition Have Failed.* New Haven, CT: Yale University Press.

Shapiro, Ian. 1999a. *Democratic Justice.* New Haven, CT: Yale University Press.

———.1999b. "Enough of Deliberation: Politics Is about Interests and Power." In *Deliberative Politics: Essays on Democracy and Disagreement,* ed. Stephen Macedo, 28–38. New York: Oxford University Press.

———. 2003. *The State of Democratic Theory.* Princeton, NJ: Princeton University Press.

———. 2007. *Containment: Rebuilding a Strategy against Global Terror.* Princeton, NJ: Princeton University Press.

———. 2010. *The Real World of Democratic Theory.* Princeton, NJ: Princeton University Press.

Shapiro, Ian, and Alexander Wendt. 1992. "The Difference That Realism Makes: Social Science and the Politics of Consent." *Politics and Society* 20, no. 2 (June): 197–223.

Sherry, Michael S. 1987. *The Rise of American Air Power: The Creation of Armageddon.* New Haven, CT: Yale University Press.

Singer, P. W. 2008. *Corporate Warriors: The Rise of the Privatized Military Industry.* Updated ed. Ithaca, NY: Cornell University Press.

Skocpol, Theda. 1979. *The State and Social Revolutions: A Comparative Analysis of France, Russia, and China.* Cambridge: Cambridge University Press.

Skocpol, Theda, and Kenneth Finegold. 1982. "State Capacity and Economic Intervention in the Early New Deal." *Political Science Quarterly* 97, no. 2 (Summer): 255–278.

———. 1990. "Explaining New Deal Labor Policy." *American Political Science Review* 84, no. 4 (December): 1297–1304.

Stears, Marc. 2010. *Demanding Democracy: American Radicals in Search of a New Politics.* Princeton, NJ: Princeton University Press.

Stiglitz, Joseph E. 2009. *Freefall: America, Free Markets, and the Sinking of the World Economy.* With a new afterword. New York: Norton.

Stiglitz, Joseph E., and Linda J. Bilmes. 2008. *The Three Trillion Dollar War: The True Cost of the Iraq Conflict.* New York: Norton.

Stillman, Sarah. 2011. "The Invisible Army." *New Yorker,* June 6, 56–65.

Strachan, Hew. 2001. *The First World War.* Vol. 1, *To Arms.* New York: Oxford University Press.

"Surveillance: A Threat to Democracy." 2013. Editorial. *New York Times.* June 11. http://www.nytimes.com/2013/06/12/opinion/surveillance-a-threat -to-democracy.html?src=xps. Accessed August 15, 2013.

Tarrow, Sidney. 1998. *Power in Movement: Social Movements and Contentious Politics.* 2nd ed. Cambridge: Cambridge University Press.

Taylor, Bob Pepperman. 2001. Review of *Deliberative Democracy and Beyond,* by John Dryzek. *American Political Science Review* 95, no. 4 (December): 976–977.

Taylor, Charles. 1975. *Hegel.* Cambridge: Cambridge University Press.

———. 1979. *Hegel and Modern Society.* Cambridge: Cambridge University Press.

Thomas, Paul. 1994. *Alien Politics: Marxist State Theory Retrieved.* London: Routledge.

Thompson, Dennis F. 2008. "Deliberative Democratic Theory and Empirical Political Science." *Annual Review of Political Science,* no. 11: 497–520.

Tobin, Elizabeth H. 1983. "Revolution and Alienation: The Foundations of Weimar." In *Towards the Holocaust: The Social and Economic Collapse of the Weimar Republic,* ed. M. N. Dobkowski and I. Walliman, 156–176. Westport, CT: Greenwood.

Trollope, Anthony. [1868] 1991. *Phineas Finn: The Irish Member.* Oxford: Oxford University Press.

Tucker, Kenneth H., Jr. 1998. *Anthony Giddens and Modern Social Theory.* London: Sage.

Wacquant, Loïc. 2008. Response to Loury. In *Race, Incarceration, and American Values,* by G. C. Loury, 57–72. Cambridge: MIT Press.

Walzer, Michael. 1983. *Spheres of Justice: A Defense of Pluralism and Equality.* New York: Basic Books.

———. 1999. "Deliberation, and What Else?" In *Deliberative Politics: Essays on Democracy and Disagreement,* ed. S. Macedo, 58–69. New York: Oxford University Press.

Warnke, Georgia. 2007. *After Identity: Rethinking Race, Sex, and Gender.* Cambridge: Cambridge University Press.

Warren, Mark. 1996. "What Should We Expect from More Democracy?" *Political Theory* 24, no. 2 (May): 241–270.

Wartenberg, Thomas E. 1992. "Situated Social Power." In *Rethinking Power,* ed. T. E. Wartenberg, 79–101. Albany: State University of New York Press.

Weber, Eugen. 1976. *Peasants into Frenchmen: The Modernisation of Rural France, 1870–1914.* Stanford, CA: Stanford University Press.

Westbrook, Robert. 1991. *John Dewey and American Democracy.* Ithaca, NY: Cornell University Press.

———. 1992. "Schools for Industrial Democrats: The Social Origins of John Dewey's Philosophy of Education." *American Journal of Education* 100, no. 4 (August): 401–419.

———. 1997. "Pragmatism and Democracy: Reconstructing the Logic of Dewey's Faith." In *The Revival of Pragmatism: New Essays on Social Thought, Law, and Culture,* ed. M. Dickstein, 128–140. Durham, NC: Duke University Press.

Williams, Bernard. 2005. "From Freedom to Liberty: The Construction of a Political Value." In *In the Beginning Was the Deed: Realism and Moralism in Political Argument,* ed. G. Hawthorn, 75–96. Princeton, NJ: Princeton University Press.

Williamson, Vanessa, Theda Skocpol, and John Coggins. 2011. "The Tea Party and the Remaking of Republican Conservatism." *Perspectives on Politics* 9, no. 1 (March): 25–43.

Wolin, Sheldon S. 1982. "What Revolutionary Action Means Today." *Democracy* 3, no. 1 (Fall): 17–28.

———. 1994. "Norm and Form: The Constitutionalizing of Democracy." In *Athenian Political Thought and the Reconstruction of American Democracy,* ed. J. P. Euben, J. Ober, and J. R. Wallach, 29–58. Ithaca, NY: Cornell University Press.

———. 1996. "Fugitive Democracy." In *Democracy and Difference: Contesting the Boundaries of the Political,* ed. S. Benhabib, 31–45. Princeton, NJ: Princeton University Press.

———. 2009. *Politics and Vision: Continuity and Innovation in Western Political Thought.* Expanded ed. Princeton, NJ: Princeton University Press.

Wood, Allen W. 1980. "The Marxian Critique of Justice." In *Marx, Justice and History,* ed. M. Cohen, T. Nagel, and T. Scanlon, 3–41. Princeton, NJ: Princeton University Press.

Writers for the 99%. 2011. *Occupying Wall Street: The Inside Story of an Action That Changed America.* Chicago: Haymarket.

Young, Iris Marion. 2001. "Activist Challenges to Deliberative Democracy." *Political Theory* 29, no. 5: 670–690.

Zimmerman, Ann, and Shelly Banjo. 2012. "Holiday Weekend Protests Begin at Wal-Mart Stores." *Wall Street Journal,* November 23. https://global.factiva .com/ha/default.aspx#./!?&_suid=14191188881230677670993913 1358. Accessed March 13, 2014.

ACKNOWLEDGMENTS

It would be strange if writing a book that is focused on strengthening common endeavors were to become an entirely isolating process. A number of people saved me from such an ironic fate. Eugene Goodheart, Jessica Goodheart, Jeffrey Isaac, John Christian Laursen, Daniel O'Connor, Mindy Peden, Corey Robin, and Georgia Warnke all read and commented on various chapters and drafts or discussed particular lines of argument with me. Carole Pateman and the participants in her democratic theory seminars engaged me in lively conversation about my ideas as they were developing. In all these cases, the usual proviso applies: they all tried to help me, but none can be held responsible for any weaknesses in the preceding pages. At Harvard University Press, Michael Aronson saw promise in an elevator talk and encouraged me as I transformed it into a book, and Kathleen Drummy provided indispensable practical guidance, especially in the later stages of this process. Kevin Pham also provided valuable assistance with the manuscript. My deepest debts, though, are to Jessica and Max, who reorganized their lives at times so I could go off to think and write, and who supported my psyche in every way over the past few years.

251